It all began with an improbable wager: ask 35 scholars to each write something intelligible about every single paragraph in one of the texts included in Jacques Lacan's magnum opus, Écrits, so as to generate a commentary on the entire 800-page volume. And yet, after years of preparation, the wager has paid off: we have here useful and at times brilliant examples of textual explication! Cryptic formulations are lucidly unpacked, and mysterious references are provided, giving the serious reader myriad keys to fascinating texts.

Bruce Fink, *translator of* Écrits: The First Complete Edition in English (2006)

Let's face it: Lacan's Écrits, one of the classical texts of modern thought are unreadable - they remain impenetrable if we just pick the thick volume up and start to read it. Hook, Neill and Vanheule provide what we were all waiting for: a detailed commentary which does not aim to replace reading Écrits but to render it possible. The three volumes do wonder, their effect is no less than magic: when, after getting stuck at a particularly dense page of Écrits, we turn to the corresponding pages in the commentary and then return to the page of Écrits which pushed us to madness, the same lines appear in all the clarity of their line of thought. It is thus a safe prediction that Hook, Neill and Vanheule's commentary will become a kind of permanent companion of the English translation of Écrits, indispensable for everyone who wants to find her or his way in its complex texture.

Slavoj Žižek

Like a Rosetta stone, this accessible and superbly-written collection superimposes three levels of translation that render legible a text that Lacan quipped was not meant to be read. Cracking the code of Lacanian hieroglyphics, we discover the genealogy of his thought. These exceptionally fresh and user-friendly approaches testify to the enduring relevance and urgency of his opus magnum.

Patricia Gherovici, *psychoanalyst and author of* Transgender Psychoanalysis: A Lacanian Perspective on Sexual Difference *(Routledge, 2017)*

These essays will be an invaluable resource not only for those approaching Écrits for the first time but also for seasoned readers. Broad in scope yet following the detail of the text, they help guide us through Lacan's difficult prose, elucidating, contextualizing and clarifying, and reminding us time and time again of the precision, power and originality of his rethinking of psychoanalysis.

Darian Leader

READING LACAN'S ÉCRITS

Reading Lacan's Écrits is the first extensive set of commentaries on the complete edition of Lacan's *Écrits* to be published in English. This third volume provides an indispensable companion piece to some of Lacan's most crucial and notoriously challenging writings, from 'Logical Time' to 'Response to Jean Hyppolite', and including 'The Function and Field of Speech', 'Variations on the Standard Treatment' and 'Presentation on Transference'.

With the contributions of some of the world's most renowned Lacanian scholars and analysts – such as Bernard Burgoyne, Marc De Kesel and Russell Grigg – this volume encompasses a series of systematic, paragraph-by-paragraph commentaries which not only contextualize, explain and interrogate Lacan's arguments, but afford the reader multiple interpretive routes through the complete edition of Lacan's most labyrinthine of texts.

As there is no existing set of exhaustive commentaries on Lacan's *Écrits* available in English, this volume acts as an essential and incisive reference-text for psychoanalysts and psychoanalytic psychotherapists in training and in practice, as well as philosophers, cultural theorists and literary, social science and humanities researchers. Considering the significance of *Écrits* as a landmark in the history of psychoanalysis, this far-reaching and accessible guide will sustain and continue to animate critical engagement with one of the most challenging intellectual works of the twentieth century.

Derek Hook is an Associate Professor and Clinical Supervisor in Psychology at Duquesne University and an Extraordinary Professor of Psychology at the University of Pretoria. He is the author of *A Critical Psychology of the Colonial* and *Six Moments in Lacan*. He is co-editor of *Lacan and Race* (with Sheldon George) and of *Fanon, Phenomenology & Psychology* (with Leswin Laubscher and Miraj U. Desai).

Calum Neill is Associate Professor of Psychoanalysis and Cultural Theory at Edinburgh Napier University. He is the author of *Without Ground: Lacanian Ethics and the Assumption of Subjectivity, Ethics and Psychology: Beyond Codes of Practice* and *Jacques Lacan: The Basics*. With Derek Hook, he edits the Palgrave Lacan Series.

Stijn Vanheule is a Clinical Psychologist and a Professor of Psychoanalysis and Clinical Psychology at Ghent University, Belgium. He is also a privately practising psychoanalyst and a member of the New Lacanian School for Psychoanalysis. He is the author of *The Subject of Psychosis: A Lacanian Perspective* and *Psychiatric Diagnosis Revisited – From DSM to Clinical Case Formulation*.

READING LACAN'S ÉCRITS

From 'Logical Time' to 'Response to Jean Hyppolite'

Edited by Derek Hook, Calum Neill and Stijn Vanheule

Routledge
Taylor & Francis Group

LONDON AND NEW YORK

First published 2022
by Routledge
4 Park Square, Milton Park, Abingdon, Oxon OX14 4RN

and by Routledge
605 Third Avenue, New York, NY 10158

Routledge is an imprint of the Taylor & Francis Group, an informa business

British Library Cataloguing-in-Publication Data
A catalog record for this book is available from the British Library

Library of Congress Cataloguing-in-Publication Data
Names: Hook, Derek, editor. | Neill, Calum, 1968- editor. | Vanheule, Stijn, 1974- editor.
Title: Reading Lacan's Écrits : from 'Logical time' to 'Response to Jean Hyppolite' / edited by Derek Hook, Calum Neill and Stijn Vanheule.
Description: Milton Park, Abingdon, Oxon ; New York, NY : Routledge, 2022. | Includes bibliographical references and index.
Identifiers: LCCN 2021045296 (print) | LCCN 2021045297 (ebook) | ISBN 9781032205755 (hardback) | ISBN 9781032205779 (paperback) | ISBN 9781003264231 (ebook)
Subjects: LCSH: Lacan, Jacques, 1901–1981. Écrits. | Psychoanalysis.
Classification: LCC BF173.L1423 R434 2022 (print) | LCC BF173.L1423 (ebook) | DDC 150.19/5--dc23
LC record available at https://lccn.loc.gov/2021045296
LC ebook record available at https://lccn.loc.gov/2021045297

ISBN: 978-1-032-20575-5 (hbk)
ISBN: 978-1-032-20577-9 (pbk)
ISBN: 978-1-003-26423-1 (ebk)

DOI: 10.4324/9781003264231

Typeset in Bembo
by MPS Limited, Dehradun

CONTENTS

CONTENTS

FIGURES

CONTRIBUTORS

Bernard Burgoyne is a psychoanalyst practising in London. He was educated at Clare College Cambridge, the London School of Economics, and the University of Paris VIII. He is Emeritus Professor of Psychoanalysis at Middlesex University and is currently interested in how frontiers of desire are determined by general topological properties of the structure of the mind.

Marc De Kesel, professor of Theology, Mysticism & Modernity, is Director Intern & Extern Affairs at the Titus Brandsma Institute at the Radboud University Nijmegen (The Netherlands). His fields of research are Continental Philosophy, Theory of Religion and Mysticism, Holocaust Reception, Freudo-Lacanian Theory, Theory of Modern Art.

Russell Grigg practices psychoanalysis in Melbourne, Australia. He is a member of the Lacan Circle of Australia, the New Lacanian School, the École de la Cause freudienne and the World Association of Psychoanalysis. He has translated several of Lacan's seminars into English.

Owen Hewitson is a Lacanian scholar and author. He runs LacanOnline.Com.

Dominiek Hoens teaches philosophy at RITCS (Brussels), where he also conducts research under the heading of 'Capital owes you nothing'. Recent publications include an edited collection on Marguerite Duras (www.lineofbeauty.org), a chapter on Jacques Lacan in *Routledge Handbook of Psychoanalytic Political Theory*, and several articles on Blaise Pascal.

Thomas Svolos practises psychoanalysis in Omaha, Nebraska. He is a member of Lacanian Compass, the New Lacanian School, and the World Association of Psychoanalysis. Svolos currently serves as Professor of Psychiatry and Associate Dean for Strategy and Accreditation at the Creighton University School of Medicine. Svolos is the author of *The Aims of Analysis: Miami Seminar on the Late Lacan* (Midden Press, 2020) and *Twenty-first Century Psychoanalysis* (Routledge, 2017). He is co-editor of *Lacan and Addiction: An Anthology* (Routledge, 2011). His writings have appeared in nine languages.

Jamieson Webster is a psychoanalyst in New York City and Part-Time Faculty at the New School for Social Research. She is a founder of the psychoanalytic collective *Das Unbehagen* and a member of the Institute for Psychoanalytic Training and Research. She is the author of *Conversion Disorder* (2018), *The Hamlet Doctrine* (2013) with Simon Critchley, and *The Life and Death of Psychoanalysis* (2011). With Marcus Coelen, she is currently writing *Remains to be Read: On Jacques Lacan* for Columbia University Press.

ACKNOWLEDGEMENTS

Editing four volumes on the *Écrits* was a challenge, which above all made clear that by translating Lacan's single most important and intimidating text, Bruce Fink had already made a tremendous first effort. His translation of the *Écrits* and generous support of our project were most helpful.

We are also grateful that the publisher W.W. Norton & Company gave their permission to reprint the original figures from the *Écrits*, and thank the Department of Psychoanalysis and Clinical Consulting at Ghent University for the financial support and acquiring this permission. We are likewise grateful to the various institutions that have supported our work on this project over the last eight years, including the Department of Psychology at Duquesne University in Pittsburgh, the Department of Psychosocial Studies at Birkbeck College, London, and Edinburgh Napier University. A special thanks to John Dall'Aglio and Dries Dulsster.

Last, but not least we want to thank all authors and reviewers. Without our authors' dedication these Volumes simply could not have been realized. Each chapter implied hard study and a continuous search for clear expression, which was achieved. Each chapter has been reviewed by at least two peers. Many thanks to those who engaged in this meticulous task.

NOTE ON REFERENCING

Given that our aim in this project has been to offer extensive commentaries on all of Lacan's papers collected in his *Écrits*, we have adopted a referencing convention whereby we include the page number followed by the paragraph number of the phrase or section being quoted, referring to the English-language edition translated by Bruce Fink, as listed above.

JACQUES LACAN'S SEMINARS

Throughout this book the following abbreviations are used when referring to Lacan's seminars:

S1: Seminar 1 (1953–1954): Lacan, J. (1975/1988) *The Seminar. Book I: Freud's Papers on Technique*, trans. J. Forrester, ed. J.-A. Miller, Cambridge: Cambridge University Press.

S2: Seminar 2 (1954–1955): Lacan, J. (1978/1988) *The Seminar. Book II: The Ego in Freud's Theory and in the Technique of Psychoanalysis*, trans. S. Tomaselli, ed. J.-A. Miller, Cambridge: Cambridge University Press.

S3: Seminar 3 (1955–1956): Lacan, J. (1981/1993) *The Seminar. Book III: The Psychoses*, trans. R. Grigg, ed. J.-A. Miller, New York NY: W. W. Norton & Company.

S4: Seminar 4 (1956–1957): Lacan, J. (1994) *Le Séminaire. Livre IV: La relation d'objet*, texte établi par J.-A. Miller, Paris: Éditions du Seuil.

S5: Seminar 5 (1957–1958): Lacan, J. (1998) *Le Séminaire. Livre V: Les formations de l'inconscient*, texte établi par J.-A. Miller, Paris: Éditions du Seuil.

S6: Seminar 6 (1958–1959): Lacan J. (2013), *Le Séminaire. Livre VI. Le désir et son interprétation*, texte établi par J.-A. Miller, Paris: Éditions de la Martinière.

S7: Seminar 7 (1959–1960): Lacan, J. (1986/1992) *The Seminar. Book VII: The Ethics of Psychoanalysis*, trans. D. Porter, ed. J.-A. Miller, New York and London: W.W. Norton & Company.

S8: Seminar 8 (1960–1961): Lacan, J. (2001/2015) *The Seminar. Book VIII: Transference*, trans. B. Fink, ed. J.-A. Miller, Cambridge: Polity.

S9: Seminar 9 (1961–1962): *Le Séminaire IX, L'Identification*, unpublished.

S10: Seminar 10 (1962–1963): Lacan, J. (2004/2014) *The Seminar. Book X: Anxiety*, trans. A. R. Price, ed. J.-A. Miller, Cambridge: Polity.

S11: Seminar 11 (1964): Lacan, J. (1973/1994) *The Seminar. Book XI: The Four Fundamental Concepts of Psycho-Analysis*, trans. A. Sheridan, ed. J.-A. Miller, New York and London: W.W. Norton & Company.

S12: Seminar 12 (1964–1965): *Le Séminaire XII, Problèmes cruciaux pour la psychanalyse*, unpublished.

S13: Seminar 13 (1965–1966): *Le Séminaire XIII, L'objet de la psychanalyse*, unpublished.

S14: Seminar 14 (1966–1967): *Le Séminaire XIV, La logique du fantasme*, unpublished.

S15: Seminar 15 (1967–1968): *Le Séminaire XV, l'acte psychanalytique*, unpublished.

S16: Seminar 16 (1968–1969): Lacan, J. (2006) *Le séminaire de Jacques Lacan, Livre XVI: D'un Autre à l'autre*, texte établi par J.-A. Miller, Paris: Éditions du Seuil.

S17: Seminar 17 (1969–1970): Lacan, J. (1991/2007) *The Seminar. Book XVII: The Other Side of Psychoanalysis*, trans. R. Grigg, ed. J.-A. Miller, New York and London: W.W. Norton & Company.

S18: Seminar 18 (1970–1971): Lacan J. (2006), *Le Séminaire. Livre XVIII. D'un discours qui ne serait pas du semblant*, Paris: Éditions du Seuil.

S19: Seminar 19 (1971–1972): Lacan, J. (2011) *Le Séminaire. Livre XIX: … ou pire*, texte établi par J.-A. Miller, Paris: Éditions du Seuil.

S20: Seminar 20 (1972–1973): Lacan, J. (1998) *The Seminar, Book XX, Encore: On Feminine Sexuality, the Limits of Love and Knowledge*, trans. B. Fink, ed. J.-A. Miller, New York and London: W.W. Norton & Company.

S21: Seminar 21 (1973–1974): *Le Séminaire XXI, Les non-dupes errent*, unpublished.

S22: Seminar 22 (1974–1975): *Le Séminaire XXII, R.S.I.*, unpublished.

S23: Seminar 23 (1975–1976): Lacan, J. (2005/2016) *The Seminar. Book XXIII: The Sinthome*, trans. A. R. Price, ed. J.-A. Miller, Cambridge: Polity.

S24: Seminar 24 (1976–1977): *Le Séminaire XXIV, L'insu que sait de l'une-bévue s'aile à mourre*, unpublished.

S25: Seminar 25 (1977–1978): *Le Séminaire XXV, Le moment de conclure*, unpublished.

S26: Seminar 26 (1978–1979): *Le Séminaire XXVI, La topologie et le temps*, unpublished.

INTRODUCTION TO 'READING ÉCRITS': *LA TRAHISON DE L'ÉCRITURE*

Derek Hook, Calum Neill, and Stijn Vanheule

What kind of book is Lacan's *Écrits*? This is a more pressing question than it may appear. Knowing what type of book the *Écrits* is would provide us with a strategy for how one might go about reading – if 'reading' is even the most appropriate imperative in this context – this baroque, intimidating, ever-elusive text.

An unwieldy, conglomerate 'urtext', the *Écrits* might appear to have no clear precedent. There is, so it would seem, no collection of writings quite like it. For Élisabeth Roudinesco (2014: 99), however, certain other equivalents can be cited:

> *Écrits* is a summa that resembles both Saussure's *Course in General Linguistics* and Hegel's *Phenomenology of Spirit*….it functions as the founding Book of an intellectual system, which, depending on the era can be read, criticized, glossed or interpreted in many ways.

While there is certainly truth to this characterization, there are nonetheless a series of qualifications that should be made here in respect of Lacan's relation both to his own *Écrits* and to writing more generally.

In comparison to Freud's oeuvre that of course exists in the collected form of the *Standard Edition*, Lacan's written work exists in a far more scattered and diffuse state. Formally, this work occupies a place in the interstices between the performative and the textual, between an oral teaching and the written word. Lacan's oeuvre, we might say, resists collection, encapsulation, just as it appears to resist writing itself.

One initial response to the above question would simply be to say that *Écrits* is not a 'book' at all, at least not in the sense of being something an author produces with the express wish of being published, understood, or even read.

DOI: 10.4324/9781003264231-101

If we are to follow Roudinsco's (2014) account, it appears that François Wahl — former analysand of Lacan's and editor at Éditions du Seuil — played a more important role in motivating and conceiving the text than Lacan did himself. Prior to the eventual November 15, 1966 publication date of the *Écrits*, Lacan's writings were in a fragmentary state, appearing in select psychoanalytic journals that few could access. And as Roudinesco intimates, Lacan preferred it that way: 'Lacan feared plagiarism….he allowed the written trace of his spoken word to appear solely so as to have it circulate in the restricted milieu of Freudian institutions and journals' (p. 94). Staggered across various periods of his teaching and juxtaposed against the oral performance of his weekly seminar, the *Écrits* thus represented the slow and apparently unwilling accretion of Lacan's writings. As Bruce Fink (2004) speculates:

> Lacan may have only reluctantly agreed to publish his *Écrits* after Paul Ricoeur published his thick volume *De I' interpretation* translated as *Freud and Philosophy: An Essay on Interpretation*….Lacan certainly did not want Ricoeur to take credit for the return to Freud that Lacan himself had been championing. Lacan claims [in Seminar XVIII] that the texts in his *Écrits* had to be pried away from him. (p. 178)

Écrits then was reluctant text — or such is the myth that has grown around it — a much delayed 'book', published, largely, it would seem, at the urging of others, late in Lacan's life (he was 65). The factor of circumvention and delay seems telling. This consideration of deferred arrival — which contrasts so strongly to Lacan's frequent stress on anticipatory/pre-emptive modes of temporality in the *Écrits* — is in retrospect, indicative less of Lacan's reticence than — perhaps — of his *desire*.

Lacan had a famously low opinion of published writing as a means of disseminating psychoanalytic knowledge — hence his dismissive reference to '*poubellication*' (a contraction combining both garbage can and publication). In Seminar XX, during a session entitled 'The function of the written', Lacan offers a pronouncement on the *Écrits*:

> There is an anecdote to be related here, namely, that one day, on the cover of a collection I brought out — *poubellication*, as I called it — I found nothing better to write than the word *Écrits*.

> It is rather well known that those *Écrits* cannot be read easily. I can make a little autobiographical admission — that is exactly what I thought. I thought, perhaps it goes that far, I thought they were not meant be read. That's a good start.
>
> (Lacan, 1988, p. 26)

Commenting on this passage, Fink (2004) notes that Lacan never characterizes his seminars as *poubellication*, adding furthermore that while Lacan claimed to find no major errors in the published version of the seminars, such errors were to be found in the *Écrits*. Not only then is *Écrits* (as *poubellication*) apparently fit for the dustbin, it is also, effectively untitled: '*Écrits*' ('writings') is, one might argue, more a *description* than name, more the avoidance of a title than a title. Lacan's gesture here calls to mind Magritte's (1929) famous *La trahison des images,* proclaiming instead: *This is Not a Book.*

The medium of the spoken word, with all its lyricism, enunciative ambiguity, and prospective revelation, was, for Lacan, a far more suitable medium than the published word for the transmission of psychoanalysis. In the opening of *The Instance of the Letter* Lacan professes concern that what he presents 'might stray too far from speech, whose different measures are essential to the training I seek to effect' (412, 1). He goes on to announce that what we are about to read will be 'situated between writing and speech...halfway between the two' (412, 1). So whereas speech is associated with what is generative and valuable, writing, by contrast 'allows for...[a] kind of tightening up' which 'leave[s] the reader no way out than the way in, which I prefer to be difficult' (412, 2).

Elsewhere, Lacan (2018) similarly refers to the written text as something that 'can only be woven by forming knots' (Seminar XIX, May 10, 1972). Writing here is presented not merely as challenging – puzzling, enigmatic – but also as willfully obstructive. These comments connote as much a celebration of the spoken word as an aversion to what is written, a suspicious relation thus – to paraphrase Magritte – to *La trahison de l'écriture.* One is left with an image of the text as an intricately and deceptively designed labyrinth. This may, in fact, be one particularly apt way of describing 'writing in my [Lacan's] sense of the term' (412, 2), that is, as precisely *labyrinthine.* The *Écrits* then, following this thinking, is more maze than the book.

In this context, Jacques-Alain Miller (2010) states that Lacan's *Écrits* actually have a provocative function in relation to his seminar. The texts within *Écrits* don't provide us some synthesis of his oral teaching, but contain 'the waste' of his teaching: elements that he didn't discuss in public because of time restraints; and, more importantly, sensitive points to which his audience would have reacted with reluctance. Significant elements Lacan's audience could not easily accept, and which they would be treated as the waste of his discourse, were condensed, and send back to them in a written form. Thus considered, the *Écrits* constitute the symptom of the seminars.

This yields an interesting strategy for reading the *Écrits*. The *Écrits*, we might argue, is pivotal to Lacan's oeuvre, but provides us with a non-'Standard Edition' of his ideas. Through Lacan's kaleidoscopic text ideas get compressed, distorted, disguised, subjected to the multiple dreamwork operations that separate latent from manifest contents of Lacan's theoretical desire. Whereas the Freudian text is a prime instance of the secondary process – contradictions are avoided wherever possible, rational clarity is attained throughout – the Lacan text is more akin to the primary process, 'structured like a language', making use of all and every rhetorical or linguistic device possible.

Lacan's description of his own style as 'between writing and speech' provides us with a suggestion regards how we might go about commenting on his texts. Rather than attempting to fix the significations put in play by his style of 'spoken writing' we might seek to stress the multiple significations apparent therein, to invoke multiple voices speaking in – or through – what is presented on the page. Rather than the Rosetta Stone that enables the unlocking of other obscure writings, Lacan's *Écrits* is far more akin to a literary Babel. A text 'not meant to be read' could, after all, mean a text that *should be made to speak*, and speak in multiple voices.

Alternatively, a text 'not made to be read' might simply mean: not to be understood. Following this logic, the *Écrits* surely works less within the pragmatic goals of comprehension or rational intelligibility than as a means of inducing in us the perplexity and the suspension of knowledge that the analysand experiences in respect of the analyst and the analytic process itself. We might conclude that Lacan's assemblage of lectures-turned-writing is possibly less book than a psychoanalytic tool – a desire – or transference-engendering device. '[W]hen all is said and done', opined Anthony Wilden,

> even if the curious mixture of penetration, poetry, and willful obscurity in the *Écrits* seems designed to force the reader into a perpetual struggle of his own...perhaps there is a method [in this] madness. Lacan has always told his readers that they must, '*y mettre du sien*. (1968, p. 311)

The *Écrits*, in this further sense, is *not* a book: it is a type of infinite text; it does not end, it cannot be finished; it continues to escape the 'imaginarization' of our attempts at assimilation. We might then agree – at least in part – with Roudinesco's idea that

> the Écrits should be viewed less as a book than as the collection of a whole lifetime devoted to oral teaching. Hence the title Écrits, to signify trace, archive, something that does not come undone, does not vanish, cannot be stolen: a letter arriving at its destination. (2014, p. 96)

If it is not a book, then what is the *Écrits*? How to view this dense, obscure, assemblage of signifiers? As a doctrinal text, perhaps, the 'Talmud' of Lacan's return to Freud? A manual of Freudian-Lacanian clinical practice. As the constitution (or more likely in Lacan's case a 'de-constitution') of his own emerging Freudian school of psychoanalysis? A hystericizing object of desire and interpretative scrutiny? An extended manifesto against the ossified norms of the ego psychologists and the International Psychoanalytic Association, indeed, a diatribe against a degraded form of psychoanalysis? Lacan's *magnum opus*? Perhaps a (love) letter to psychoanalysis and those allegiant to Freud's own inaugural psychoanalytic desire? The Lacanian answer to this extended line of questioning must surely be: Yes.

References

Fink, B. (2004) *Lacan to the Letter: Reading Écrits closely*. Minneapolis: University of Minnesota Press.

Lacan, J. (1998) *The Seminar of Jacques Lacan, Book XX, Encore: On Feminine Sexuality, the Limits of Love and Knowledge, 1972-1973* (edited by Jacques-Alain Miller, translated by Bruce Fink). New York and London: W.W. Norton.

Lacan, J. (2018) *....or Worse: The Seminar of Jacques Lacan, Book XIX*. Cambridge: Polity Press.

Miller, J.-A. (2010) *Orientation Lacanienne – La vie de Lacan*. Unpublished Seminar. Available at: https://viedelacan.wordpress.com/2012/11/19/iv-lacan-contre-tous-et-contre-lacan/.

Ricoeur, P. (1965) *De l'interprétation*. Paris: Seuil. (Translated as *Freud and Philosophy: An Essay on Interpretation*, trans. D. Savage (New Haven: Yale University Press, 1970)).

Roudinesco, É. (2014) *Lacan: In Spite of Everything*. London: Verso.

Wilden, A. (1968) *Speech and Language in Psychoanalysis: Jacques Lacan*. Baltimore & London: The Johns Hopkins University.

1

LOGICAL TIME AND THE ASSERTION OF ANTICIPATED CERTAINTY: A NEW SOPHISM

Dominiek Hoens

Context

One can hardly overestimate the importance of *Logical Time* for Lacan's thought. Although this short text was originally published quite early in his career as an author (Lacan, 1945) and nearly a decade before the public Seminar started (1953), Lacan returned or alluded to it in almost every text in his *Écrits* and in each year of his teaching. Even the mere place of *Logical Time* within the corpus of the *Écrits* can be considered as an additional argument for paying special attention to it: the text is not included at the 'right,' that is chronological, place where one would expect it. Following the chronology of Lacan's writings, it should have been a part of Section II of the *Écrits*, and included amongst texts such as *Presentation on Psychical Causality* and *The Mirror Stage*. In the actual edition of the *Écrits*, however, it forms, together with *Presentation on Transference*, a separate Section III, where it takes on the function of mediating between earlier texts and later ones. Or, as Lacan put it in *Seminar II* (1954–1955), the sophism discussed in *Logical Time* is 'designed to draw out the distinction between language applied to the *imaginary*...and the *symbolic* moment of language, that is to say, the moment of the affirmation' (Lacan, 1991: 290–291; my italics).

The odd place of the text illustrates one of the text's major arguments: if we try to understand human subjectivity in its relation to time, relying on a plain, and simple chronological conception of time does not suffice. This questioning of chronology and the struggle to theorize another conception of time is already present in Freud's work. As has been well documented before (Forrester, 1990: 192–206), Freud frequently used the common German substantive and adjective, *Nachträglichkeit* and *nachträglich*, but in doing so, gave them a specific meaning. Freud used *Nachträglichkeit* to refer to the phenomenon that an event at a moment in time, $t2$, connects to a memory at $t1$ and turns it into a traumatic one as if it had always been traumatic. Yet, the

DOI: 10.4324/9781003264231-1

connection between the event (at *t2*) and the memory (at *t1*) is not established randomly, but through an association of representations (*Vorstellungen*), which allows one to consider the memory as *anticipating* the event that will turn it into a traumatic signifier. This active awaiting of a future event that will give a specific meaning to a (past) memory and, *vice versa*, the determination of the past through an event yet-to-come allows for a speculation on subjective time which is different than the usual conception of time as a unidirectional line, an arrow, onto which events can be precisely and unambiguously located. In this respect, *Logical Time* consists of an argument against chronology and in favor of a conception of time that can do justice to the strange idea that something may be chronologically posterior, yet logically anterior (and *vice versa*). More generally put, in *Logical Time* one finds the elements of a psychoanalytic theory of causal determination, far removed from the psychoanalytic cliché according to which infantile experiences determine adult psychic life.

The question of time never left Lacan, and tellingly the titles of his two last seminars – *The moment of concluding* (1977–1978) and *Topology and Time* (1978–1979), both unpublished – take up questions stemming from *Logical Time*. In between *Logical Time* and the very last phase of his teaching, Lacan had singled out *Nachträglichkeit* – often obfuscated by loose and differing English translations of Freud's works – as an important notion, which eventually leads to its inclusion as *après-coup* in Jean Laplanche and Jean-Bertrand Pontalis' classic vocabulary of psychoanalytic notions (Laplanche and Pontalis, 1968/1988: 111). While the authors do credit Lacan explicitly for drawing attention to Freud's thoughts on *Nachträglichkeit*, at one occasion he objected to not being credited (Lacan, 2006: 394).

This highlighting of an, at the time, obscure Freudian notion leads Lacan to consider the time of the subject as the *future anterior*, as that which 'will have been.' This implies that the subject is not to be considered as a substance unaffected by change, but as determined by time on a fundamental level. When Lacan famously stated that the subject is a lack-of-being (*manque-à-être*), this needs to be related to its temporal nature: the subject *is* not, for it has to realize itself through a dynamic of an anticipated future and a retroactive determination of its past.

Yet, in *Logical Time* one finds neither a reflection on trauma and its double inscription on a timeline nor much discussion of linguistic tenses. The article mainly consists of the analysis of a riddle that Lacan was told at a party in February 1935 (Roudinesco, 1999: 176). A prison warden summons three prisoners, shows them three white and two black disks and puts a white one on the back of each prisoner. The first one able to tell the color of the disk on his back, solely relying on logical reasoning, will be released. After some time looking at each other, the three prisoners all walk up to the warden and use an identical argument to explain why the color of the disk on their back is white. The question is: what is the argument made by the prisoners? The interest of *Logical Time* does not reside in Lacan's solution to this problem. Moreover, the '(new) sophism' as Lacan names it, can hardly be considered to be an original logical puzzle, since it is known in many variants – 'the muddy children,' 'three wise men,' etc. – which have been discussed in various sources and contexts, including mathematics (Bollobás, 1986: 25), epistemology (Fagin et al., 2003: 4–7), philosophy of mind (Floridi, 2005), and literature (Tahan, 1999: 220–226). The novelty of Lacan's discussion resides in his discrimination of three different times. Here, the word 'time' refers first and foremost to the three different ways the prisoners can possibly relate to the given situation. What at the end of the game is presented as a logical argument with a certain conclusion can, according to Lacan, only be reached if the prisoners go through three different, yet tightly interconnected 'moments of evidence,' three steps implying three different subjective positions and three different ways in which time is experienced. Lacan emphasizes that time, as something one can lose – as it is for human beings by definition finite – emerges from within the logical process and propels the latter to a conclusion.

This insight had consequences for the Lacanian view on psychoanalytic practice, in the sense that the psychoanalyst uses the time to make the analysand experience his existence as temporal. This eventually led Lacan to argue for the variable length of the psychoanalytic session. Deviating from the standard 40 or 50 minutes session allows, on one hand, the analyst to end the session at a moment that makes the last word(s) said to resonate with something that was said earlier and, on the other hand, it prevents certain analysands from dutifully sitting through the standard duration and makes them experience time as inherently limited by an end they cannot foresee.

Commentary on the text

161, 1

The introduction sketches the context within which *Logical Time* was published. The article was originally published in the first post-war issue of *Cahiers d'Art*, of which only a thousand copies were published. It contained contributions by, amongst others, Fernand Alquié, Gaston Bachelard, and Georges Bataille, lavishly illuminated with reproductions of works by, mainly, Pablo Picasso, Georges Braque, and Henri Matisse. Lacan highlights the significant dates on the cover of the issue, 1940–1944, one of the references to the Second World War in this article. As mentioned already above, the article's particular inclusion in the *Écrits* illustrates its main argument: the past anticipates a future within which it can retroactively find a place.

A logical problem

161, 2

A prison warden states he has to release one of three prisoners. In order to determine who will be set free, they are invited to participate in a test. The warden takes five disks, three white ones, and two black ones. Each prisoner gets a disk on his back, which means he cannot see this disk, yet the other prisoners can. The first to deduce the color of the disk on his back will be released. There are two important rules to the game the prisoners need to observe: they cannot communicate with each other, and the solution should be based on exclusively logical grounds, merely calculating the most probable case is not acceptable.

162, 1–2

Having agreed to participate, each of the prisoners has a white disk attached to his back, which means that no use is made of the black disks. How can the prisoners solve the problem?

The perfect solution

162, 3

After spending some time looking at each other, the three prisoners walk together to the door and give a similar explanation. Let us take the perspective of one prisoner, A. He makes the following hypothesis: 'I am black.' If this were the case, a second prisoner, B, could make the same hypothesis, 'I am black,' which would imply that the third prisoner, C, is facing two blacks and should leave at once. For, if C sees two black disks, he knows immediately that the disk he is wearing is white, as there are only two black disks in the game. As C does not leave immediately, B could conclude he is not wearing a black disk and walk to the door. Yet, as B is also not leaving, A can conclude that his initial hypothesis – 'I am black' – has been proven wrong. Hence he knows he is wearing a white disk and has a logical argument underpinning this knowledge.

Sophistic value of this solution

162, 4–5

Lacan relates the situation of the prison to the general political context within which the article was written. During the Second World War, a large part of France was occupied by the German national-socialists, a situation which made daily life prison like, with its specific rules and regulations, and its division between the imprisoned and the imprisoners. As the translator, Bruce Fink, notes in an editorial comment (2006, p. 782), this situation made Jean-Paul Sartre conclude that the French never were freer than under the German occupation. This paradoxical statement can be explained if one relates it to Sartre's conception of freedom. Freedom is not about the absence of external limitations to one's inclination to do this or that – it is obvious that under the occupation, as in a prison, a lot of things cannot be done or are difficult to do – freedom is a matter of choosing where and how one positions oneself with regards to a given situation and acting accordingly. A prison, therefore, does not limit one's freedom, but rather highlights it, forcing each prisoner individually to consider his position within it. This leads to dilemmas such as 'Will I completely identify with the role I am given as a prisoner or rather oppose it?' and 'Will I collaborate with those in power, or rather become a member of the resistance, or remain passive?' On an existential level, this means that one is always free in the sense that existence lacks any positive content except the one that is chosen.

Here, Lacan takes distance from Sartre, who wrote *Huis Clos (No Exit*, a play written in 1943 and first staged and published in 1944) which describes a situation similar to the one analyzed by Lacan: three people locked up and dependent on the others for determining their identity. Despite this similarity, Lacan does not think that being imprisoned actually helps one to discover freedom as the fundament of one's existence.

163, 1

Lacan states he tried out the game with various groups of people, 'appropriately chosen, qualified intellectuals,' which may have been the people he met at the meetings of the *Collège de Sociologie*, founded in 1937 by Georges Bataille, Roger Caillois, and Michel Leiris (Roudinesco, 1999: 136).

163, 2–3

Whatever the results obtained by an experimental testing and however the sinister situation of a prison may reflect (post-)war France, Lacan's sole interest resides in the logical value of the sophism. What was first presented to Lacan as a riddle – what argument do the prisoners use to conclude that the color of the disk on their back is white? – is now qualified as 'a sophism' for it includes the solution, which sounds acceptable, yet also raises questions regarding its soundness. Like any sophism, it contains a seemingly correct reasoning, whose conclusion is nonetheless not convincing. The problem with a sophism is thus that one is at the same time seduced by the argument *and* not able to accept the conclusion. It challenges our trust in reason and forces us to both look for the hidden mistake and to question the rules of sound logical reasoning. Lacan will take on the role of the logician – not unlike Edgar Allan Poe's detective Dupin in *The Purloined Letter* (see pp. 6–48) – and deal with both aspects, i.e. the possible objections and the logics used to reach the conclusion.

Discussion of the sophism

163, 4–5

The first objection to the sophism can be formulated as follows: if A is black (that is his hypothesis), then B and C have to remain undecided. For as soon as C (or B) would move (thinking the other sees one black and one white disk), B (or C) would have to doubt his conclusion based on C's (or B's) standing still. Hence A cannot conclude that his initial hypothesis is wrong and therefore he cannot determine the color of the disk on his back. Lacan replies to this objection that this is a logical supposition on behalf of A. The conclusion A derives from this supposition does not refer to B or C's actual departure (as the first prisoner who found out the color of his disk), but, indeed, on their mutual hesitation. Everyone has to hesitate, for only the situation of wearing a white disk and seeing two black disks on the other prisoners' backs allows one to know immediately one's own color and to leave prison at once. Therefore, B and C's indecision is not a counter-argument to A's reasoning, for the latter is precisely based on their standing still.

164, 1

Yet, the objection returns at the second stage of A's reasoning: the moment A has reached a conclusion, the other two prisoners, B and C, move as well, which should make A doubt whether his conclusion is valid.

164, 2

This second objection resembles the first one, yet the difference resides in the fact that the first objection concerned a hypothesis regarding B and C's thought process, whereas this second objection concerns B and C's real behavior; that is, they both move. This movement is actual and real, and therefore it does falsify A's conclusion, which, as we have seen, relies on B and C's standing still.

164, 3

Lacan repeats that all three prisoners are identical: they are in the same situation – seeing two white disks, wearing one on their back – and make the same reasoning ('if I were black, etc.'). Hence, the three prisoners reach the same conclusion, yet, need to doubt it as soon as they see the other two move as well. Having concluded, they all move towards the door, notice the others' movement too and stop, doubting the correctness of the conclusion ('I am white'). What will happen then is that A (and B and C) will go through the same reasoning again. The fact that B and C stopped and now hesitate allows him not only to make the same reasoning, but also to reach the same conclusion.

164, 4

Now the obvious question is whether this process of reasoning, concluding, moving, and halting will ever stop. Will the prisoners actually ever be certain about their conclusion and reach the door?

165, 1

Yes, after two halts, the three prisoners know for sure that they are wearing a white disk. Let us imagine that A would really be wearing a black disk and consider B's perspective. B has reached a conclusion, yet he sees C moving too. Which makes him doubt the validity of his conclusion. Yet, the fact that C stops as well, means that C does *not* see two blacks (A and B) – for when one sees two blacks, there is no doubt whatsoever possible –, therefore B is not wearing a black disk. If A is wearing a black disk, the other two prisoners only need one halt to gain certainty about their color. Therefore, the fact that B and

C halt a second time proves that A is not black, which allows him to conclude with certainty that he is wearing a white disk.

One can formulate the same idea in a slightly more abstract way: the halts objectify the hesitations A relies on his logical reasoning. As we have seen, A imputes a hesitation to C (he does not leave at once, for he does not see two blacks), and one to B (he sees C hesitating, yet still postpones his departure). These two hesitations, which were merely supposed and imputed by A to B and C, become subsequently objectified (in the sense of a positive datum one can actually see) in the two halts. In the first halt, C's hesitation becomes evident (he does not see two blacks), in the second one B's doubt (he can derive from C's hesitation that the latter does not see two blacks, yet B still doubts).

165, 2

If one includes the two halts or 'suspensive scansions' as Lacan names them, in the sophism, it shows the rigor of a sound logical reasoning.

Value of the suspended motions in the process

165, 3

Is it, however, correct to integrate the two 'suspended motions' into the sophism?

165, 4

Here, Lacan starts an argument in favor of the view that the suspended motions do *not* belong to the logical process. It is only after a conclusion is reached, made clear by the prisoner's moving, that the two suspensive scansions take place. As such they do not add anything to the logical process itself.

165, 5–6

The suspended motions may be crucial to end the game, but they do not verify a hypothesis, and thus are not internal to the logical process. Given the fact that there are three prisoners, three white and two black disks, three combinations are possible: two blacks, one white; one black, two whites; three whites. The prisoners immediately see that the first option (two blacks, one white) is not the case.

The possibility of choosing between the other two options arrives with the data provided by the suspended motions. In that sense, the halts can be qualified as unintentional signals, for the prisoners are not allowed to communicate about what they see. The fact that they halt, tells every participant something about what the others are actually seeing (either one black and one white disk, or two white disks). But, again, despite their importance, Lacan emphasizes that the suspended motions are not part of the logical process.

166, 1

The reason why Lacan rejects the idea that the suspended motions would be about the verification of a logical process (and are as such to be considered as part of it), is to be found in his idea of a logic including time, which cannot and should not be conceived of in spatial terms. Hence, the idea that our prisoners perform a logical reasoning, which results in a hypothesis to be verified by the suspended motions, misses a crucial aspect.

166, 2

Although *Logical Time* does not refer to other versions of the test the prisoners undergo – the muddy children, three wise men, etc. – here, it is helpful to point out the difference with Lacan's version. In Malba Tahan's story 'In Black and White' (1999: 220–226), King Cassim the Uncertain wants to choose the best amongst three princes courting his daughter, Princess Dahize. He is afraid of making the wrong choice and asks his daughter who she prefers, a question she responds to by affirming that her preference would be for the most intelligent of the princes. As the three princes all seem to be very, yet equally, intelligent, the king decides to follow the advice of a dervish, namely to subject them to a test. This test is the same as the one our *Logical Time* prisoners need to undergo, with one major difference: they need to answer the question one after the other. The first two princes give the incorrect answer, which allows the third prince to answer the question correctly (and marry Dahize). His reasoning goes as follows: as the first prince answered incorrectly, he was not facing two blacks (for this would have excluded the wrong answer), and the fact that the second competitor could not come up with the correct answer, this proves he made the wrong choice between two remaining options, one black and two white disks, or three white disks (that is, he opted for the former). The errors of his fellow contestants lead to the certainty with which the third prince can determine the color of the disk on his back.

The difference between Lacan's argument and the one presented in Tahan's story is striking. In *Logical Time* all the prisoners are in the same situation, whereas in the story it is clear that only the third prince can reach a logically sound conclusion, basing his reasoning on the objective fact of the mistakes the two others make. In that sense, the errors belong to the situation the third prince is in and function as unintentional signals – they too are not allowed to communicate – of what they are able to see.

That is why Lacan emphasizes the particularity of his version and differentiates it from any spatialized understanding of it. A spatialized conception of the logical process solely relies on what is seen by the prisoners: the white disks on the other prisoners' backs and the consecutive suspended motions occurring later in the process. Tahan's and many other versions are in that sense spatialized, that they stage a situation within which one prisoner (prince, wise man, or child, etc.) can be absolutely certain about the answer to the question asked. As long as they are able to perform basic logical operations, they can 'see' the solution clearly. Lacan relates this immediate clarity to the eternal prestige of the forms of classical logic: no time is needed to go from a certain set of premises to a certain conclusion. Classical logic deals with forms, which consist of the right connections between premise and conclusion, and which as such can be seen 'at once.' Human beings may need time to go through the steps of a logical reasoning, but this time is not inherent to logic itself, which deals with eternally and universally correct forms of thought.

Therefore Lacan will continue to look for the sophistic aspect of his *Logical Time* argument. If one integrates the suspended motions as 'data' into the process, as facts the prisoners can rely on, then the reasoning is ultimately correct and in accordance with logical rules. Yet, this approach misses the sophistic character of the reasoning, for how did the prisoners, first of all, come to a conclusion? How can one possibly reach a conclusion (which can be verified afterwards), when facing two white disks and being asked to find out the color of one's own disk?

166, 3–7

Like each text in the *Écrits*, *Logical Time* was edited by Lacan before inclusion. Yet, this article is probably one of the most heavily redrafted chapters, quantitatively (see Porge (1989: 203–211) for a list of modifications) and qualitatively. With this, we mean that in this case Lacan did not simply rephrase sentences or reorganized paragraphs, but added expressions and words only used later in his work. In this paragraph we find a striking example of this, as the original 'the function of the phenomena here contested' (Lacan, 1945: 36) is replaced by 'the coming into play as *signifiers* of the phenomena here contested' (my italics). The phenomena here referred to are the two halts. Calling them 'suspended motions' indicates one quality that Lacan will later (in the 1950s) attribute to the signifier: it retroactively bestows meaning onto the signifiers that came before. A signifier does not mean anything in of by itself, it is only through its combination with other signifiers that meaning occurs. As this combination may be endless in principle, each signifier can function as a temporary endpoint in the ongoing process of signifying. Relating this to the process the prisoners go through, this means that the halts are *interruptions*, which do not verify or make visible an earlier hypothesis, but refer to the steps in the logical reasoning made before.

In these particularly dense paragraphs, Lacan prepares the second part of the article. The first part consists of a detailed commentary on the sophism, its logic, and the possible objections, the second part focuses on time as emerging within the logical process.

The suspended motions do not add data to what one can see at the beginning. If it were merely about choosing amongst three possibilities (two black + one white, one black + two whites, or three whites), the first one can be ruled out from the start and the second one gets excluded by the first halt. This way of looking at the logical process amounts to, indeed, *looking* from an outside perspective at the problem. Yet, there are *two* suspended motions, which relates to the fact that the prisoners included in their argument two hypotheses: 1) A thinks he may be black (hypothesis 1), and 2) A thinks that he is wearing a black disk and that B may think the same (hypothesis 2). This means we actually have three steps in the logical process: hypothesis 1, hypothesis 2, and the conclusion (based on the consecutive denials of both hypotheses). These three steps correspond to three 'times of possibility' inherent to the logical process.

166, 8

These three instances of time need to be qualified in further detail and explained through the logical form within which they appear.

The modulation of time in the sophism's movement: the instant of the glance, the time for comprehending, and the moment of concluding

167, 1

There are three evidential moments (*moments de l'évidence*), which should not be considered as chronologically succeeding each other. Despite the fact that time plays in each of these moments a different role, which separates one from the others and makes them discontinuous, the moments can be considered as a musical modulation, that is changing from one key to another. In that sense, the three times identified in *Logical Time* constitute a development in which each time implies the other and is resorbed by it. Lacan's description sounds thoroughly Hegelian: one moment (of evidence) is different from another moment, yet it can only find and 'be' itself *via* this other 'modulation of time.'

The genesis of these moments in the logical movement operated by the three prisoners can be understood when formalized in three rigorous statements.

I Being opposite two blacks, one knows that one is a white.

167, 2–4

Taking into account the facts of the situation, this statement can only be true. One can see and one knows this immediately. Yet, there is some sort of subjectivity involved – 'one' – and the logical implication (two blacks: one white) can be reformulated as the connection between a protasis and an apodosis, between the condition and its consequence.

These paragraphs suggest a fundamental relation between subjectivity and time. The subjectivity may be considered as minimal – every*one* knows that... –, yet this one needs the time of *the instant of the glance* in order to connect protasis (condition) to apodosis (consequence). Although factually excluded, the reformulation of this statement as a conditional one – *If one...then...* – starts the logical movement as it suggests that one can start a process of reasoning *with* a hypothesis that may lead to a conclusion.

II Were I a black, the two whites that I see would waste no time realizing that they are whites.

168, 1

The second moment of evidence can only occur if prisoner A (and B and C) adds something to the facts of the situation, to wit the hypothesis 'Were I a

15

black.' In that case, the two others need some time to deduce that they are white, a conclusion that is, as we have seen, based on the other's standing still. This time is *the time for comprehending*, during which the other two prisoners make use of the other's standing still to interpret it as a *hesitation*, that is a standing still which means that the other is not facing two blacks.

168, 2

Lacan raises the following question: how long does the time for comprehending take? If the others are facing a black disk and a white disk, they may possibly find out their color just as quickly as when seeing two black disks, which would reduce *the time for comprehending* to *the instant of the glance*. And how can the two reciprocal subjects, B and C, ever reach a conclusion, for they are in exactly the same situation and are, from A's point of view, totally dependent on each other's hesitation. This mirroring of each other will however get surpassed by the third time that is accompanied by a different form of subjectivity.

> III *I hasten to declare myself a white, so that these whites, whom I consider in this way, do not precede me in recognizing themselves for what they are.*

168, 3 – 169, 1

The time for comprehending finds its conclusion in the form of a judgment, an *assertion* about oneself. This judgment is based on the hypothesis made in the time for comprehending and which involved the others as each other's mirror image. Both the comprehending and the reflexive subjectivity involved are left behind the moment the subject realizes he is lagging behind the other two, for they do not need to make the supplementary hypothesis of being black. If the others (B and C) really see a white and a black (A), and yet, they are still standing still, then A should haste himself to arrive at the conclusion that he is white. The haste is not motivated by the fear of losing the game or other external circumstances, but emerges *within* the logic of the reasoning: if the hypothesis is truly the case, then A, about to reach the conclusion that he is white, should speed up and actually conclude his reasoning, for the others do not need to make this hypothesis and are ahead of A in understanding the situation.

One should note here that A's conclusion (being white) negates the hypothesis (being black), which may in retrospect – once the conclusion has been reached – make the haste seem unnecessary. Yet, Lacan adds another important argument in favor of a conclusion made in haste. If A does not conclude and lets the other proceed he will no longer be able to determine his color. For what to conclude when the others would actually precede him: is their moving proof of the correctness of the hypothesis (A = black) or rather effect of a swiftness A lacks (implying A, like B and C, is white)? Put differently, as A's conclusion of the logical reasoning is entirely dependent on B and C standing still, he needs to conclude before they move; as soon as they move the conclusion no longer holds and the time for comprehending loses its end and meaning.

As we have seen, Lacan argues that the three times are different from each other, yet dialectically connected. This becomes more clear in the movement from *the time for comprehending* to *the moment of concluding*. The comprehending of (meditation or speculation on) the situation does result in a conclusion, yet only when the subject is able to grasp the certitude of its conclusion in a moment of haste. Despite its difference with the time for comprehending, both qua subjectivity and qua modality of time involved, *only* the moment of concluding can give meaning to the time for comprehending, *because* it gives an end to it.

Moreover, having concluded the subject will be able to understand the two subsequent halts as proof for the correctness of his reasoning and conclusion. He who did not conclude will not participate in the 'suspended motions' and cannot learn anything from them.

In the next section, Lacan will discuss the conclusion again in relation to its verification in the two suspended motions.

Temporal tension in the subjective assertion and its value manifested in the demonstration of the sophism

169, 2–3

Lacan focuses on the third statement as an assertion that concerns the subjectivity of the one who formulates it. He repeats that the conjunction of the hypothesis with a consequence motivates the subject to reach a conclusion. This conclusion is based on the reasoning made in the time for comprehending, yet the latter would never find an end if the subject were not seized by the fear that the others will precede him (and make any possible conclusion impossible). This fear, however, is not (only) to be understood as a psychological emotion, but as 'the ontological form of anxiety.' The qualification as ontological reminds one of Martin Heidegger's analysis of *Dasein* in the context of an exploration of the intimate relation between being and time in *Being and Time* (Heidegger, 1927/2000).

The similarities between Heidegger's argument and Lacan's commentary on the sophism are striking. According to Heidegger human beings are not to be understood as subjects who find themselves separate from and in front of a world constituted by objects. That is why he introduces the notion of human beings qua *Dasein*, that is as a being-there that is always already thrown into the world. *Dasein* finds itself in relation to others (*Mitsein*) and as having access to a meaningful world. This being part of a pre-constituted world gets put into question when this world appears as strange and uncanny, when the usual and meaningful organization of our world is suspended. Whereas *Dasein* as being-there is situated and can be analyzed *spatially*, the moment of anxiety reveals *temporality* at a more fundamental level. Meaning and meaningful relations are

17

not just there, but are thoroughly marked by the anticipation of them. We continuously anticipate meaning as it is hardly ever totally evident. Heidegger's crucial point here is that this anticipation refers back to *Dasein*'s fundamentally temporal way of being as it anticipates its own death. Being-there is a being-towards-death (*Sein-zum-Tode*) and death is that one event one can both be certain of and one is unable to give meaning to or to know what it is. This does not mean that one finds in *Sein und Zeit* a reflection on the mortality of all living beings and on human beings as that species that knows it is doomed to die sooner or later. The anxiety Heidegger refers to is not the anxiety for one's own disappearance in death. That sort of meditation would give too much positivity to death. The anxiety Heidegger discusses – and which Lacan calls 'ontological anxiety' – does not arise in life-threatening situations, but when our anticipation of meaning fails. Precisely because this anticipation fails it becomes clear to us how we are always already in the mode of anticipation, of *being* beyond a mere coincidence with the present. This continuous ec-stasy can ultimately be referred to our *being-towards-death*. That is why, according to Heidegger, anxiety can give way to resoluteness (*Entschlossenheit*), a term whose meanings refer to both 'to loose' or 'to free (from)' and 'to be resolved' or 'to be set (on).' This resoluteness emerges when one is free from pre-existing meaningful scenarios and interpretations and is able to grasp the future as an open possibility. When acting in resoluteness, I anticipate the future not as a meaning, there to discover, but as an open possibility. That is why anxiety does not have an object, for in anxiety *Dasein* discovers the absence of (sufficient) ground for its own acts and interpretations, and understands its being as thoroughly marked by time, that is as *Entwurf*, as a project(ion) onto an open, indeterminate future.

This digression on Heidegger – whose philosophy became known and discussed in France in the Thirties – shows the existentialist-phenomenological background to Lacan's analysis of the sophism. In both authors, we find a similar move from spatiality to temporality, from being caught in an inter-subjective logic of interpretation to discovering the task of freeing oneself from it and choosing one's destiny in the absence of any guarantee or ultimate meaning. Whereas the *logic* may be Hegelian – one time gets succeeded and taken up by another one – the *time* involved is a temporality which can only be experienced *subjectively* and which does not occur necessarily. This time emerges within a logical process, yet cannot be reduced to it.

170, 1

This leads Lacan to name the third statement a '*subjective assertion*' involving a knowing subject that is *personal*. Differing from the other two subjectivities, the impersonal 'one' of the first statement (I) and the 'undefined reciprocal subject' involved in the second one (II), this subject is an '*I*' (*je*). This personal subject (*je*) may be different from the other two forms of subjectivity, but it still has to assume these two other forms as leading up to the third moment of a personal and hasty conclusion. This also implies that concluding *requires* a

preceding time for comprehending, and its integration in the conclusion. Put differently, concluding is not about blindly jumping to a conclusion, but grasping the right moment when the time for comprehending reaches its end.
170, 2

The 'one' of 'one knows that…' can be anything that functions as the subject of a statement; the knowledge could be attributed to God, a table, or a wash-basin. The second form of subjectivity can be qualified as specular. The one prisoner functions as the mirror image of the other, to the point that they are, in A's reasoning, indistinguishable from each other. As Lacan had explained before (1938/2007: 36–45) this reciprocity is required for any form of subjectivity (different from the generic 'one') to appear. In that sense jealousy, competition and rivalry contain both the reciprocity (and, hence, the disappearance of my 'self') and the constitution of an 'I' to the extent that jealousy concerns an object that is lost, as the other is supposed to possess it. Via the lost object, the object of rivalry and competition, an 'I' is formed as different from the other, my rival. Mapped onto *Logical Time*, this means that the third form of subjectivity arises out of competition and emerges as the 'I' who is lagging one time or one step behind.

The last sentence is of particular importance to Lacan's theoretical project in general. As we have seen, Lacan draws heavily on Heidegger's analysis of *Dasein* and its French reception in the works of Kojève and Sartre. Although the sophism can be read as an existentialist parable, a moral tale describing how human subjectivity needs to free itself from a determination by others ('*L'enfer, c'est les autres*' – 'Hell is other people' – as Sartre famously wrote in the afore-mentioned *Huis Clos*), Lacan rather emphasizes the *logical* form of the subjective 'I,' and qualifies this form as *essential* instead of existential. This anticipates Lacan's later game theoretical and other mathematical approaches to the subject, that is as an x that can be calculated. In that sense, *Logical Time* presents the essential (read: universal and timeless) form of the psychological 'I,' instead of exclusively focussing on the temporality and nothingness characteristic of subjectivity. It is only through a long structuralist and game-theoretical phase (the 1950s to mid-1960s) that Lacan will consider a non-essential, non-universalizable, singular (or existential) element around which human subjectivity gravitates, first as object *a*, later as *not-all* (Hoens, 2019a).
170, 3

The external observer is of course unaware of the division into three mo-ments of evidence and cannot tell whether the subject has seized the moment of concluding. One can imagine that one of the prisoner's simply walks, along with the other two, towards the door thinking he is wearing a black disk. The only thing one can predict is that there can only be one prisoner arguing that he is black – for, as we have seen, one black equals two whites.
170, 4

The assertive judgment (formulated in the moment of concluding) equals an act. Lacan relates this to modern thought, which may refer to Descartes for whom the subject is derived from thought (I think, therefore I am), or to Kant's argument in *Critique of Pure Reason* (1781/1999) that different forms of judgment consist in *actively* bringing together sense data and the categories of understanding, or to existentialist philosophy (see above).

The subject's judgment is an act to the extent that if one were to stick strictly to the facts present within the situation, one can never conclude anything. That is why Lacan refers to the logical time argument as a sophism: logic does not suffice to reach a certain, inevitable conclusion. In order to arrive at a conclusion, one has to make a judgment for which there are good reasons, yet not sufficient ones. The certainty of the conclusion is anticipated, or wagered upon, and only this active anticipation makes it possible to find out later, because of the subsequently suspended motions, the correctness of one's conclusion. As we have seen, *Logical Time* moves from the impersonal one to the reciprocal, interchangeable subjectivity in order to arrive at the personal subjectivity of the 'I.' The latter moment gets desubjectified again after the moment of concluding, when one gains an *impersonal* certainty about one's conclusion, for, as we have seen, two suspended motions equals three whites for and only for those who acted for fear that the lagging behind might engender error (170, 1).

171, 1

The first suspended motion corresponds to the time for comprehending and objectifying it. Initially, the time for comprehending was part of A's speculation on the significance of the others' standing still. Now the standing still can objectively be understood as a hesitation or a time needed by the others to reflect upon the situation. This proves that each of them needs *more* time than the instant of the glance (when facing two blacks) and that *their* time for comprehending will end again in *my* moment of concluding.

171, 2

Although doubt may have been the starting point of a modern, Cartesian idea of subjectivity, Lacan argues that the logical value of the assertive judgment (*I hasten myself to declare...*) depends less on doubt than on the anticipated certainty inherent to it. Before a conclusion can be doubted, one first needs to conclude in haste and to anticipate certainty.

171, 3–4

Because the three prisoners hesitate, even an outside observer is allowed to think they doubt their initial conclusion. Yet, what this doubting means and what the collective hesitation is proof of, depends on each individual participant's assessment of the situation. Of crucial importance is the hasty conclusion preceding doubt: if one did not conclude or came to the erroneous conclusion that one is black – and made one's own identity entirely depend on what the others do (see the second moment of evidence) –, one will misunderstand the others' hesitation as (further) proof that one is black. As Lacan underlines, one needs to have subjectively *appropriated* the conclusion, instead of letting it depend on what the others do (moving), in order to be able to doubt and reaffirm it in the first suspended motion.

172, 1– 173, 1

The second suspended motion objectifies the moment of concluding and only lasts an *instant*. As soon as one sees the other two hesitate again one should be absolutely certain that they are not seeing a black and a white, and therefore conclude one is white as well. This is also clear to an external observer and *a fortiori* to the prisoner who may at first have thought of himself as wearing a black disk. That is why at the second scansion the assertive judgment gets desubjectified 'to the utmost' (*au plus bas*): it is clear for all and everyone that the three prisoners have white disks on their backs. The third moment of evidence (see (III)) formulated a subjective assertion that can here be replaced by the desubjectified, that is objectively true insight: 'One must know that one is a white when the others have hesitated twice in leaving.' Therefore, it is possible that one (but only one) prisoner accompanies the two others, merely copying their moving and hesitating, and is finally able to gain the same certainty about his color.

The truth of the sophism as temporalized reference of oneself to another: anticipating subjective assertion as the fundamental form of a collective logic

173, 2–3

Truth, according to Lacan, depends on a tendency that aims at it, which in *Logical Time* emerges as the haste with which one concludes. Therefore, truth is not a-temporal or eternal, but develops itself in a (logical) process. Contrary to what Hegel argued, truth does not arise out of a long history of errors, but precedes error and can only occur via an act. Error avoids the act, remains inert, and can only be corrected when it follows and adjusts itself to the insight deduced from the two suspended motions or 'truth's conquering initiative,' as Lacan prefers to name it.

173, 4–6

We have seen how truth needs different steps and the assertive judgment in particular in order to become evident. Here the question raised by Lacan concerns the specific relation this subjective 'I,' capable of the assertive judgment, entertains with the reciprocal subjectivity discovered in the preceding time for comprehending. As explained before, the anteriority of the time for comprehending can only be understood logically, that is as a necessary part of the moment of concluding, which is the time for comprehending's end. As such the moment of concluding only lasts an instant, 'the instant of the glance.' This also implies that the 'I,' discovered through the hypothesis of being different from the others (*if I were a black...*), is not so much a solitary and heroic individual following his unique course, but an 'I' that not only depends on others to find its own identity, but adapts to the common measure of the time for comprehending. Only if some (2) or all (3) prisoners make the same reasoning and take an equal quantity of time to arrive at a conclusion, only then some (2) or all (3) may get to the truth.

174, 1–2

The emphasis on the dependence of others in order to arrive at the right conclusion regarding the color of the disk on one's back leads Lacan to introduce the notion of 'collectivity.' Adding one person to two others does not only change it quantitatively, but also qualitatively, as three make up a collectivity. A collectivity is a group defined by (1) a limited number of people and (2) reciprocal relations.

Lacan's interest in the dialectic between a group and its individual members was provoked during a five-week stay in England in September 1945 (Roudinesco, 1999: 172). In a text, discussing the work of, amongst others, Wilfred Bion and John Rickman, he praises English psychiatry and how it managed to treat large groups of patients during the Second World War (Lacan, 1947/2001). What interested Lacan, in particular, was the idea that a group does not need to depend on a leader or an ideal in order to show some organization and coherence. Freud had discussed this issue before in his *Group Psychology* (Freud, 1921/1981), although he made the horizontal, mutual identifications and emotional ties depend on a logically anterior and more important vertical identification with a leader or more abstract ideal. While Lacan, like Freud, is not interested in the *generality* of a collection of an indefinite number of people, he disagreed with Freud regarding the formation of groups. Lacan questioned the necessity of a 'point' (leader, ideal,…) outside of, yet required for any mutual, 'horizontal' identification (Hoens, 2019b). Although *Logical Time*'s sophism contains a prison warden, who has the power to set prisoners free and distributes the disks, the prisoners' reasoning, which determines their identity, does not include any reference to him and he remains entirely outside the game played. Yet, one could speculate that the prison warden anticipates the Lacanian Other in its dimension of distributing places and identities in a symbolic order (Hook, 2013: 126–128). At this stage of Lacan's thought, however, the emphasis is on mutual identification between members of a collectivity who do not identify with a particular trait incarnated by a leader or with an ideal as a pre-existing signifier that would be the condition of possibility of any mutual recognition. An emphasis which should be related to Lacan's basic assumption of the social decline of the paternal 'imago' (Lacan, 1938/2007: 60) and the exploration of an (inter)subjectivity without a 'head,' or 'acephalous' as his friends at the *Collège de Sociologie* put it.

174, 3

In principle the prisoner's sophism can be applied to larger groups, the only requirement being that the number of black disks should equal the number of members of the group minus one (three subjects-two black disks, four subjects-three black disks, etcetera). Yet, one can easily imagine that the temporality discovered whilst discussing the sophism with three prisoners may become less evident when applying the test to a larger group. Even with a relatively small group of 15 prisoners, it is hard to imagine prisoners going through all the steps of the reasoning and, after concluding, to gain the de-subjectified certainty of being white at suspended motion number 14. Lacan may have been able to demonstrate how classical 'spatial' logic should be supplemented by a differentiating between three logical 'times,' it remains hard to see how the notion of collectivity can become part of logic, or, *vice versa*, how a collectivity can be approached from a logical point of view.

174, 4–6

These closing paragraphs give a particular twist to the collectivity introduced above. From a definition of collectivity as a group containing a *definite* number of members who discover their identity in a logical process involving mutual identification, here Lacan moves to the *general* logic sustaining 'man.' Throughout history, man has been defined in various ways, and Lacan mentions one of the most famous: man is a rational animal (Aristotle, 1995: 1741; for an overview of other definitions of man, see Clemens, 2009: 84). Defining man implies that one knows and applies the distinctive feature that distinguishes man from anything non-man. This positive feature, however, can only be used to define mankind on the basis of an anterior exclusion: (1) A man knows what is not a man. In the second step (2), similar to the time for comprehending, men mutually recognize each other as men. This recognition needs to be assumed and subjectified in the third step: (3) I declare myself to be a man for fear of being convinced by men that I am not a man. With this Lacan suggests that humanity as the collectivity of men is not a given but relies on a complex dialectic involving exclusion, mutual recognition, and a subjective or 'hasty' identification. All men may think they are men, yet this comfortable certainty is only gained on the basis of an (unconscious) logical process. Beyond the common self-evidence of being a man, one does not find a realm of animal or barbaric drives, but a collective logic that creates the possibility of being a man. This is succinctly formulated in footnote 6 to the text (175): the collective is nothing but the subject of the individual. This statement, added in 1966, is influenced by Lévi-Straussian anthropology and game theory, to which Lacan was introduced by his friend Georges Théodule Guilbaud. Although Lacan's remarks on this issue, both in *Logical Time* and in the contemporaneous *Number Thirteen* (1946/2001) are minimal, they still allow us to conclude that the collective or a collection needs to be distinguished from a class. Whereas the latter determines its elements via the external criterion of either possessing a particular quality or not, a collection is formed by an internal process of comparison which leads to either in- or exclusion. The excluded is *operative* as the element that allows the other elements to mutually recognize each other as identical. The result is a set of, in one respect, identical elements, yet without one's knowing precisely the quality that makes them belong to it. It is only known that they are alike and that they differ from the element(s) excluded from the collection. On that note, *Logical Time* not only anticipates Lacan's future reflections on time and temporality, but announces his definition of the unconscious as the discourse of the Other: any imaginary identity is made possible by an unconscious and thoroughly social symbolic order governed by logical operations.

Conclusion: no subject without an object

The three logical formulae, corresponding to the three times Lacan differentiates, imply three different forms of subjectivity: an impersonal 'one,' a personal 'ego,' and a subjective 'I' (*je*). Additionally, Lacan points out how the latter time concludes the logical process, yet precedes, logically speaking, the two earlier times. The last time, i.e. the moment of concluding, is anterior to the other times as their final cause, reducing them to necessary yet 'sublatable' steps in a logical process. The conclusion, therefore, both ends and motivates the entire reasoning. To the philosophically informed this cannot but sound Hegelian and, indeed, Lacan's logical time argument is cloaked in dialectical language and reads like a 'ruse of reason' unbeknownst to the prisoners involved. The crucial difference, however, resides in how the 'objective' logical statements, not unlike speech balloons floating above the prisoners' heads, are turned into subjective statements. The three formulae may very well create space for the formation of three different forms of subjectivity – one, ego, and I – but the dialectical movement from one time to the other is not without an objective supplement. Shifting from the instant of the glance (1st time) to the time for comprehending (2nd time) is only possible if one *adds* to the visible givens of the situation the hypothesis of carrying an odd, black disk; and turning this second time into the moment of concluding (3rd time) involves the *exclusion* of the hypothetical identification with this object. Therefore, as much as the logical time argument emphasizes the logico-linguistic determination of the subject – the 'thing' that is being spoken about, even before it can and is allowed to speak (cf. the prisoners' silence up and until the moment they can present their conclusion) – one should not overlook the presence of a virtual object, appearing at the junction between two consecutive logical statements (from the first to the second, and from the second to the third).

However, referring to the second formula – 'Were I a black, etc.' – one may object that this object (the black disk), *qua* hypothesis is part of the logical reasoning and therefore nothing more than a logical element. To answer this objection, one only has to refer to the shift from the second to the third formula, which involves time constraints and is based on the insight that one can conclude *nothing* from sticking to this hypothesis of carrying a black disk. The moment of concluding is an anxious moment in which one surmises what the implications of being the object of the others' gaze are. In order to conclude, one has to leave behind what one hypothetically *is* in order to *become* the subject of the third, concluding formula. Becoming, indeed, is here the adequate word, for while the conclusion may eventually involve a substantial, socially recognized individuality, its basis (its *subject*) is logically speaking insufficient.

This explains why Lacan repeatedly stressed the subject's anticipatory nature: it appears in the mode of the future anterior ('will have been') and is not entirely grounded upon a watertight logical movement from one proposition to the other. Here, the suggestion is that the subject qua gap in the logical process only gains an identity through the exclusion of the objective position in the time for comprehending. Or, put into logical terms, the *implicans* of the hypothesis 'Were I a black…' is not negated by a *modus tollens*. This would mean that if the *implicatum* is false, then its antecedent, the *implicans* ('Were I a black') is also false; but that is not what happens (the other prisoners do *not* leave). The conclusion of being white is not the result of a *modus tollens*, but is arrived at by choosing the third proposition. This proposition is based upon the second one, but not in any logically strict way. The hypothesis of the second proposition, therefore, may be considered as irrelevant as soon as one has reached the moment of concluding, yet it does not get negated *within* the logical process leading up to the conclusion. The subject, emerging in the moment of concluding, may coincide with the gap in the logical process – the anticipatory leap from comprehending to concluding – yet the hypothetical object can only be *excluded from* and not negated within the logical process. Therefore, (1) to the extent that the subject is the unconscious (because repressed) gap in a logical process, and (2) because the latter does not negate the object position that the time for comprehending starts with, the subject's logical identity – the place it occupies in the third formula – is and continues to be accompanied by an excluded object.

Acknowledgements

For the pleasure of discussing *Logical Time*, at different times and places, I wish to thank David Blomme, Andrew Cutrofello, Lucca Fraser, Lieven Jonckheere, Alexi Kukuljevic, Eric Laurent, Clare Murphy, Ed Pluth, Erik Porge, Jacky Santy, and David Schrans.

References

Aristotle (1995) Nicomachean Ethics. In Barnes, J. (ed.) *The Complete Works of Aristotle: Volume Two*. Princeton, NJ: Princeton University Press, pp. 1729–1867.

Bollobás, B. (ed.) (1986) *Littlewood's Miscellany*. Cambridge: Cambridge University Press.

Clemens, J. (2009) Man Is a Swarm Animal. In Hoens, D., Jöttkandt, S. and Buelens, G. (eds.) *The Catastrophic Imperative: Subjectivity, Time and Memory in Contemporary Thought*. Basingstoke: Palgrave Macmillan, pp. 83–113.

Fagin, R., Halpern, J., Moses, Y. and Vardi, M. (2003) *Reasoning About Knowledge*. Cambridge, MA/London: MIT Press.

Floridi, L. (2005) Consciousness, Agents and the Knowledge Game. *Minds and Machines*. 15, 3-4, 415–444.

Forrester, J. (1990) *The Seductions of Psychoanalysis: Freud, Lacan and Derrida*. Cambridge: Cambridge University Press.

Freud, S. (1921/1981) *Group Psychology and the Analysis of the Ego*. Trans. James Strachey, *Standard Edition*, vol. XVIII. London: The Hogarth Press, pp. 67–143.

Heidegger, M. (1927/2000) *Being and Time*. New York: Happer & Row.

Hoens, D. (2019a) The Logic of Lacan's Not-All. *Crisis & Critique*, 6, 1, 130–155. Available at: https://crisiscritique.org/april2019/hoens.pdf.

Hoens, D. (2019b) Jacques Lacan. In Stavrakakis, Y. (ed.) *Routledge Handbook of Psychoanalytic Political Theory*. New York: Routledge, pp. 44–56.

Hook, D. (2013) Towards a Lacanian Group Psychology: The Prisoner's Dilemma and the Trans-subjective. *Journal for the Theory of Social Behaviour*. 43, 115–132.

Kant, I. (1781/1999) *The Critique of Pure Reason*. Trans. Paul Guyer. Cambridge: Cambridge University Press.

Lacan, J. (1938/2007) Les Complexes Familiaux dans la Formation de l'Individu. *Autres Écrits*. Paris: Seuil, pp. 23–84.

Lacan, J. (1945/2006) Le Temps Logique et l'Assertion de Certitude Anticipée: Un Nouveau Sophisme. *Cahiers d'Art*. First post-war issue: 1940–1944, pp. 32–42.

Lacan, J. (1945/2007) Logical Time and the Assertion of Anticipated Certainty: A New Sophism. In Lacan, J. (ed.) *Écrits: The First Complete Edition in English*. Trans. B. Fink, New York: Norton & Co., pp. 161–175.

Lacan, J. (1946/2001) Le Nombre Treize et la Forme Logique de la Suspicion. *Autres Écrits*. Paris: Seuil, pp. 85–99.

Lacan, J. (1947/2001) La Psychiatrie Anglaise et la Guerre. *Autres Écrits*. Paris: Seuil, pp. 101–120.

Lacan, J. (1991) *The Seminar, Book II: The Ego in Freud's Theory and in the Technique of Psychoanalysis (1954–1955)*. In Miller, J.-A. (ed.), Trans. S. Tomaselli. New York: Norton & Co.

Lacan, J. (2006) *Le Séminaire, Book XVI: D'un Autre à l'autre (1968-1969)* (ed.) Miller, J.-A. Paris: Seuil.

Laplanche, J. and Pontalis, J.-B. (1968/1988) *The Language of Psychoanalysis*. Trans. D. Nicholson-Smith. London: Karnac Books.

Porge, E. (1989) *Se Compter Trois: Le Temps Logique de Lacan*. Paris: Erès.

Roudinesco, E. (1999) *Jacques Lacan: An Outline of a Life and History of a System of Thought*, Trans. B. Bray. New York: Columbia University Press.

Sartre, J.P. (1944) *Huis-Clos*. Paris: Librairie Gallimard.

Tahan, M. (1999) *The Man Who Counted: A Collection of Mathematical Adventures*. Trans. L. Clark and A. Reid. New York: Norton & Co.

2

PRESENTATION ON TRANSFERENCE

Bernard Burgoyne

Context

Lacan's presentation has the form of an intervention. His intervention was made at a Congress that can be seen as constituting one of a number of high points of the redevelopment of psychoanalysis that was undertaken across Europe after the ravages of the Second World War. The Congress took place in 1951, it was held in Paris, and its topic was transference: Lacan's constructions in his intervention were put forward as a response to a paper given by Daniel Lagache. There were several such responses – Lacan's was not unique, although it did turn out to have a unique quality. Lagache's presentation itself constituted a *tour de force*: it had been intended to be encyclopedic and to contain an exhaustive account of the state of problems and theories concerning transference since the beginnings of the psychoanalytical movement.

This fourteenth meeting of the Conference of French-Speaking Psychoanalysts was held on 1 November 1951. It provided a forum for reflections and proposals concerning problems of transference, re-opening, as it did so, questions of the nature of psychoanalytical technique. The field of the relations between analytical concepts and analytical technique had lain fallow since before the War, and this too was reworked in an extensive way as the meeting proceeded. Two main proposals are found at the center of the intervention made by Lacan at this Congress. The first concerns the structure of the analytical relation, or what at the time he would call the subject-subject relation; the second was the determination of the relation of Socratic dialectic to psychoanalytic technique. The second element was a *nouveauté*: no other contribution came at all close to grasping this new perspective introduced by Lacan in his intervention. Both these proposals contain consequences as regards the question of the status of the science of psychoanalysis.

Transference is a phenomenon of love; it is the appearance of the residues of lost love within the paraphernalia found in everyday life. It causes a slight shift in the analytical relationship: in responding to this shift, the analyst can either

DOI: 10.4324/9781003264231-2

seek the historical origins of its appearance or attempt rather to survey its outlines in the present. This second tack – in large measure – characterizes a considerable fragment of contemporary Anglo-Saxon psychoanalysis; the first represents the direction of work proposed by Lacan. Beyond this basic difference, there are many additional aspects of the transference that receive no common interpretation across a wide variety of schools of psychoanalysis.

One aspect of the transference is a love transference to the analyst: the transference relation draws new material into the neighborhood of infantile loves – in this process, some aspect of the analyst is taken into the circle of lost and broken relations of childhood love. An additional aspect is a repetition – or remembering – of these infantile loves in the material of the analytical session. Both of these aspects raise a number of questions: does the reproduction of elements of archaic love represent a resistance to analytical work, framing it within fixed clichés of love? Or does it rather function as a motor of the analysis, giving access to otherwise deeply repressed material? Is the transference primarily an affective phenomenon, or is it rather a linguistic effect, displaying a shift at play in the representational world of the analysand? Again, the Anglo-Saxon and the Latin responses to these questions tend to differ: in the Anglo-Saxon world, the affective component of love is given predominance, whereas Lacan maintains a focus on the signifying structure that provides a frame and a boundary to the deployment of love.

Freud held to two notions of transference: the first that it is an affective phenomenon, and the second – one that he proposes in the Dora case – that the transference is a 'new edition or facsimile' of a previous text. The shift of connotation that takes place in this movement from one text to the other, I have elsewhere called Dugald Stewart transference (for some detail of this see my article (Burgoyne, 2002) in Glynos and Stavrakakis 2002). This *DS* shift, as it may be called, is a theory of transference that was held by Freud – he had taken it from Dugald Stewart *via* John Stuart Mill, and it constitutes what might be called a 'philosophical' formulation of his second – linguistic – account of the structure of transference. There remain today many conflicting schools within psychoanalysis as regards the relations of philosophy to psychoanalysis, and of the affine relations of psychoanalytic concepts and technique to the methods of the sciences. At the time of Lagache's report then, there were many conflicting theories of transference, together with conflicting recommendations for the handling of transference in analytical techniques.

Lagache's report comes in two parts: the first is an extensive and detailed account of the concept of transference since its appearance in *Studies on Hysteria* in 1895. He divides Freud's work on transference into two phases – from 1895 to 1920, and 1920 to 1929 – two phases separated by the publication of *Beyond the Pleasure Principle* in 1920. In parallel to this, he adds the elements of the theories of transference proposed in the contributions of the first generation of psychoanalysts: by Karl Abraham in 1908, and by Sandor Ferenczi in 1909. The 'second period' of Freud's work indicates a going beyond the pleasure principle to introduce the repetition compulsion as a further factor at work in the underlying dynamics of any transference phenomena. Lagache then ranges widely over the history of the analytical movement, finally moving from the panel on the relations of psychoanalytic concepts and technique at the Marienbad Congress in 1936 to Melanie Klein's presentation at the Amsterdam Congress in August 1951. He follows this survey of the history of the field with an equally extensive account of what he took to be the main problems raised for psychoanalytical work in the present. In this section, called 'Elements of the Theory of Transference', Lagache starts by distinguishing three 'systems of reference' where one finds the term transference – in everyday discourse, in psychology, and in psychoanalysis. In starting in this way he is already placing at the center of his argument a series of problems for which Lacan would produce completely different solutions in his own response to Lagache's presentation.

The direction of Lagache's research is to see the transference effect as a form of behavior, while Lacan sees its production – and its analysis – as being dependent on what he calls the subject-to-subject relation, and what Lagache manages to perceive as a 'discursive analysis'. Lacan bases his notion of discourse – and even, or particularly, scientific discourse – on a classical theory of dialectic: Lagache however refuses any initiative of this kind. But beyond this, the notion of dialectic rejected by Lagache is at the heart of Lacan's formulations of Freud's theory of the relations of psychoanalysis and science. This raises a particular question of the relation of transference to dialectic, as well as a more general question of the relation of dialectic to science (for an account of Freud's view of the relations of psychoanalysis to science see Burgoyne, 2003). When Lagache's report was published, it was buttressed by other articles: by Freud, by Schlumberger, by Klein, and by a article by Melitta Schmideberg on shifting signification in transference, and on the implication of this for the question of psychoanalysis becoming a science. When it came to his response to the comments of his other colleagues, Lagache (1951b/1952) chose to particularly address two of these colleagues, Maurice Bénassy and Jacques Lacan: in each of these responses he raised the problem of the position that psychoanalysis could take up within the field of science.

In 1879, Freud translated a lengthy review – it takes up some 80 pages – of a text on Socratic dialectic. The author of the review, John Stuart Mill, had taken care to investigate in detail the arguments put forward by his friend George Grote, as part of their common project of establishing Socratic dialectic as the format for the investigation of human nature, and as a proposed framework for the construction of the methods of the sciences, as well as the organization of the relations between civil society and the State (for details of this see Burgoyne (2000) and Burgoyne (2007)). Freud may well have taken up this framework as a protocol for the analysis of human subjectivity: Lacan in later perceiving the veins of dialectic structuring Freud's technique with Dora may have discovered the elements which Freud took into his program several decades earlier.

Socratic dialectic operates within a set of words: 'in ein Netz von Worten' (Freud, 1880); its aim is to change opinions – in psychoanalysis particularly, opinions about sexual love; and its method is to allow people to gain access to the absurd consequences of what they hold to be true. In the text that Freud translated, the strongest of these opinions are taken to be the class of constraints that earlier generations impose on their children: the children suffer from these opinions, according to Grote, and they 'give an entirely wrong direction to their desires'.

In the problem situation as constructed by Mill, as he takes up Grote's argument (Mill 1866), the starting point for the dialectic is an 'ignorance which takes itself for a knowledge'; elements of this ignorance are then reversed by means of a questioning which opens up pathways connected to it; these paths lead to an abandoning of the initial 'false persuasion', and to 'a sorrowful conscience of ignorance' being installed in its place. Grote frequently calls this process a 'negative analysis': in the form in which it was taken up by Freud, it represents a 'testing by analysis' of opinions on sexual love.

There are many steps in the process of the dialectic: in each of these moments, by means of a series of indirect pathways, a connection is established which weakens the old attachments, and which thus leads to a new access to the truth. In the early years of his clinical work, Freud occasionally – as at the end of his work with Dora, as he is becoming aware of one of his mistakes – took it that the analyst has a better grasp on the dialectic than does the analysand: after all, as Mill had put it, the dialectic constitutes a 'sifting of opinion ... (that can be) victorious over any logical objection'. Such a haste to assume the truth is – at least in Freud's case – an infrequent error on the part of the analyst: but Freud's great achievement is to formulate the production, the maintenance, and the challenging of psychic defense as a process of dialectic. The analysand has many reasons to maintain defense – questioning, after all, causes 'Scham und Unbehagen' – shame and discontent; but Socratic dialectic allows an entire apparatus to be brought to bear on the weakening of such defenses. Freud uses the notion of a dialectic form of analytical discourse from the beginning of his work: even in his work with the less dialectical Breuer, representations of suffering can be changed, his text says, only through the agency of discourse – 'durch die Rede gestattet' (Breuer and Freud, 1893-5/1955). But Freud was never explicit about the dialectic foundation of analytical technique: much to his merit – and to the benefit of psychoanalysis – Lacan was the one to perceive this foundation after it had been latent for 70 years.

Before the Congress, both Lagache and Lacan had presented papers to the British Psycho-Analytical Society. Lagache read his contribution on 4 April 1951 – from the start, it aimed to relate his own work to that of the British School. He presented psychoanalysis as a theory of behavior – where transference, repetition, and the rectification of knowledge are all delineated in a behavioristic framework. Verbal activity – as he called it – as well as having a symbolic dimension, was also 'a piece of concrete behaviour', a way of dealing with the psychoanalytic situation. In choosing this direction, he drew in Susan Isaacs to help him – not the Isaacs of the structuring effects of phantasy, but the Isaacs of what he called the 'compatibility of psychoanalysis and the psychology of behaviour'. It was a tendentious reading: Isaacs herself had said that her aim was 'to emphasise the key significance of method', and within this context, she claimed, 'words have the greatest possible dynamic influence' (Isaacs 1939). Certainly, she did not ignore behavior – Freud has taught us she said 'to appreciate sequences and connections in behaviour' (but sequences and connections belong to the Freud-Herbart domain of mathematical elements within the field of representation); what she wanted to investigate she claimed, was how 'the testing and verification' of the perceptions of the analyst have a central role in the 'reconstruction of the patient's *past history and past feelings*'.

Both in London and seven months later in Paris, Lagache was attempting to extend the scope of the surveys of transference that had been produced by Silverberg (1948) and Macalpine (1950) in the previous two or three years. In his London presentation – large sections of which are recapitulated in his Congress presentation in November – he interpreted the transference as a particular piece of behavior, as a repetition replacing a remembering 'by thought and language'. He claimed that any attempt to explain this by construing an 'automatism of repetition' within the field of language and thought missed what he took to be the key to the explanation – that behind this automatism there must lie a 'more dynamic explanation' in terms of the psychology of behavior. So transference – and with it, repetition – is then to be explained by the lines of force that are discovered within 'forms of behaviour'. Despite Lagache's claim to an affiliation with the themes discussed by Isaacs, the direction taken up by Lacan will have much more in common with the way that Isaacs formulates the problems, than will this orientation to behavior introduced by Lagache.

One month after Lagache – on 2nd May – Lacan gave his own presentation in London. It developed a theme much ignored by the British School – although present in a central position in Freud's work, and in the work of a number of the first generation of psychoanalysts, Nunberg, for example: the theme was that of misrepresentation by the ego. This paper that Lacan read to the British Society also separates his program from that of Lagache. So we have four texts which together distinguish these two orientations: two London texts – from April and May – and two Paris texts from November 1951.

Lacan started his London presentation with one of his central claims: reality is a construction of the ego and organized around a function of misrecognition. He warned his audience that with this notion – that he had called *méconnaissance*, and that in Freud appears as the agency of 'false connection' – there is a need to revise any 'naïve conception of the reality principle' (Lacan

1951/1953, p. 11). If there are errors and illusions everywhere, then how can anyone find an orientation to what is real? This an old philosophic query – first answered in an extensive way by Socrates, with what he built out of the earlier Eleatic theory of dialectic.

Next, he stressed the mediating effects of language in finding any pathway that is able to approach what is real. Misrecognition, he claimed, is an operation that is central in the functioning of the ego: 'the ego is very nearly that systemic refusal to acknowledge reality (*méconnaisssance systématique de la réalité*)' (Lacan 1951/1953, p. 12) – where this translation into French was given by Lacan in his original presentation. Rather than the misrepresentation being something minor and eliminable – Jones went so far as to label it 'rationalisation' – this 'alienation of the ego is one of the preconditions of human knowledge' (Lacan 1951/1953, p. 12). So there is a need for a dialectic to operate on the forms given to reality by the ego, and a necessity to gain access to its underlying subjectivity. Lacan put this in terms of basic relations between negation and desire: his claim was that it followed 'that the recognition of objects and of the ego must be subjected to constant revision in an endless dialectical process' (Lacan 1951/1953, p. 12).

'Just such a process was involved in the Socratic dialogue': this is how to analyze any form of misrecognition, he claimed, ' ... whether it dealt with science, politics, or love' (Lacan 1951/1953, p. 12). Lacan then contextualized his solution within the culture of classical Greece: 'Socrates taught the masters of Athens to become what they must by developing their awareness of the world and themselves through 'forms' that were constantly redefined. The only obstacle he encountered was the attraction of pleasure' (p. 12). This obstacle is one example of inertia, taking the form of a 'resistance to the dialectical process of analysis' (p. 12): these forms are then subject to dialectic, not to styles of behavior. Lacan continued: analytic technique actually uses this dialectical movement, giving it a modern setting. Analysis 'substitutes the strange detours of free association for the sequence of the [original formulations of Socratic] Dialogue' (p. 12); and it is with this aperçu that Lacan will approach Freud's presentation of Dora.

The structure of the psychoanalytic relation, and the nature of psychoanalytic technique, is grounded in a dialectical relation between subjects: 'the psychoanalytic dialogue enables us to re-establish a more human relationship' (Lacan 1951/1953, p. 17). Lacan continued: 'Is not the form of this dialogue determined by an impasse, that is to say, by the resistance of the ego?' (p. 17). 'Indeed, is not this dialogue one in which the one who knows admits by his technique that he can free his patient from the shackles of his ignorance only by leaving all the talking to him' (p. 17). This is the starting point of a (Socratic) dialectic – and it was the starting point of Freud's work with Dora. It is an indicator of the power of the counter-transference – invoking Freud's illusory perception of Dora's choices in love – that Freud, in the final minutes of the analysis, had started to do all the talking himself.

Referring to Plato's *Meno*, Lacan claims that in a Socratic dialogue, knowledge is elicited from the one who is questioned. At the start of the work, the analyst knows nothing about the psycho-sexual history of the analysand, but one of the things that the analyst needs to know is that this advance from ignorance is vehicled by Socratic dialogue. This technique brings with it a supposition by the analysand of knowledge on the part of the analyst – the transference can then be seen as effectuating this perception of the analyst as the one who knows the ways through what were previously impasses in the relations of infantile love.

Lagache had proposed the analysis of the individual by means of concepts of personality, ego, and general psychology. Lacan rather focussed on the dialectic at play in the constitution of subjectivity: like Freud, he was then led to investigate the way in which psychoanalysis proposes a reformulation of the classical sciences. In doing so, Lacan – like Isaacs – focuses on method. It is novel theories, he says, that 'prepare the ground for new discoveries in science' (Lacan 1951/1953, p. 14); in the field of transference, as in other regions of what can become the science of psychoanalysis, such theories allow the facts to be grasped better – being indeed 'what make it possible for them to be observed in the first place' (Lacan 1951/1953, p. 14). The resistance of the ego is opposed to the deployment of any dialectic – 'here we see the ego, in its essential resistance to the elusive process of Becoming, to the variations of Desire' (Lacan 1951/1953, p. 15): analytic dialogue seeks out this desire, while being founded on dialectic. Given this centrality of dialectic in Lacan's formulations, what remains to be further examined is the function of dialectic in analytical technique.

Two papers written by Lacan in the years running up to the 1951 Congress help to throw light on this. Both had been presented at earlier meetings of the same Conference – the first, at the XI Congress in May 1948; the second at the XIII Congress in May 1950 (Lacan 1950/2006): there are many allusions to the material of these texts in Lacan's presentation, and I will refer to the texts in what follows as [Ag] and [Cr].

Commentary on the text

At the start of the text published in the *Ecrits*, Lacan introduces a sub-title and four preliminary paragraphs. Lacan's comments in these paragraphs take the form of a retrospect: they were written 15 years later, at the time of the publication of the *Ecrits*. They function as an introduction to Lacan's argument, and I will discuss them before I move on to the text of his intervention.

(176['66], 1). The sub-title: a few weeks before the Congress took place, the Conference had decided to extend its reference and to change its name, from 'the Conference of French-Speaking Psychoanalysts' to 'the Conference of Romance Language-Speaking Psychoanalysts'. Some of their proceedings were subsequently described under the old name, but this new name was taken up by Lacan. This in itself is a transference, a *DS* transference: a term – and this term is concerned with speech – is given a shift of meaning, moved into a wider sphere. From *French* to *Romance* is an extension, a linguistic shift, which in the classical theory of tropes would have been called a transitive extension or transference.

(176['66], 2). Lagache at this time was attempting to organize psychoanalysis around an expansion of the themes of behavioral psychology. In contrast to this, Lacan's subject-to-subject relation was a notion that was comparatively new. Already, in London in May, Lacan had tentatively introduced the notion of subject, still however within a focus on Socratic dialectic, in relation to the misrecognitions of the ego. The colleague who in 1966 was to 'remain anonymous' was Maurice Bénassy.

(176['66], 3–4). The Zeigarnik effect was discovered in 1927 by Bluma Zeigarnik, a Russian research student working in the laboratory of Kurt Lewin in Berlin. Her work had shown that uncompleted tasks are remembered significantly better than ones that have been allowed to reach their completion. At the 1951 Conference, both Bénassy and Lagache had invoked this effect: Lagache in order to be able to perceive the rememberings – and the repetitions – of the transference as Zeigarnik effects of unresolved conflicts of childhood. But Bénassy had proposed taking the transference out of its setting in the analytical relation, perceiving it rather to be more generally an underlying explanation of Zeigarnik effects in everyday life. Bénassy then chose to explain such 'wild-transference' by means of an appeal to the 'structure of the personality'. Here, Lacan drew the line: the transference relation is an element of a network of relations, part of a body of subject-to-subject relations, and analyzed within the psychoanalytical setting, using the resources of the analytical dialectic. For Lagache too, Bénassy's claim was a little too much; he drew back from Bénassy's hypotheses, preferring to see the analytical transference – in its Zeigarnik manifestations – as being an attempt to disengage the ego from unresolved unconscious conflict (Lagache 1951b/1952).

Lagache pointed out that he had put forward – already in 1949 – 'the idea of establishing a connection' between transferential repetition and the Zeigarnik effect. He made no mention of the Zeigarnik effect having been taken up in relation to psychoanalysis well before this – by Heinz Hartmann. In 1933, Hartmann had proposed using the Zeigarnik effect as an instrument that might explain the effectiveness of the psychoanalytical technique. In her original work, Zeigarnik had found that almost twice as much material was remembered in situations where subjects had worked on tasks that had remained incomplete, compared to situations where the tasks had been completed. Hartmann attempted to see if he would obtain the same results with obsessional subjects; he found that although his results for 'healthy' subjects were in the same region as those obtained by Zeigarnik, for obsessional subjects, the amount of increased recall was considerably lower. Hysterics, on the other hand, rate highly in this field of Zeigarnik recall: so if the psychoanalytical process in part hystericises people, then Zeigarnik's effect ought to have a bearing on the determination of the protocol of the setting.

Bénassy's presentation had contained an algebraic formulation of the relations that he assumed to be active in the analytical relation: the analysand he called – 'algebraically' – an "O", and the analyst another "O" – an "O"'. The analytical field of force is then given 'essentially as the – if I may put it this way – algebraic sum of these two lines of pressure with opposite signs'. In fact, this algebraically constructed field he took to be equivalent to 'what Lacan calls the dialectic' between the analyst and the analysand. It was after this attempt at a mathematization of the psychoanalytical relation that Bénassy moved on to an extended commentary on the Zeigarnik effect. He admitted a close similarity between the Zeigarnik and 'certain aspects of the transference' – he included in this the effect produced by ending the session, thereby interrupting the analysand in the middle of a chain of associations. He then raised the question of whether or not the Zeigarnik result is itself produced by the transference. This presented him with an alternative that then took his theorizing quite outside the field of the analytical relation.

(176['66], 5). Lacan addressed these themes of dialectic and transference in the material of his first two Seminars: he had asked Alexandre Koyré to present a seminar on Socratic dialectic on the eve of the second session of Seminar II (on 16 November 1954) – it forms the central leitmotif of the first sessions of this Seminar, leading on to the theme of the activity of dialectic within circuits of repetition in the subsequent development of the Seminar. In the session of 1st December, Lacan says 'without a radical position being taken on the functioning of speech, transference is purely and simply inconceivable'; and throughout Seminar I – addressing Freud's papers on technique – Lacan had repeatedly claimed that the analysis of transference constitutes a historical discourse – one which reconstructs, in moving to ever deeper layers, the psycho-sexual history of the analysand. And almost ten years after his original intervention, Lacan took transference as the theme of the Seminar that he gave from November 1960 to June 1961. In this Seminar, he reformulated the early work of Ferenczi and Abraham in terms of his own reading of Abraham's later theory of 'forms of organisation' of the libido (Lacan 1960–1961/1991). In the sessions of 1st and 8th March, he drew classical notions of dialectic and reality into relation with contemporary psychoanalytical work: in these sessions, Lacan recapitulates the theme stressed by Grote – 'entire regions of society have been given an orientation in their practical action', he claimed, by the Socratic discovery of an inter-subjective dialectic.

(176, 6). Bénassy (and Lagache) had looked for a causal relation between repetition in the transference and the Zeigarnik effect. Lacan, on the other hand, seeks conditions that are found in an inter-subjective dialectic. Socratic dialectic breaks apart previously established knowledge; a break is evocative of broken and lost childhood loves; dialectic, therefore, produces a transference effect, as it evokes the material of lost childhood loves. This theme will be a major element of Lacan's later investigation into analytical technique – particularly of the relations between transference and interpretation (Lacan 1958/2006).

(176, 7–8). One of the interventions at Lagache's presentation – that of Sacha Nacht – had contained the term 'the presence of the analyst' (Nacht 1951). This notion had been invented by Nacht, as part of his proposal to supplement the neutral screen (or position of absence) of the analyst by this function of presence. He intended it to be a form of active technique – a series of actions by the analyst within the sessions – that he hoped would bring about a 'liquidation' of the transference. Lacan ironically uses this phrase, as he recalls that what is actually brought into being by the mere 'presence' of the analyst is a predisposition to dialectic, the 'dimension of dialogue'.

(176,9). The disposition to dialectic involves the navigating of pathways, the 'crossing of certain dams' put into place as forms of resistance to the analytical work.

(177, 1). Lacan stresses that there is a dialectic that is proper to the analytical situation; that this is other than an 'everyday' dialectic; and that this raises questions about how dialectic operates within analytical technique. That psychoanalysis is a dialectic experience can be found already in Lacan in 1948: 'I have emphasised ('souligné') that the analyst cures through dialogue' ([Ag]; 86, 6).

The field within which the analytical dialectic operates has its own 'gravitation': there are accordingly some questions that 'only psychoanalysts' can answer, since 'only they have a dialectical experience of the subject' ([Cr]; 114, 5). In terms of this new field of the analytical dialectic, Lacan puts the question as follows – 'What virtue ... did Freud add to dialogue?' ([Ag]; 86, 6).

Verbal dialectic has frequently met an impasse ([Ag]; 86, 5). The dialectic that was introduced at the time of Socrates had been intended to act as a new force – the force of argument: it changed opinions without having recourse to the force of arms. The analyst, in this Socratic mode, is trying to loosen attachments to certain opinions – everyday opinions about sexual love, including daydreams, and fantasies of love. The unconscious fantasies that underlie these dreams have a more inert structure, so that this replacement of violence by persuasion has not always worked; the analyst encounters forms of resistance, the dialectician within the city encounters the fixity of tradition and ideals. Lacan stresses that the aim of dialectic is to discover the foundation of the law ([Cr]; 103, 2). The law that the analysis uncovers is the law of desire.

Despite the *impasses* and the negative responses to the work, there is a direction introduced by the dialectic: this new direction, Lacan says, 'is called 'truth'.

(177, 2). The urgency of the times: Lacan had engaged with Politzer's 'psychology of the concrete' in the 1930s. His own program also was developed within the shadow of the War: a central element of it is the relation between dialectic and violence.

(177, 3). It is a twist of history – a modern ruse of reason – that Lacan, in casting light on the dialectic foundations of psychoanalysis, was seen as the only proponent of it. When Freud claimed that psychoanalysis rests on 'the methods of the sciences', he was not taking these to be in any sense antagonistic to Socratic dialectic. In psychoanalysis, as in the sciences, what brings about the organization of truth is not a body of facts, 'but rather a dialectic' ([Cr]; 118, 2).

At any particular moment of the dialectic, there are limits to its action – limit is one of the elements of the topologies that bring the dialectic into being. And objectification in science – wherever it operates – leads to the loss of recognition of truth.

(177, 4–5). A perversity in the politics of the psychoanalytical movement: rather than working within the reorganization of (post–Herbartian) psychology by the analytical movement, a reorganization of psychoanalysis by psychology had been proposed. Lacan ascribes this to fear at hearing a voice that has been stilled. In the process of psychoanalysis, and in the construction of theories of psychoanalysis, 'nothing is to be feared more than saying something that might be true' (515, 2).

Socratic dialectic searches for the truth; it is the tradition that 'conditioned the appearance of all our sciences' ([Cr]; 105, 3), and that Freud – from his extensive study and translation of Socratic dialectic in 1879 – placed at the center of his work. Dialectic discovers limits – in the case of Plato's *Gorgias*, limits that are 'marked by the reality of the Slave' ([Cr]; 105, 2). In this reference to the limits to freedom, there is already latent a topology of psychic space; dialectic explores the structure of such space – its elimination brings with it the danger of a retreat to the acceptance of forms of suffering whose truth has been elided.

(177, 6). Psychologism, far from being a mere conceptual mistake, 'reifies' the condition of human beings, threatening a loss of access to the causes of suffering. According to Lacan, it constitutes a radical misrepresentation of human nature, as well as a misunderstanding of the nature of the sciences, making its dangers greater than those of the threat of the physicists' bombs.

(177, 7). Underlying social structuring there are 'the radical structures that language transmits in the unconscious' ([Cr]; 105, 5). This division gives people two sorts of interests, each kind accompanied by a corresponding dialectic – one that allows for the servicing of social realities, and the other that gains access to underlying subjective realities. Lacan talks of the alienation of being cut off from this underlying dialectic.

(178, 1–2). Homo psychologicus: Lagache had hoped to produce a new psychoanalysis, transforming it by means of the science of psychology. In Freud's view, the process would need to operate in the opposite direction: the psychoanalytical theory of subjectivity reformulates all the existing sciences. This would be necessary because psychoanalytical assumptions about subjectivity and knowledge are radically different from those found in the

37

traditional – or even established – sciences; Françoise Balibar has produced a fascinating account of Freud and Lacan on these questions of science – see Balibar (2007). In effect, for Freud, the orientation of psychoanalysis is that given to it by the 'method of the sciences'. So Lacan proposes this remedy against psychologism: allow the orientation that is found within psychoanalysis to reformulate the subject of science.

(178, 3). Lagache had seemed not to grasp the extent of the distance between his own psychology program and the program brought into being by the directions initiated by Lacan: it was left to Pasche (1951/1952), in his comments on Lagache's presentation, to remind him. Lagache had claimed that failure plays a part in the generation of tension within the ego. He had focussed on the failure of oedipal loves – 'infantile experience is a series of trials and errors which end in failure and … injury': these injuries he took to be narcissistic wounds. And he was able to conclude: 'In the light of the Zeigarnik effect, transference (and in particular repetition) can be considered as the activation in the psycho-analytic situation of an unsolved conflict'. For him, these repetitions are secondary effects: attempts by the ego to repair the injury. Pasche (1951/1952) on the other hand took repetition to be a primary functioning, and he held that the investigation of its automatism would lead to establishing 'the limits' of the psychoanalytic field. In asserting this, he referred his audience to comments made by Lacan on the differences between the fields of psychology and psychoanalysis. For Lacan, repetition is a primary factor, and access to its working can be gained by means of a dialectic between the analyst and the analysand. Lacan will next aim to show that this dialectic is present in Freud's work with Dora.

(178, 4–5). Lacan presents the case as progressing by a series of dialectical interventions. Each of these successive moments of the treatment redefines truth for the subject, shifting somewhat the framework and organization of the world of their object-relations. In terms of the network of connecting pathways – the structure, that is, of what Freud calls logical threads, and what Lacan calls the signifying chain – this progression of truth operates by means of a recognition of what were previously unavailable or lost pathways. These pathways are contoured by the tension of desire – as new pathways are made, the subject experiences the impact of desire. Interpretations made within the transference allow for missing oedipal pathways to be brought into the material of the work: an error on the part of the analyst in operating this dialectic will result in what is commonly called 'a negative transference'.

(178, 6–7). Truth is not a 'given that one can grasp in its inertia', but rather is at first constituted by the dialectic, and then again reconstituted by the dialectic in successive moments ([Cr]; 118, 2). Lacan is introducing the first moment of this process: this first development allows for the deployment of a space where the analysand's current opinions on sexual love can be explored. Reconsiderations of this – and subsequent – moments of the analysis can allow for the rectification of any error on the part of the analyst in the handling of the transference.

There are affective and conceptual obstacles to dialectic – 'sincerity is the first obstacle encountered by the dialectic in the search for true intentions, the first goal of speech apparently being to disguise them' ([Cr]; 115, 1); the corresponding goal of the analyst is to act against the grain of these obstacles, to take them by surprise. As he listens to Dora, Freud is led to make a Socratic response, alerted by what Lacan here calls the constancy of the social lie. This initial listening allows for what Lacan terms 'the first development of truth'.

At the center of her development, Dora had placed a somewhat over-complete 'file full of memories'. Freud, in his account of his work with Dora, explains that this is hardly what one would expect from such a first development of truth. The first narrative account given to him when he asks the analysand for an initial version of their history is more likely to be full of absences: at the start, he says, the analyst is lacking a 'well-rounded case-history, without gaps'. Freud presents the first account produced by the analysand as an 'unnavigable river whose stream is at one moment choked by masses of rock and at another divided and lost among shallows and sandbanks … leaving gaps unfilled, and riddles unanswered'. The connections in an initial version are incoherent, and the sequence of events described is uncertain.

Freud comments further on the patient's inability to give an ordered history of their life: he describes how such a loss of access can be brought about. In cases where 'the events have actually been maintained in memory' the loss of access can be achieved 'by nullifying one of the connections'. Now, this is a very particular kind of 'nullifying': a negation, certainly, but a destruction and a cutting also. The term that Freud uses is 'Aufhebung' – the term used by Hegel for the transformation of one state of consciousness as it is replaced by another in the deployment of his dialectic. So Freud is indicating the presence of such dialectical operations in the transformations of everyday life. Lacan will take this claim further, finding in the relation that determines the analytical situation, a particular dialectic that allows for transformations in analysis.

In Dora's first presentation of her relationships, there were no gaps to be found in her memory. A series of connections in these relationships had been cut: as part of this, she had 'nullified' aspects of her father's relation to Frau K, and had 'dismissed from her mind every sign which tended to show its true character'.

(179, 1–2). Dora had told Freud that she was a puppet in the hands of the others, innocent of any active role, and merely manipulated by them in their games of love. Lacan points out that Freud's response to her had taken the form of a Socratic intervention: he said to her that she had already described to him her regular complicity in these games of love. Freud's pointing out this contradiction operates a key moment within the first development of the dialectic. It weakens somewhat Dora's attachment to the opinions that she first proffered to Freud: it allows access to previously discarded connections – 'look, what is your own part in this disorder of which you are complaining?': it brings about what Lacan has called 'the first dialectical reversal'.

(179, 3–4). Some further connections are revealed in the next development of Dora's account of her world: Freud puts it as follows – a 'new light is shed on her relationship with the other partners'. This next development of her relations with the others is a dance of love: Lacan reconstructs it as a quadrille – or quadrilateral. Within the movements of the dance, four pairings of love take their steps in the representations that she gives to her prospects of love: her father and Frau K – Frau K and Herr K – Herr K and Dora – and Dora and her father. Lacan points out that at this stage of things, the mother is reduced to being merely hitched onto this network of relations. But what is commonly referred to as the circle of Dora's love relationships already takes the form here of a geometry of love.

(179, 5). Underneath this new version of things, lie connecting pathways that lead to the oedipal material. These new versions of conflict in love contain a covering ruse, and what this ruse hides is betrayed by semantics. By semantics here Lacan means connections within the signifying chains: in particular those implicated with condensation and displacements between her father's riches (Vermögen) and impotence (Unvermögen). These connections betray an identification on the part of Dora with her father, one that is operative in all of her conversion symptoms. Freud does not at this point intervene – as he later will – with an account of these underlying oedipal connections: he responds instead with a yet further dialectical intervention.

(179, 6–7). There is still something that is puzzling in Dora's new account of her loves: the intensity and the insistence of her thoughts about her father's love for Frau K. 'The unrelenting repetition of the same thoughts' about this love relation Freud took as a signal that underneath Dora's interest in the rival for her father's love there was something that could not be assimilated into the constructions that she had already made. Freud then made another dialectical intervention – in the form of a question: What had been the intensity of her earlier relations with Frau K? He had grounds when asking this question to think that an answer of 'very little' was incompatible with the overriding nature of the jealousy that Dora had displayed.

(180, 1–2). This question initiated a second reversal, which in turn led to the third development of truth. The closeness of the relation between Dora and Frau K is central to this third development: it had been close, it seems, since she was a young girl: 'When Dora stayed with the K's she used to share a bedroom with Frau K, and the husband used to be quartered elsewhere'. Over this period, the 'scarcely grown girl' was the 'confidante and adviser' to Frau K on her love conflicts with her husband. The amatory confessions that Dora received – at the heart of which lie questions about her feminine sexuality – are touched on in this third development, while their full extent remains unplumbed: the two women in this version are complicit as 'mutual ambassadors of their desires in relation to Dora's father'.

(180, 3–5). But this further development itself leads to another question: one that Freud had difficulty with. Dora's adoration of the 'lovely white body' of Frau K raises a question about her own sexual life: she had already discussed love secrets with Frau K. What secrets of her own sexuality – of what it means to be a woman – were raised for Dora as she engaged in the relationships portrayed in this third development of the truths of her engagement with the world? We shall see later that this is where Freud hesitated to proceed: Lacan finds that he has to formulate for Freud a pair of questions, by means of which he can point out Freud's direction. With the bringing to light of this secret, we would be 'led to the third dialectical reversal'. Lacan comments that 'the real value of Dora's object' – of Frau K – would be revealed by this reversal: that Frau K represents 'not an individual, but a mystery, the mystery of Dora's own femininity'.

(180, 6–7). But there is another limit that must be reached: the incorporation of an image from Dora's childhood. She had 'a clear picture of a scene' from her childhood, when she was with her brother – who was 14 months older. She was sitting on the floor sucking her thumb, while with the other hand she was plucking at her brother's ear lobe. In relation to this scene, Freud discusses the distance and separation from her brother, the distance and separation between daughter–father and mother–brother, and the childhood sexuality that it contained. Freud uses the damned up and dry river-bed metaphor again here: he raises the question of irrigating these dried beds, and the new knowledge that comes from it.

Lacan finds in this a matrix – an imago – of what 'man' and 'woman' mean to her. This structure appears in the imaginary framework given to all the symbolic forms of repetition that in her later life she is subject to. Lacan comments that it is a natural part of the dialectic operated by Freud, to be able to catch such formative scenes in its net.

(180, 8). Dora was speechless in the scene of her love-tugs on her brother; she nevertheless was satisfying a 'primitive oral desire'. As long as she has no access to the question of her sexuality, she will remain subject to this imago of the fragmentation of her body, and to the conversion symptom of her coughs.

(181, 1–2). The dependence on the actual presence (and potential or actual absence) of 'the masculine partner' leads Dora into the quadrille that Lacan has already described. An identification is a misunderstanding of who one is: Dora has identified with her father, with her mother, and with Frau K. As long as these identifications are maintained, she remains subject to the effect of such early imagos, and to the impossibility of discovering who she is.

(181, 3). Aggressiveness is part of the narcissistic image. The dominance of imaginary identifications in the ideal form of the ego gives rise to resistance to a continued dialectic. It is the analyst's function to overcome such resistance: the responsibility of the analyst is to overcome resistance by establishing fresh connections to archaic loves. It is at this point in his work with Dora that Freud began to waver.

The dialectic encounters resistance. Where Freud pictured this resistance in terms of contours on a hillside, Lacan is content to describe it as the effect on the dialectic of a 'backcloth of inertia' ([Ag]; 87, 2). The inertia of the resistance is employed in bringing about a 'negative therapeutic reaction' ([Ag]; 87, 4). In this history of the halting of dialectic, Lacan perceived the effects of the death drive, and already at this time − 1948 − he gave it a topological formulation: a transference, and particularly its 'negative' aspect, he termed 'the inaugural knot of the analytical drama ([Ag]; 87,8). At these moments, imaginary forms interfere with the following of symbolic paths: 'opposition, negation, ostentation, and lying' being 'characteristic modes' of the ego as they are introduced into the structure of the dialogue. ([Ag]; 88, 7). The dialogue, in other words, is on the side of the realization of the subject, while the misrecognitions of the ego insinuate into the structure of this dialogue an agency of inertia and confusion. The archaic image identified here by Lacan produces an 'imaginary transference' ([Ag]; 87,9), which will be maintained as long as the resistance is allowed to 'oppose … the subject's realisation' ([Ag]; 89,1).

(181, 4–5). 'A regression with respect to the relations that she had begun to set up with Herr K': the relation that she maintains with a man not her father diminish the action of the more archaic imagos of love. But this 'hommage' (the esteem that she gives 'à l'homme'), although it will introduce the allegiances establishing the pathways of her sexual life, will acquire its power of action only after she has exhausted the meaning of what she was looking for in Frau K.

(181, 6). There is a subjective impasse − Freud missed it.

(181, 7–8). Freud failed at what could have been this third moment of reversal brought about by dialectic. 'I failed to discover in time and to inform the patient that her homosexual (gynaecophilic) love for Frau K was the strongest unconscious current in her mental life'; 'I ought to have guessed … '. Guessing − making a hypothesis − is an everyday activity in the operation of a dialectic: it is even at the heart of the scientific method. The same Greek philosophers who discovered this dialectic discovered also the apparatus of the scientific method. From problem to attempted solution; from problem to conjectural theory; from problem to further questions: analysis has always worked in this way with knowledge. Freud recognized that Dora had a problem of knowledge: 'remarkable … that she had all this scandalous knowledge … and never wanted to know where her knowledge came from'. And he recognized that his mistake lay here: 'I should have picked up the thread of this riddle … and looked for the motive'. If I had done this, he says, Dora's second dream would then have disclosed its secret. 'The ruthless craving for revenge … was suited as nothing else was to cover over the contrary current … the magnanimity with which she forgave the treachery of the friend she loved': too late Freud realized that his lack of dialectical response left Dora's dialectical conflict hidden away.

(182, 1–2). 'The action of the transference': Freud claims that a transference always brings with it material concerning sexual love. He takes this to be a theorem of psychoanalysis, but admits that he is incapable of giving it a proof. He would have done better to present it as an axiom: instead, he waits for a contradiction ('Aufhebung') of this theorem to come to light – or at the very least, something that would limit its scope. But effectively both of Freud's explanations address the same point.

(182, 3–4). Synthesis is difficult – since analysis is difficult, but each step in an analysis eliminates some erroneous solution. Lacan proposes a classical movement towards synthesis: his aim is to take up Freud's two explanations and subject them to some further analysis, before finding a point at which the kernels of the two remaining versions become compatible. What Lacan here seeks to make compatible are, on the one hand, a lack of interpretation, and on the other, a refusal to advance towards Dora's love for another woman.

(182, 5–6). Freud claims that at the time of the analysis of Dora, when he was faced with a homosexual current of love, he would enter into a state of 'complete bewilderment'. Lacan's comment is that this distress is indexed by the amount of time that it took Freud to revise his theory of the Oedipus Complex. Only in the mid-1920s was Freud able to account for the differing trajectories taken by men and women as they navigated the oedipal conflicts: at the center of this revision is Freud's becoming able to locate the oedipal starting point for the girl as a homosexual love attachment to the mother.

(182, 7–8). The 'triumph of love': if Herr K, in his relation with Dora, had returned to his 'strongly reasoned passion', the result might have been that the inclination of the young girl would come to brush aside all internal difficulties. But even as this Hollywood ending is envisaged by Freud in a moment of reflection on his failure with Dora, he continues to maintain the thesis of the irredeemable conflict between reality and the structure of fantasy in neurosis. Despite this, however, in the last phrases of the main body of his text, he raises the prospect of this love conflict being resolved through 'an overcoming of the neurosis' by reality. Outside of Freud's counter-transferential mood, both he and Lacan agree that the cure is by reason, and not by love. 'Dialogue in itself seems to involve a renunciation of aggressiveness; from Socrates onward, philosophy has always placed its hope in dialogue to make reason triumph' ([Ag]; 86,5).

(182, 9–10). Lacan takes this even further: Freud, he says, takes himself to be 'in M K's shoes'. This counter-transference position not only means that he ignores certain pathways that he would otherwise have followed, and that he mis-understands the direction of other material, but that he also, Lacan claims, focuses too regularly on the love 'inspired in Dora' in this drama by Herr K.

The consequence of this is that Freud's position in the dialectic is lost: his style moves from a dialectic to a didactic, and from there to an almost hec-toring attempt at mastery in what was to be the final session. 'Dora disputed the fact no longer'; 'Nor does his conduct … contradict this view'; 'To prove to you how deeply impressed you were ... let me draw your attention'; 'She listened to me without any of her usual contradictions'; 'Now I know ... '; 'You have not even got the right to assert that it was out of the question'. Rather than continuing the dialectic, he now takes himself to be asserting the truth: assertative proof is very different from what is often called 'indirect' dialectic. The first works by an assumption of knowledge; the second by drawing attention to absurdity. But rather than working with contradiction, Freud is now seeking assent – and he is so far away from his coordinates, that he is surprised by it: 'here she nodded assent, a thing which I had not expected'. In the final sentences, he loses his grasp of his position.

These last few sentences are filled with representations of Freud's own (counter-transferential) predicament: as he describes her relation with Herr K 'you did not let him finish his speech' – he clearly knows that this is about to happen to him. The hortative tone increases: 'you ... do not know what he meant'. Nuances and alternatives are eliminated: 'this would have been the only possible solution'. Freud's own disillusionment with his position is offered to Dora 'it must have been a bitter piece of disillusionment for you'. His last phrase 'Now I know, what it is that you do not want to be reminded of' is a repudiation of what Freud himself did not know: it has a consequence 'Dora had listened to me without any of her usual contradictions'. Analysts infrequently publish their failed analyses: Freud had the courage to include in his case report the moment when the dialectic left him.

(183, 1–2). The dialectic has effects: the intra-psychic dialectic, that is, has effects on the dialectic – or lack of it – in Dora's social relations with the others. In everyday social relations, the position that people take up is frequently consolidated by a luring stage-setting made up by the ego. The conflicts of everyday life can upset this stage, but only within analytical work is the movement towards an underlying truth continued. The encounter by the lakeside between Dora and Herr K can have as its initial effect the inability to continue with a series of symptoms, but an analytic interpretation will be needed in order to introduce new connective elements into the 'long-joined thread of connections' that link this arena of every-day symptoms to the underlying strata that gave rise to them.

(183, 3–4). The topology of Dora's loves has one of its pathways broken; Herr K's words – discovered by Freud in the analysis of Dora's second dream – took away from Dora some of her means of access to the love of Herr K's wife.

(183, 5–6). Freud also, in his final didactic interpretations, had cut off any further access into the fabric of her love relations with Frau K.

(183, 7). Dora knew that her love secrets remained beyond the range of Freud's interpretations. The outcome of this blockage of the analytical dialectic seems to be a drawing back, but the new positions that Dora takes up are supported only by her ego. Such a defense against love is more likely to allow an occasional unguarded insight, than are the effective screens constructed by the batteries of words with which she first approached Freud.

(183, 8). The analytical dialectic itself constitutes a method of demonstration or proof. Freud proposes that the counter-transference can get in the way of such demonstration and that this aspect of the transference relation 'evades proof'. Even if – as Freud claims – the effects of counter-transference are to be eliminated, Freud asserts that since 'no psychoanalyst goes further than his own complexes and resistances permit' there are limits to the scope of the dialectic. Both Lacan and Freud include 'material of which the analyst is in ignorance' as an aspect of this limitation of scope. In doing this, both seem a little severe in their attitude to proof: even where something 'invisible' is operative, conclusions can be reached which shift previously held views of the world.

(183,9) and (184, 1). 'Transference is nothing real in the subject, if not the appearance, in a moment of stagnation of the analytical dialectic, of the (fixed) permanent modes by means of which the subject constitutes their objects'. This could be taken as an axiom for the handling of the transference.

(184, 2). 'What then does it mean to interpret the transference?' The transference acts as a motor that offers to deeply repressed material an access to consciousness. But as it does so this analytical productivity is opposed by a series of stereotypes of love. Lacan gives a mathematical organization – 'series', 'envelopes' – to these stereotypes that suspend the operation of the dialectic ([Ag]; 90, 5). Any transference then has at least four elements to it: as an agent of the progress of the analytical work, the transference moves in one direction, augmenting the analytical dialectic. This direction is opposed, however, as repetition and archaic modes of love move the work into a second – opposing and regressive – direction. But the reality can be approached by an analysis of forms of love – so the transference-as-motor finds itself accompanied by Repetition, Resistance, and the Real: this third 'R' – as long as access to it can be maintained – augments the motor of the first direction.

(184, 3–4). Lacan proposes for Freud a mode of intervening that would have protected the direction of analysis; Freud had actually conjectured this mode of intervening for himself. Lacan suggests that had Freud responded to Dora by means of an interpretation that within her transference to him there was a love relation to Herr K, this would have allowed the analysis to continue. The interpretation would have functioned as a 'lure', allowing for the further analysis of what it actually means for Dora to love a man, and what it means for her to love a woman.

(184, 5–6). The transference is not primarily affective – its coordinates are primarily dialectical. Wanting what is good is a position that had been proposed to Freud as a possible position for the analyst. Freud's response was that there were very many ways of construing the good – even many differing philosophies of morality and good – none of which formed any part of the structure of analysis. The analyst is not indifferent to this question of the good: when Lacan talks of an error he talks of 'wanting the good too much', and the main issue here is that such a concern deflects from maintaining the dialectic.

(184, 7). Lacan's reading of 'analytical neutrality' is the taking up a position of dialectician. Refutation of previous assumptions about love force a search for other solutions – other than those that the analysand has assumed to make up their history. Lacan had claimed that the analytical dialogue, as it 'reaches the most radical significations intersects with the universal', it gains access, in fact, to 'the universal that is included in language' ([Cr]; 104,6). Socratic dialectic, he had claimed, constructs pathways that lead to 'formerly unknown limits' in love; and it gains access in this way to a 'first symbolism' that 're-verberates' in the body ([Cr]; 105,4). Elements of this primary symbolism can then take on a form of conscious representation by means of the linguistic mechanisms of the transference.

(184,8). There are universal constraints on love: the structure of desire is at the kernel of the unconscious. But conflicts in love can either be accessible or deeply hidden away. For an obsessional, some time can pass before such conflicts leave the screen of the ego (*moi*), and become available as material for a dialectic. But for a hysteric, whose relations are organized around conflicts in love, in between the symptoms and the beginning of the conflicts that underlie them there is no great distance. So in hysteria, there is more transparency: but even here, the work revolves around what Lacan calls 'a demonstration', a demonstration constructed within a dialectic, and made possible by moving from the *moi* to the *mot*.

(184,9). If the analyst allows their attention to lie within the stereotypes of the representations of love, then there will be at least a local 'going astray and loss of orientation'. If, in addition to this, analysts take themselves at times to be addressed by the material that they listen to, then there will be a more global loss of bearing. But whether transference or counter-transference leads astray, the analyst can rectify this by questioning themselves as to their position within the drama being recounted: such a shift in positioning allows for the reintroduction of a dialectic into the subject's history.

What did Freud himself claim about the presence of stereotypes of love within the transference dynamic? The transference, he claimed, introduces 'a stereotype plate' of love 'which is constantly repeated'. Some commentators have taken this to be an effective discounting of transference love. But conflicts of love are at the center of the human condition: so Freud continued 'It is true that the love consists of new editions of old traits, and that it repeats', and he added, 'but that … is not what is essential'. What is essential is that the transference gives an access to the conditions and limitations of love, and that by working within the transference, an analytical dialectic can discover these limits, and move beyond them.

References

Abraham, K. (1908/1927) The Psycho-Sexual Differences between Hysteria and Dementia Praecox. In *Selected Papers of Karl Abraham*. London: Hogarth.

Balibar, F. (2007) La Vérité, Toute la Vérité, rien que la Vérité. In Plon, M. and Rey-Flaud, H. (eds.) *La Vérité*. Toulouse: Editions Erès.

Bénassy, M. (1951/1952) Intervention sur le Transfert. *Revue Française de Psychanalyse*. XVI, 1-2, Janvier-Juin, 1952, 118–122.

Breuer, J. and Freud, S. (1893-5/1955): *Studies on Hysteria*. In *The Standard Edition of the Complete Psychological Works of Sigmund Freud*. London: Hogarth.

Burgoyne, B. (2000) Autism and Topology. In *Drawing the Soul: Schemas and Models in Psychoanalysis*. London: Rebus Press, 190–217.

Burgoyne, B. (2002) What Causes Structure to find a Place in Love?. In Glynos, Jason and Stavrakakis, Yannis (eds.) *Lacan and Science*. London: Karnac.

Burgoyne, B. (2003) From the Letter to the Matheme: Lacan's Scientific Methods. In Rabaté, J.-M. (ed.) *Cambridge Companion to Lacan*. Cambridge: Cambridge University Press.

Burgoyne, B. (2007) Socratic History. *Journal of the Centre for Freudian Analysis and Research*. 17, 108–133.

Ferenczi, S. (1909/1952) Introjection and Transference. In Ferenczi, S. (ed.) Sex in Psychoanalysis. New York: Basic Books.

Freud, S. (1880: translator) Plato. In Mill (1880).

Freud, S. (1912/1958) The Dynamics of Transference. In *SE* XII.

Freud, S. (1915/1958) Observations on Transference-Love. In *SE* XII.

Freud, S. (1920/1955) Beyond the Pleasure Principle. In *SE* XVIII.

Glynos, J. and Stavrakakis, Y. (2002) *Lacan and Science*. London: Karnac.

Hartmann, H. (1933/1964) An Experimental Contribution to the Psychology of Obsessive-Compulsive Neurosis: on Remembering Completed and Uncompleted Tasks. In *Essays on Ego Psychology: Selected Problems in Psychoanalytic Theory*. New York: International Universities Press.

Isaacs, S. (1939) Criteria for Interpretation. *The International Journal of Psychoanalysis*. 20, 1939, 148–160.

Lacan, J. (1936/2006) Beyond the Reality Principle. In *Ecrits the First Complete Edition in English*. Trans. from the French by B. Fink. New York and London: W.W. Norton, pp. 58–74.

Lacan, J. (1948/2006) Aggressiveness in Psychoanalysis. In *Écrits the First Complete Edition in English*. Trans. from the French by B. Fink. New York & London: W.W. Norton. pp. 82–101.

Lacan, J. (1950/2006) A Theoretical Introduction to the Functions of Psychoanalysis in Criminology. In *Ecrits the First Complete Edition in English*. *Trans. from the French by B. Fink. New York and London: W. W. Norton*, 102–122.

Lacan, J. (1951/1952) "Presentation on the Transference" – originally "Intervention sur le Transfert". *Revue Française de Psychanalyse*. XVI, 1-2, Janvier-Juin, 1952, 154–163.

Lacan, J. (1951/1953) Some Reflections on the Ego. *International Journal of psychoanalysis*. XXXIV, Part 1, 1953, 11–17.

Lacan, J. (1958/2006) The Direction of the Treatment and the Principles of its Power. Trans. from the French by B. Fink. *Écrits the First Complete Edition in English*. New York: Norton. pp. 489–542.

Lacan, J. (1960–1961/1991) *Jacques Lacan, Le Séminaire*. Livre VIII: Le Transfert, Paris, Editions du Seuil.

Lagache, D. (1949) De la Psychanalyse à l'Analyse de la Conduite. *Revue Française de Psychanalyse*. XIII, 1, 97–118.

Lagache, D. (1951/1953) Some Aspects of Transference. *International Journal of Psychoanalysis*. XXXIV Part 1, 1953, 1–10.

Lagache, D. (1951a/1952) Le Problème du Transfert. *Revue Française de Psychanalyse*. XVI, 1-2, Janvier-Juin, 1952, 5–115.

Lagache, D. (1951b/1952) Réponse. *Revue Française de Psychanalyse*. XVI, 1-2, Janvier-Juin, 1952, 167–169.

Macalpine, I. (1950) The Development of the Transference. *The Psychoanalytic Quarterly*. XIX, 501–539.

Mill, J. S. (1866) Grote's Plato. *The Edinburgh Review*. CXXIII. April 1866, 297–364.

Mill, J. S. (Ed. Gomperz, T.) (1880) *Gesammelte Werke*, Vol, 12, Leipzig, (R. Reisland) Fues's Verlag.

Nacht, S. (1951/1952) Intervention sur le Transfert. *Revue Française de Psychanalyse*. XVI, 1-2, Janvier-Juin, 1952, 163–166.

Pasche, F. (1951/1952) Intervention sur le Transfert. *Revue Française de Psychanalyse*. XVI, 1-2, Janvier-Juin, 1952, 153–154.

Politzer, G. (1928) *Critique des Fondements de la Psychologie – I: La Psychologie et la Psychanalyse*. Paris: Les Editions Rieder.

Silverberg, W. V. (1948) The Concept of Transference. *The Psychoanalytic Quarterly*. XVII, 303–332.

Zeigarnik, B. (1927) Über das Behalten von erledigten und unerledigten Handlungen. *Psychologische Forschung*. 9, 1–85.

3

ON THE SUBJECT WHO IS FINALLY IN QUESTION

Thomas Svolos

Context

Most of the texts in the *Écrits* were papers published or presented previously by Lacan. There are four texts that Lacan wrote specifically for the *Écrits*. 'On the Subject Who Is Finally in Question' is one of those texts. The location of this short text is immediately prior to one of Lacan's most well-known works, 'The Function and Field of Speech and Language in Psychoanalysis'.

The placement of this text prior to 'The Function and Field' is significant. As Lacan will allude to (189, 1) in the beginning of 'On the Subject', there is a specific context to the delivery of the paper on 'The Function and Field'. The context was the first split that the French psychoanalytic group underwent in the early 1950s, a split that led to the formation of the Société Française de Psychanalyse. Following a dispute on a variety of issues, most manifestly on Lacan's practice regarding the punctuation of psychoanalytic sessions, a group of French psychoanalysts that included Lacan left the Société Parisienne de Psychanalyse in 1953 and formed the Société Française de Psychanalyse. The subsequent paper in the *Écrits* on 'The Function and Field' lays the theoretical groundwork in part for Lacan's practice of the punctuation of sessions, ending sessions at a moment that is not dependent on an artificial measure such as a clock (i.e., the standard 50 minutes session), but at a time propitious for the psychoanalytic work (thus, the term variable-length session). I would like to highlight two aspects of those debates in France that inform both this critical paper from 1953 and the paper 'On the Subject' from 1966, which I suggest we read as an echo of the earlier text. One relates to the issue of the language or logic used to express something about the psychoanalytic experience. For Lacan, in the early 1950s, it is quite clear that he wishes to use the scientific findings in fields such as anthropology and linguistics as ways in which to say something more precise about the psychoanalytic experience. This was one innovation of his that met resistance from his colleagues and which is highlighted in 'On the Subject'. The second matter relating to questions regarding

DOI: 10.4324/9781003264231-3

the formation of the psychoanalyst was also a subject of debate at that time. There too, some of Lacan's final formulations around psychoanalysis – such as the Pass – a new mechanism for defining the end of analysis; or, the breakdown of the distinction between a therapeutic analysis – one pursued by a patient for some therapeutic benefit – and a training analysis, sometimes called a didactic analysis – one pursued because the analysand or patient wished to become a psychoanalyst – were also topical issues around 1966.

Both of these issues, namely, one having to do with the status of truth or knowledge in psychoanalysis and its relationship to science, and, two, that of the question regarding psychoanalytic formation, are issues addressed most directly in the text in question.

Thus, we find this text interesting in its concise formulation of several critical dimensions of Lacan's particular contributions to psychoanalysis, in that it is addressing issues raised previously from a slightly different perspective. Indeed, some of Lacan's comments about training analysis, as we will see, recapitulate what he developed in 1964 in the 'Founding Act' and will further describe a year later, in the 'Proposition of 9 October 1967 on the Psychoanalyst of the School' about the way in which psychoanalysis will advance through the experience of those who take their analysis to the ultimate end.

Commentary on the text

A good place to start here might be to further specify what Lacan is alluding to with the notion of a subject. On page 190, he writes 'namely, the subject whom we qualify (and significantly so) as a patient, which is not the subject as strictly implied by his request, but rather the product that we would like to see determined by it' (190, 8). The subject is not the person demanding analysis as such, but something that Lacan described as a product of the analytic experience, or something 'extracted' from or 'append[ed] to' (191, 1) the person requesting help. Such specification is certainly classic in the way in which it separates Lacan's notion of the subject from that of the ego, or, the body of the person asking for analysis. The subject is not a given, but something obtained through or resulting from the psychoanalytic experience. These formulations of the subject are linked both theoretically to Lacan's fundamental thesis from the 1950s of the subject as an effect of the signifier and also prefigure the point to be developed later as the subject as that which can be extracted through the mechanism of the Pass.

And, in this regard, this specification sets up the next point Lacan wishes to develop in this paper. This relates to the importance of training analysis to the psychoanalytic experience. Note here that Lacan will continue to use the term training analysis through this paper, though conceptually he is in the process of moving away from this notion. Indeed, close to the time of this text, in the 1964 'Founding Act', Lacan elaborated a distinction not based on the intent of the analysand or patient at the outset – treatment, or path to becoming a psychoanalyst – but rather on the basis of the psychoanalytic experience itself, in that any psychoanalysis could result in the creation of a new psychoanalyst, one ratified by the School through the procedure of the Pass. But here, in 1966 in this text, rather than look upon training analysis in the usual fashion of that era, as some type of modification of the usual psychoanalytic practice – which brings to light the question that Lacan states is not frequently asked regarding when a psychoanalyst could be a training analyst – Lacan will pose the problem differently, echoing the texts of 1964 and 1967 alluded to above:

> Shouldn't we, rather, conceptualize training analysis as the perfect form which sheds light on analysis itself, since it provides a restriction to it?

> Such is the reversal that never occurred to anyone before I mentioned it. It seems to force itself upon us, nevertheless. For while psycho-analysis has a specific field, the concern with therapeutic results justifies short-circuits and even tempering modifications within it; but if there is one case in which all such reductions are prohibited, it must be training analysis (191, 5–6).

Thus, for Lacan, it is training analysis – one which does not include any of what Lacan refers to as short-circuits to achieve any certain therapeutic gain – that will allow us to most clearly elucidate or extract or produce the subject, the psychoanalytic subject. The implications of this are clear: namely, that if one wants to understand (though that word or concept 'understand' is certainly problematic) the subject, the psychoanalytic subject, we will obtain what we can know most precisely through a training analysis. This conclusion certainly specifies more clearly the development of Lacan's distinction, from the 'Founding Act' in 1964, between pure and applied psychoanalysis. Pure psychoanalysis is psychoanalysis pursued to its absolute end. Any use of psy-choanalysis for therapeutic purposes is what Lacan will identify as applied psychoanalysis. And, it is through pure psychoanalysis that we are able to learn something about the subject. This lays the groundwork for all the later de-velopments associated with the Pass. The Pass is the process through which a psychoanalyst will relate his or her experience of analysis to two other in-dividuals also at the latter moments of their analysis, those two referred to as passers. The passers then present the analysis, serve as bearers of the description of the psychoanalysis, to a Jury, who will determine if the individual has completed the Pass and is then in a position to present testimony of their analysis to the community of psychoanalysts (the School, in psychoanalytic terms). It is through the experience of the Pass and the transmission by the analysand to the passers of a discourse about the experience of analysis that something about subjectivity can then be extracted and passed on to the community of psychoanalysts. This small point that Lacan develops in the paper, thus, has significant implications for his later work and for the developments of Schools, such as those of the World Association of Psychoanalysis, that practice the Pass. The idea here is that something of the subject can be extracted from the psychoanalytic experience and placed into words or a logical form that can be transmitted from person to person and the wider psychoanalytic community.

Indeed, it is that issue of a logic or language for psychoanalysis that Lacan will next address in 'On a Subject'. What are the ways in which one might express something about the psychoanalytic experience?

Moving to the next section of this paper, Lacan states 'It is obvious that psychoanalysis was born from science. It is inconceivable that it could have arisen from another field' (192, 1). Lacan writes about how it is clear that for those who hold to Freudianism, there is a belief that psychoanalysis has its support in science, and that 'there is no possible transition to psychoanalysis from the realm of the esoteric' (192, 2).

Lacan then briefly alludes to various post-Freudian departures from psychoanalysis, divergences such as Ferenczi and his 'biological delusions' (192, 4) regarding *amphimixis*; or, Jones and his notion of *aphanisis*. *Amphimixis*, the embryological concept of the fusion of two gametes in sexed reproduction to form a zygote, was appropriated by Ferenczi as a model for a successful sexual interaction based on a fusion of partial drives and grounding of sexuality in biology – both features presupposing a certain harmony or balance in sexuality and also a harmony based on some notion of a harmony in nature. Jones developed *aphanisis* in the arguments in the 1920s over feminine sexuality. Against Freud, Jones described this concept of a fading of sexual desire as more fundamental than the castration complex, with its asymmetry between the male and female positions. Lacan at this point in his career remained with Freud with regard to the central place for the phallus in sexuality and in his final development on sexuation in *Seminar 20* affirmed an asymmetry in sexuation that Jones argued against. Regarding all of these post-Freudian developments, Lacan noticed that they all remain centered on a notion of the 'subject's completeness' (192, 4). For Lacan, and for his reading of Freud, the subject is incomplete, which is manifest in multiple ways. The subject is divided into language and speech, which has a traumatic impact on the subject and separates the speaking being from language. The subject is divided from the other sex through the process of sexuation, linked to castration, a loss that cannot be recuperated, thus, one of the most aphoristic phrases of Lacan that 'there is no sexual relationship'. The post-Freudians wish to avoid or to veil that incompleteness.

He further adds to this that these post-Freudians attempt to say something about psychoanalysis with 'myth-like sketches' (193, 2). In other words, these analysts will take certain notions and develop myths or pull in material from mythology to support their theoretical arguments. But, he adds, that authentic myths 'Never fail to leave visible the subject's decompletion' (193, 3). For

Lacan, any true myth does not give a complete subject at the end. Post-Freudians, however, will take folklore-like fragments of the myth as imaginary corroboration for what they wish to say about the psychoanalytic experience. Thus, Ferenczi's use of *amphimixis* uses embryology to create a myth-like explanation of human sexuality.

Corollary with their turn to the esoteric and the avoidance of castration are the ways in which post-Freudian analysts approach the transmission of knowledge. Lacan talks about how, in the best sense, these analysts compare psychoanalysis 'to those trades in which, for centuries, transmission occurred only in a veiled manner, maintained by the institution of apprenticeship and guild' (193, 5). This is, for example, found in the institutional structures of the International Psychoanalytic Association, with the supervising and training analysts as the masters and didactic psychoanalysis and control analysis a process of apprenticeship. Lacan rejects this notion of transmission and states that even this notion of transmission is possible only in the case of a very different subjective position, or different relationship, we might say, of the subjects of knowledge, which I read as a very defined knowledge that can be passed more straightforwardly. In contrast to this, Lacan proposes 'an algebra that tries to correspond, in the place thus defined, to what the sort of logic that is known as symbolic does when it establishes the rights of mathematical practice' (193, 8). What Lacan is alluding to here is that psychoanalysis must lean on science and the logic derived from science, as we see in all of Lacan's efforts over his career to use notions from linguistics and anthropology, or a formal logic of the mathemes, or notions from geometry such as topology or knot theory for the transmission of psychoanalysis. Later on (193, 5) he states that in its youth, psychoanalysis used notions from the liberal arts for its transmission. This is certainly something that he will develop further, as I stated above, with his notion of the Pass.

Lacan then moves on to talk about how this transmission of psychoanalytic experience is linked to a transmission of something of the subjective experience as articulated in the symptom itself. This is how Lacan will reformulate the question of truth in psychoanalysis. Lacan will state that a symptom 're-presents the return of truth as such into the gap of a certain knowledge' (194, 4). In this regard, truth is not a 'failure of representation', but rather truth is 'a truth of another reference than the one, whether representation or not, whose fine order it manages to disturb' (194, 5). We might simplify this a bit by saying that in as much as a symptom is meaningless, it represents a certain failure or lack of knowledge. In other words, when many analysands present for help, they don't know why they have a certain symptom – it is troubling to them, but without meaning. However, through psychoanalysis, one establishes that the symptom does indeed carry meaning, a meaning that represents the truth itself, at least with regard to the subject. That can be seen very clearly in one of the first Testimonies of the Pass published in English, the Testimony of the Argentinian psychoanalyst Mauricio Tarrab (2007) in New York. Tarrab is troubled by various symptoms of paralysis, inability to move or act linked to a sense of menace, and eventually panic-like difficulties breathing. These symptoms are linked in a very precise and singular way to a set of experiences of Tarrab through his life. Initially, the symptoms are present but meaningless. Through the process of psychoanalysis, these symptoms are revealed to have a very specific meaning for Tarrab and speak some fundamental truth about which he was previously unaware.

Put in more classical linguistic terms, Lacan states that

> Unlike a sign—or smoke which is never found in the absence of fire, a fire that smoke indicates with the possible call to put it out—a symptom can only be interpreted in the signifying order. A signifier has meaning only through its relation to another signifier. The truth of symptoms resides in this articulation. [As can be seen most clearly in the Testimonies of the Pass, of those who have taken their analysis to the point where they have something to transmit to others.] Symptoms remained somewhat vague when they were understood as representing some irruption of truth. In fact they *are* truth, being made of the same wood from which truth is made, if we posit materialistically that truth is what is instated on the basis of the signifying chain. (194, 10 − 195, 1)

Thus, for Lacan, one way in which one might say something about the subject is through their speech about the symptom, something spoken through the psychoanalytic experience. To simplify − the 'truth' that Mauricio Tarrab (2007) was looking for in his psychoanalysis was found, as it were, in what his symptom had to say. Indeed, Lacan will specify this a little further by stating that

> by taking one's bearings from the joint between the consequences of language and the desire for knowledge − a joint that the subject is − perhaps the paths will be more passable regarding what has always been known about the distance that separates the subject from his existence as a sexed being, not to mention as a living being. (195, 5)

This definition of the subject as a joint between the consequences of language and desire for knowledge clearly articulates the subject as residing within the psychoanalytic experience. As a speaking being, we suffer the consequences of language, one of which is certainly castration. And, it is the suffering of the symptom that leads to a desire for knowledge that passes within the psychoanalytic experience. Through a desire to know more about our symptoms, analysands seek out psychoanalysts and through that process are led to find that their truth as the subject is a consequence of language (or the consequence of the encounter of language with the body). The subject is the result of that encounter.

Lacan will finish with remarks on what is referred to as the end of the analysis. He talks about a construction necessary regarding the ways in which unconscious fantasies screen the real. He talks about the resistances that are overcome on the basis of structural reference points that must be elucidated over the course of an analysis. And he notes that

> all of these verification values will not stop castration – which is the key to the subject's radical dodge by which the symptom comes into being – from remaining, even in a training analysis, the enigma that the subject resolves only by avoiding it. (195, 9)

Avoiding it, one presumes, through the responsibility the subject has for being well-spoken, as Lacan will allude to in the next paragraph.

Lacan closes with a comment on how training analysis and psychoanalytic teaching must remain 'identical in their scientific openness' (196, 2). He speaks about how psychoanalysis must constitute itself as a science by itself, noting as well that this is a science raised to the second power. Indeed, for Lacan, the issue was not so much whether psychoanalysis could fit within the scientific paradigms of his age, but whether someday we might have a science adequate for psychoanalysis. The experiences of the subject that develop in every psychoanalysis, especially those most 'well spoken' exemplars of psychoanalysis that we hear and read in the Testimonies of the Pass, are the very stuff with which any science must be able to make an account of.

References

Lacan, J. (1964). Founding act. Available at: http://www.amp-nls.org/page/gb/59/fouding-act

Tarrab, M. (2007). Testimony of the Pass in New York. *Lacanian Compass*. 1, 11, 26–36.

4

THE FUNCTION AND FIELD OF FUNCTION AND FIELD OF SPEECH AND LANGUAGE

Derek Hook and Marc De Kesel

By way of introduction ...

'It is up to you to be Lacanians ... I am a Freudian', said Lacan (2011, p. 18), in 1980, in one of his last public statements.[1] The celebrated 'Return to Freud' underpinned Lacan's theoretical innovations until his final days. We could put a date to the formal inauguration of this project: 26 September 1953, the day that Lacan presented an abbreviated version of his paper *The Function and Field of Speech and Language in Psychoanalysis* (henceforth *Function & Field*). This lecture, commonly referred to as the *Rome Discourse*,[2] was delivered just months before the beginning of Lacan's annual series of seminars, which would last until 1980.[3] *Function & Field* is thus both a manifesto – the Magna Carta of Lacan's Freudian contributions to psychoanalysis, as Muller & Richardson (1982) put it – and a blueprint for years' worth of teaching. This goes some way to explaining a notable feature of the text: while Lacan clearly advances a general thesis, he does so without fleshing out many of the subsidiary arguments that he introduces. Ultimately, a systematic, step-by-step line of reasoning is not provided.

What overarching thesis then does *Function and Field* defend? The idea, seminal to Lacanian theory, is that psychoanalysis operates only within the domain of language and speech. Analysts, at this point in the historical development of psychoanalysis notes Malcolm Bowie, needed 'to be reminded that the unconscious is available ... only in the form of language', particularly so given the temptation 'to think of the unconscious as a place, a force ... a collection of wordless drives or as-yet unworded thoughts or ideas' (1991, p. 48). Lacan insists thus that psychoanalysis must limit itself to the function and field of language; analysis should not look to or focus upon something beyond the remit of the signifier. What is helpful for the analysand must be sought *in their speech*, and in the way they relate to their own speech, i.e. in how they are realized as the subject (in Latin, *subiectum*, the 'bearer', 'support', 'ground') of what they say about themselves.[4]

DOI: 10.4324/9781003264231-4

Despite the emphasis on the 'real', which is so characteristic of today's reception of Lacan, *Function & Field*'s thesis concerning the primacy of language and speech remains the most provocative aspect of Lacan's work. To appreciate the rationale behind this, it helps to understand a series of psychoanalytic ideas not explicitly discussed in *Function & Field*. To this end, we will present a brief overview of Lacan's thinking pertaining to the concept of the subject before launching into a close reading of the text. We can begin by stressing an axiom of psychoanalysis. Human life is not governed solely by instincts of preservation. It takes form also in relation to the demand for pleasure, and in relation to the libidinal imperative to *enjoy* beyond the limits of the pleasure principle, which is to say, beyond biological goals of homeostasis or life-sustaining adaptation. Such libidinal enjoyment – or, to use Lacan's preferred term, *jouissance* – routinely subverts the aims of self-preservation.

Pleasure and enjoyment thus both destabilize human existence from the very outset. Pleasure is destabilizing inasmuch as what matters to the infant is less the reality of the world, the accuracy of their perceptions, etc., than gratification itself. Or, in terms which more directly invoke Freud: primordially, the child is not primarily interested in the other or in anything else as opposed to immediately satisfying their requirements for pleasure. *Jouissance* is also destabilizing: libidinal enjoyment routinely over-rides instinct; it perverts optimal biological functioning. One recalls here Freud's (1905a/2001) characterization of the sexuality of the infant as polymorphously *perverse* – such that a variety of life-sustaining activities come to be continued, *enjoyed*, far beyond the satiation of an organic need.[5] We need bear in mind, moreover, that the infant is always born 'prematurely' in the sense that they are clearly lacking in self-sufficiency; their needs must be tended to by an Other, to whom demands – and subsequently desires – must necessarily be directed.

We have at least three levels of disconnection here then: (1) pleasure is at odds with reality, (2) enjoyment is at odds with biological homeostasis, (3) and needs cannot be directly met but require the intervention of the Other, an Other to whom demands and desires will, of necessity, be addressed. We understand better now how, according to psychoanalysis, each of the above areas of human experience is destabilizing, conflictual, and more than just this, *intrinsically traumatic* insofar as each is marked by an inherent division or impossibility, by an irresolvable incompatibility. Let us focus for the time being on the first of these incompatibilities. In order to live and to build an identity – or, more accurately, an *ego* – the infant will need to repress the radical non-reconcilability between their demands for pleasure and the actual circumstances of their given reality. It is here that reality becomes the 'real', in the Lacanian sense of the term: in so far as it is incompatible with the human economy of pleasure. Lacan calls this basic condition '*le manqué-à-être*', a difficult to translate the term, which can be understood as 'the lack of being' (524, 3; 595, 1; 614, 7), or, as Lacan himself translated it, precisely so to stress the role of desire: 'want-to-be' (Miller, 1996a, p. 11). Human existence is always, in this sense, off-kilter; one exists not simply in an uncomplicated state of (actual, balanced or self-integrated) being but precisely as *lack* of being. The subject *is* lack of being, a state which entails a *longing* for being which will never be attained. This is Lacan's re-formulation of what Freud (1900/2001) defined as the primacy of the '*Wunsch*', the 'wish': the subject lives their identity as a *wish* to be identical to themselves, a wish that is never realized (even though it will, of course, be tirelessly re-enacted in fantasy).

The insistence that language plays a crucial role here is foundational to Lacanian theory. Language, however – like the subject him or herself – is constitutively marked by lack. It remains always incomplete. There is no totalizing way of saying it all. This is a structural impossibility given that signifiers, by their very nature, refer constantly on and on to other signifiers. No perfect translation is possible between one set of signifiers and another, hence the Lacanian mantra: 'there is no metalanguage' (688, 7). Signifiers, moreover, never fully coincide with what they are taken to signify (that is, with their signifieds); this is a disjunction, as structural linguistics tells us, that holds for language as such. This dimension of lack should not be read in a fatalistic way, as evidence of irremediable failure. The lack within language is, by contrast, of a *productive and operational sort*. Language works *thanks to* its lack: we keep on talking because of the impossibility of ever fully conveying something. It is this factor that ensures that language becomes the universe within which the speaking libidinal being lives.[6] Repressing their lack of being by language, and thereby also by *the lack of language*, the libidinal subject endeavors to transform impasse into linguistic/symbolic productivity. This makes it possible for the speaking subject to realize themselves as *wishing* (as constantly propelled by the primary process, to put it in Freudian (1900/2001) terms), to realize themselves as the subject of (unsatisfiable) desire.

Having emphasized the foundational role of lack, it helps to say a little more about another crucial leitmotif of Lacanian theory, desire, and how it emerges through the speaking being's relation to language. We can do this by considering the very earliest engagements with language. The infant is acquainted with the language first as an unending flood of articulated sounds, which they do not understand – or even *want* to understand – focused as they are on the goal of immediate satisfaction. Immediate satisfaction is not possible given the infant's state of pre-maturation and their absolute dependence on caregivers. The infant's only way forward is to rely on mediation: they are dependent on others and upon the interactions – always accompanied by language, signifiers, symbolizing activities – that accompany the caregivers' attending to their needs. Symbolic activity is always well underway by the time of the infant's arrival, so much so that in Lacanian theory there can be no pre-symbolic world. This is not, of course, to say that the infant understands the stream of words that washes over them. Yet there is something that the child quickly begins to grasp: all these articulated sounds uttered by caregivers have a prospective value or meaning, and that meaning seems to concern them, the child him or herself.

Although lack undeniably characterizes the existence of the infant, at the earliest months of life – during the narcissistic period of 'His Majesty the Baby' (Freud, 1914/2001, p. 91) – the infant acts as if it were only *others* who are marked by lack, a lack which would explain why they are talking all the time. Consequently, the child supposes themselves to be the answer to that lack, i.e. that which makes the world in which they live – in Lacanian terms, *the Other* – complete. Inevitably of course the child comes to realize that they are neither the answer to all of the Other's questions nor the center of meaning within the world. Neither the child's ('little') others – those who provide the basis of its imaginary ego – nor the symbolic ('big') Other are exclusively preoccupied with them. Destined however to a relation of identification with others, to a symbolic location relative to the Other, and to being a subject of speech and language, the child will necessarily undergo a shift. They will no longer consider themselves to be the *subject as answer* to the lack *of* the Other, but as *subject as bearer of* that very lack. Here, the libidinal being becomes the subject of the desire of the Other, a fact which implies that, now, they – even if only unconsciously – acknowledge themselves as also marked by a fundamental lack. This shift is only possible given a context of language, a context, we might add, which is indispensable to human social existence as such. The libidinal being thus becomes a subject of language, a subject that lacks, a subject whose lack is reverberated in each signifier that refers (never fully, always incompletely) *to them*, and does so in a way which necessarily entails a succession of referrals (one signifier relating always differentially back to other signifiers). We have, in short, entered the territory of desire, that place – or perhaps better yet, the scene – in which the subject assumes a relation to the desire of the Other.

All of this has an immediate bearing on the clinic. The demand of the neurotic analysand is of an imaginary nature, says Lacan. The analysand seeks to avoid their condition as the divided subject of language, as the lacking subject of the Other (indeed, as *the subject of the desire of the Other*), precisely by fortifying their ego. They cannot stand their condition as the subject of desire, i.e. the fact that they do not coincide with a full 'self' (a coherent, self-knowing undivided ego) but rather, far more fundamentally, with a condition of lack. The existence of unconscious wishes, the fact of being split and overdetermined by the symbolic Other of language, these facets of their existence must be kept at bay by whatever means possible. The irony of the situation is that the remedy being sought, namely the replacement of a condition of lack with the utopian goal of a whole 'self' (a fantasmatic ideal image the ego has of itself), merely deepens the state of alienation. Such a demand for a full 'self', illusory and futile as it for Lacanian theory – the ego is always based on images taken from others – remains nevertheless both a powerful and seductive demand. Such a fantasmatic goal is understandably enticing; it makes us believe that a resolution of lack (of castration, of a condition of dividedness) is possible. And this is what the analysand's symptom – and their demand, more generally – is about: 'If my symptom is healed, if my demand is answered, I will be delivered from this bothersome lack of desire that keeps me incomplete'. Language enables the patient to play such a game, to attempt such a 'solution', namely that of inventing a full 'self' – a 'self' that is supposed to be the fulfillment of their desire.

This is why, for the analyst, the most difficult challenge in an analytical cure, is not so much the patient's, but *their own* desire. The analyst is constantly seduced into assuming the position of whatever imaginary object/persona might fill in or compensate for the lack of the analysand. Hence the Lacanian imperative according to which the analyst must avoid providing an answer to the patient's demands or offering a diagnosis that links the patient's problems to facts, to anything beyond language itself.[7] Such a diagnosis would maintain the patient in the imaginary position.[8] The aim of psychoanalysis is to shift this imaginary position into one in which the analysand assumes their position as the subject of the symbolic, their position as the subject of the desire of the Other.

Now we understand why it is so important that the analyst – and psychoanalysis more generally – must remain within the function and field of speech and language. It is true, on the one hand, that it is by means of language and speech that the analysand denies their status as lacking, as desiring (hence, as we will see, Lacan's notion of empty speech). And yet, on the other hand, it is only within the realm of language that the analyst can lead the patient to an encounter with – and, optimally, the subjective assumption of – the fundamental lack that characterizes them as the subject of desire. The analysand's confrontation with the split condition of their status as subjects can only happen via language and speech. Every appeal to what lies beyond language results in the analyst falling into the imaginary trap set by their patient.

The analyst and the analysand are involved in a 'dance' that occurs in the medium of speech in the structural domain of language.[9] This is a dance that oscillates between the imaginary denial of lack (the lack that desire is based upon), and the symbolic assumption of that lack. This is a dance, moreover, choreographed not merely for two but for *four* dancers given the fact that both the patient and the analyst oscillate between the functions of an imaginary ego and that of a symbolic subject – or, in the concepts utilized within *Function & Field*: between a '*moi*' (ego) and a '*Je*' (I). While *Function & Field* does not fully establish the structure and procedure of such a choreography,[10] it does provide selected components for the project of directing a treatment and, speaking more generally and historically, for the rejuvenation of a truly Freudian form of psychoanalytic practice. In what follows we will adhere closely to the meandering path that Lacan forges, detailing his references to other texts and theories, while trying all the while to provide an overview of the implied line of reasoning.

Context

Lacan begins *Function & Field* with a quote, 'an inscription for a psychoanalytic institute in 1952' (197, 1), whose methodological and conceptual priorities he could not be more opposed to: '[I]t should not be forgotten that the division into embryology, anatomy, physiology, psychology, sociology, and clinical work does not exist in nature and that there is only one discipline: a *neurobiology* to which observation obliges us to add the epithet human' (197, 1). These are the words of Sacha Nacht, a leading Romanian-French analyst who represented the orthodoxy of psychoanalysis as it was then practiced. It is regrettable, from a Lacanian perspective, that such a perspective might still be endorsed by many psychoanalysts even in the twenty-first century; this fact gives a renewed urgency to studying *Function & Field* today.

In late 1952 and early 1953, disputes concerning psychoanalytic theory and practice had split the French analytical society, the *Société Psychanalytique de Paris* (SPP) (founded in 1925), of which Lacan had been a leading member. In June 1953, a new society – *Société Française de Psychanalyse* (SFP) – was created when Lacan and Daniel Lagache led a secession from the Paris group. As a result, Lacan and all the other members of SFP were declared unwelcome at the planned 1953 biannual Congress of French-Speaking Psychoanalysts. The SPP 'proclaimed', as Lacan puts it, 'that it would prevent the person who, along with others, had tried to introduce a different conception of analysis from speaking in Rome' (197, 4–198, 1). '[D]ifferent conception' is a notable understatement, given the disdain Lacan held for any form of psychoanalysis willing to subscribe to the above cited inscription (and indeed, to any privileging of the biological in respect of psychoanalytic theorization or practice).[11]

Lacan had been invited to speak at the Congress prior to the split from *Société Psychanalytique de Paris*. While the Italian hosts of the Congress wished to accommodate the analysts of the newly formed *Société Française de Psychanalyse,* they could not prevent the dissident voices from being excluded from the platform. Lacan was replaced by another speaker, but was nonetheless given an occasion to speak at a different time. He did not read the text of *Function & Field,* opting instead – in line with the practice of psychoanalysis as a verbal modality – to deliver a series of extemporaneous remarks on select themes within his paper. And so, as Lee observes, while

> Lacan could no longer represent the SPP at the Rome meeting; nevertheless he did speak on the 26 September, and he used this occasion to launch his own ongoing challenge to the international psychoanalytic community, a challenge that henceforth took the form of his weekly or biweekly seminar ... [which continued] from autumn of 1953 to the spring of 1980, and it is not at all unfair to see Lacan's teaching career as a sustained elaboration and rethinking of the fundamental positions articulated in Rome in 1953.
>
> (Lee, 1990, p. 31)

Jacques-Alain Miller (1996a) affirms this, noting also that Lacan effectively consigned all his work prior to 1952 to the status of his 'antecedents'; *Function & Field*, stresses Miller, was '[t]he starting point of his teaching' (p. 4).

Commentary on the text

Preface

After relating fragments of the institutional split described above, Lacan begins the *Preface* by locating himself – and his situation – by means of an etymological reference. Lacan seems in fact to console himself, saying that he felt 'assisted … by a certain complicity inscribed in the place [of the Universal City] itself' (198, 4). How so? Well, in his *Noctes Atticae,* Aulus Gellius, the second century Roman grammarian, associated *Mons Vaticanus* (a hill located across the Tiber River from the traditional seven hills of Rome), to the word *vagire* 'which designates the first stammerings of speech' (198, 5). If Lacan has been reduced then to such stammerings, 'to be nothing more than a newborn's cry' (198, 6), then, he avers, it is worth exploiting the historical resonances of his location – which draws attention precisely to the dimension of speech and enunciation – so as 'to revamp the foundations our discipline derives from language' (198, 6). Lacan insists, moreover, that he has broken with tradition so as to adopt an ironic style suitable to a radical questioning of the foundations of psychoanalysis. It is for the benefit of his students that he has broken the rules of the 'high priests' (198, 8) in charge – his former colleagues from *Société Psychanalytique de Paris* – because they had become overly fixated with rules and neglectful of the autonomy of those they sought to train. With respect to the formation of new analysts, formalism is fatal; this, for Lacan, was one of the most pressing reasons why a return to – and clarification of – the principles of psychoanalysis is so urgently required.

Lacan makes it clear, however, that holding on to underlying theoretical principles does not exclude the possibility of disputes or divergences of opinion. On the contrary, fidelity to principles requires a 'dialectical testing of contradictory claims' (199, 4), which in turn requires reflection upon the conceptual supports of Freud's theory. We must retain Freud's concepts because it would be 'premature to break with the traditional terminology' (199, 8). However, that terminology needs clarification, and here, current anthropological studies and many of the 'latest problems in philosophy' prove immensely helpful (199, 9).[12] Such points of guidance and inspiration will not only prevent the practice of psychoanalysis from deteriorating to a technical set of procedures; they will foreground the meaning and value of traditional psychoanalytic concepts currently in danger of 'being deadened by routine use' (199, 10). Psychoanalysts, for Lacan, had become so lacking in curiosity as to the principles underlying the efficacy of their analytical skills and techniques, that the power of the treatment to induce change had come to seem virtually magical to them. So disconnected had they become from any rigorous attention to the materiality of everyday psychoanalytic practice – the workings of language and speech – that they were content to credit neurobiology as being the underlying foundation of psychoanalysis. This, for Lacan, is an error akin to a driving school imagining itself 'in a position to supervise car construction' (200, 5). The discipline of psychoanalysis was thus in danger of letting itself down, for, surely, 'a method based on truth and demystification of subjective camouflage' should 'apply its principles to its own corporation ... ?' (200, 10) Psychoanalysts, in other words, had forgotten the foundational tools of psychoanalytic inquiry when it came to assessing psychoanalysis itself as an institution.

At the end of the *Preface*, using a concept he has yet to explain, Lacan stresses a 'symbolic action [that] becomes lost in its own opacity' (201, 1). 'Symbolic' announces the field in which both the analyst and the patient have to operate: a field of signifiers in which the patient has always already lost him or herself – i.e. their imaginary 'ego' – and where, in that very loss, he or she will find themselves as a 'subject', i.e. as *subiectum* of desire (desiring, amongst much else, a remedy – a 'self' – to the lack that defines them). In the last sentences, Lacan apologizes for the 'haste in which [his discourse] was written' (201, 2). This too, he suggests, is not without direct reference to the psychoanalytical field and praxis. He refers here to his 1945 essay *The Logical Time and the Assertion of Anticipated Certainty* (see Chapter 1 in the current volume) where he describes 'haste' as the temporal condition in which the patient must come to conclusions during the analytic cure. He will return several times in *Function & Field* to that essay, treating it as a crucial precursor to his current concerns.

Introduction

Lacan begins with two epigraphs that announce the main theses of *Function & Field*, even if only in an elliptical manner. The quotation from Georg Christoph Lichtenberg ('We shall determine this while we are still at the aphelion of our matter, for, when we arrive at the perihelion, the heat is liable to make us forget it' (201, 6)) directs our attention to questions of location. It tells us: we need to determine our position *now* given that, in our voyage around the sun, we are at the farthest point (the aphelium); once we have reached the nearest point (the perihelicium), this will no longer be possible. Whether things are possible or not for someone, we can thus say, is a matter of *topology*, i.e. of where they are located. Although abstract, this idea gives us a sense of what Lacan will argue in what follows: the problem that both the analyst and analysand face during the cure is a *topological* one, a matter of *where they are located* in the intersubjective field they share. This field is not so much constituted by the patient and the analyst, as by what they share with one another – language, considered in the materiality of spoken signifiers. This is also what the second quotation, another celestial musing, taken from the nineteenth century poet Robert Browning, points to. In the context of a fictitious discussion with Bernard de Mandeville,[13] we hear the interlocutors talk about the constellation of Orion. There we read:

> Is, joint by joint,
> Orion man-like, — as these dots explain
> His constellation? Flesh composed of suns —
> How can such be?' exclaim the simple ones.
> Look through the sign to the thing signified.
>
> (Browning, 1887, p. 30)

This quasi-ontological discussion moves from considering whether the constellation of Orion is humanoid in its arrangement – as various ancient astronomers had decided it was – to debating a very different proposition: that flesh might itself be composed of stars. Not only then do we have a rival sense of what the underlying materiality/substance of things might be (that is, the properties and proportions of the human as opposed to the carbon or cosmic matter underlying the very possibility of human existence). There is also a sense – especially in the lines following those quoted by Lacan – that a subtle change in the symbolic ordering of a pattern might fundamentally alter our understanding of it, and the ontological status that it has hitherto been afforded:

> Look through the sign to the thing signified —
> Shown nowise, point by point at best descried,
> Each an orb's topmost sparkle: all beside
> Its shine is shadow: turn the orb one jot —
> Up flies the new flash to reveal 'twas not
> The whole sphere late flamboyant in your ken!
>
> (Browning, 1887, p. 30)

Those lines, 'twas not/The whole sphere late flamboyant in your ken!' convey something of Lacan's message to the more orthodox and ego psychology supporting variants of psychoanalysis of his (and our) day: What you have taken as central to psychoanalysis (its ostensibly biological underpinnings or the central role of the ego) is misguided inasmuch as it reads and prioritizes a gestalt (the visual impression of a constellation) over the symbolic operations of language and speech which are of far greater importance. From the perspective that insists on the primacy of the signifier (understood here as inclusive of the symbolic order and the multiple functions of language as such), human beings might well be composed of stars in the precise sense that both their identity and that of the sun is the first and foremost a matter of signifiers.

Lacan now properly begins, invoking Prometheus, and stating – in uncharacteristically clear and direct terms – that just as human beings have historically turned fearfully away from their most important discoveries – discoveries revealing 'the true face of ... [their] power' (201, 8) – so have psychoanalysts. Indeed, one can trace 'a growing aversion regarding the functions of speech and the field of language' which has negatively impacted proposed 'changes in aim and technique' within the discipline (201, 9). To turn away from language is to turn away from the medium in which human intersubjectivity occurs; it is to bypass the means through which the subject might find their truth. It is hardly surprising then that we are witnessing, as Lacan puts it, a 'general decline in therapeutic effectiveness', and the trend for analyzing resistances – which Lacan clearly pinpoints as a culprit here – should instead be approached via an analysis of the dialectical play of the analytical process. In this dialectical play, the emphasis on the 'the object's resistance' (a reference to the analysand) must be scrutinized; one will subsequently 'recognize in this emphasis the attempt to provide the subject with an alibi' (201, 9). This suggests that a technical fixation on the analysis of resistances in fact buttresses rather than questions the ego of the analysand. It provides the analysand with an effective escape-clause when it comes to assuming their position as a subject of language, as a subject of desire. Lacan provides a 'topography' of how psychoanalysis has turned away from speech and language, offering a short overview of the psychoanalytic literature of the time which identifies how 'the current problems in psychoanalysis ... fall into three categories' (201, 10):

A   The domain (or Lacan puts it '[t]he function') of the imaginary (202, 1). This is somewhat misleading because although Lacan uses a term from his own conceptual lexicon, he is in fact differentiating his own prioritization of speech and language from trends that centralize fantasies in 'the technique of psychoanalytic experience' (202, 1) and which foreground the importance of stages of psychological development and the corresponding type of object that tends thought to predominate at each of these stages. Worse yet, from Lacan's perspective, such trends, having arisen 'from the analysis of children' – Melanie Klein is the obvious target here – are much preoccupied with 'preverbal structurations' (201, 1) – a clearly oxymoronic phrase for Lacan – and thereby necessarily sideline the role of language. While the domain of the imaginary may appear to be preverbal, it necessarily calls for symbolization ('symbolic sanction' (201, 1) as Lacan puts it) in interpretation. Hence the repeated emphasis Lacan places on the symbolic register.[14]

B   The realm of libidinal object relations theory – typically represented by the work of Melanie Klein, W.R. Fairburn and D.W. Winnicott – which has asserted the idea of 'treatment progress' (202, 2) and thereby influenced how a psychoanalytic treatment should be conceptualized. The object relations approach has also enlarged the domain of psychoanalytic treatment to include psychosis. Lacan makes reference here to psychoanalytic theories that consider the libidinal vicissitudes of the drive as following an ostensibly *natural* evolution toward attaining the right attitude in relation to the right object (Maurice Bouvet's (1972) notion of the genital object, being a prime example of such thinking). Here, psychoanalysis is reduced to a kind of 'orthopraxis', a praxis aiming at a 'right' way of living. It is in this sense that psychoanalysis is reduced to 'existential phenomenology', and even 'an activism activated by charity' (202, 2). And again, Lacan announces 'symbolization' to be the remedy here.

C   A sphere in which countertransference – that is, the transference of the analyst with regard to the patient – has been prioritized in conceptualizations both of treatment 'and, correlatively … [within] analytic training' (202, 3). This obsessive attention to the lived experience of the countertransference had resulted in a series of complications in respect of the termination of a treatment and the ending of a training analysis. The idea that the analysis of the analyst's unconscious reactions to their analysand's should be a crucial factor 'in the effects of an analysis' or 'brought out into the open at the end of the game' (203, 3) was anathema to Lacan.[15] Likewise problematic for him was the requirement that there needed to be some 'unconscious mainspring' located *beyond* the inter-subjective field of speech and language (202, 3).

Psychoanalysts have thus attempted 'to abandon the foundation of speech' (202, 4) – precisely in domains where speech should be most carefully examined: in 'the child's education by its mother [firstly], Samaritan-type aid [secondly] and dialectical mastery [thirdly]' (202, 4). In the following paragraphs, Lacan indicates some other positive attempts to consider the role of symbolization in psychoanalysis (for example Ferenczi's (1949) study on the 'confusion of tongues' in the child/adult relation), yet he concludes that 'only an appropriate return to the study of the function of speech' will suffice (203, 2). It is precise via speech and language that Freud approached the libidinal problems of, amongst others, Little Hans (Freud, 1909a/2001) and Daniel Schreber (Freud, 1911/2001) (203, 3). After Freud, such an approach had been almost completely abandoned. Rather than approaching psychoanalysis as a dialectical play in the field of language, the treatment has become a set of formal procedures similar in many ways to what Freud diagnosed as 'obsessional neurosis' (203, 5).

All of this, according to Lacan, is due to an 'ignorance of the origin of terms' (203, 6) within the broader context of Freud's thinking. The meaning of psychoanalytic concepts had come to be determined by the way the psychoanalytical community (the important American group included) was using them. By criticizing analysts, says Lacan, he is only applying the 'analytical method [i.e. the primacy of language and discourse] to the collectivity that sustains it' (203, 9). It is in this historical context – of conceptual vagueness and imprecision – that Lacan formally introduces the triad of 'symbolic, imaginary, and real' (204, 2) although without affording the terms much by way of explanation.[16] Referring to the American psychology and psychiatry of his day as dominated by ahistoricism and behaviorism, Lacan distinguishes his approach as being primarily symbolic/linguistic in its foundations, i.e. as recognizing the primacy of the 'symbolic order' (i.e. the field of language, the realm of signifiers). Yet, once again, instead of explaining the term, he refers to an effect of that symbolic order, and more specifically, to something he once labeled as the 'c factor' (at a Congress of Psychiatry in 1950) (204, 4). This is a reference to the fact that the subject – contrary to the tenets of behaviorism – needs to be viewed as fundamentally cultural and not simply as a natural or adaptational entity.[17]

It seems indisputable, Lacan claims, that, under the influence of the American group, psychoanalysis has moved in the direction of a psychological adaptation theory (204, 6–204, 7). This is the reason for the 'eclipse in psychoanalysis of the liveliest terms of its experience – the unconscious and sexuality' (204, 7). A correct understanding of these concepts is a *sine qua non* for psychoanalysis despite that these concepts have not been considered essential to a 'true mastery' (205, 1) of psychoanalytic practice or the teaching of psychoanalysis that some training institutes demand of their senior analysts (Lacan is sarcastically referring here to the American psychoanalytic community obliging their new analysts 'to give at least one class' (205, 1)). And yet, Lacan qualifies, the emphasis on a correct understanding of the concepts is not a plea for a new orthodoxy. It is, by contrast, a means of announcing that 'these concepts take on their full meaning only when oriented in the field of language and ordered in relation to the function of speech' (205, 3).

In the last paragraph of the Introduction, Lacan refers at length to an author who is alleged to have reduced Freud's thinking to merely a theory of instincts. This, as Lacan makes plain, is a crass misunderstanding worsened by the fact that this author refers to the work of Marie Bonaparte as being at the same level as that of Freud himself.[18] Added to these egregious errors is a complete denial of the importance of language and speech in psychoanalysis and the reduction of psychoanalysis to little more than a form of neurology. Lacan's disdain is on full display here. This author considers the psychoanalytic concept of the drive to be 'reducible to the reflex arc' (205, 4). They maintain that Freud's complex work of theory construction – which, Lacan reminds us, moves from discovering the libido in the erogenous zones to an understanding of the pleasure principle and the death drive – amounts to little more than 'the binomial of a passive erotic instinct, modeled on the activity of lice seekers' (205, 4). (The reference here is to Rimbaud's poem *The Seekers of Lice*). The unnamed author that Lacan so thoroughly disparages – someone we will hear more of as we progress – is Maurice Bénassy. Bénassy's writings are, for Lacan, a travesty, a patchwork of misunderstandings that don't rightly deserve to be called psychoanalytic. They are most useful to us as an example of what psychoanalysis should *not* be.

I Empty speech and full speech in the psychoanalytic realization of the subject

The first section of *Function & Field* is focused on the topic of speech, and Lacan, accordingly begins with two further epigraphs, each of which includes an incitement to speak. The first epigraph is taken from *L'Enternelle Consolacion*, a contemporary French version of the fifteenth century text on spirituality, *De Imitatione Christi*: 'Put true and stable speech into my mouth and make of me a cautious tongue'.[19] This is not only a plea for speech; it also contains an implicit reference to truth. Hence its relevance here: for Lacan, psychoanalysis is not only a matter of language and speaking but of the speaking subject's *relation to truth*. This challenges commonplace presumptions about the aims of a psychoanalytic treatment. The goal is not the banal agenda of restoring a state of happiness. It concerns the subject's realization of themselves as the bearer or subject of a truth of desire, a truth that can only be found in what he or she shares and exchanges in language and speech with others, with the analyst in this case. In order to attain a cure, analysands will have to talk and, by means of the 'talking cure', as Anna O. so famously defined her analytic cure (Freud, 1910/2001, p. 13), search for truth. Speech is the 'method' of psychoanalysis; its aim is the truth of desire.

'Keep talking', the second motto, is by Lacan himself and is left untranslated in the English edition. The French version, '*cause toujours*', allows one to appreciate the semantic link to the fictitious origin of the quote: 'Motto of a 'causalist' thought' (206, 3). 'Causalist' refers to theories that locate the origin of the patient's problem in an ostensible cause outside the field of language, beyond the parameters of the speaking process of an analytic cure. Later in *Function & Field* Lacan will discuss this position by criticizing an unnamed representative of that theory (208, 5). Here he uses the word 'causalist' in reference to the French word '*cause*' in '*cause toujours*' ['always speak'/'keep talking'], insinuating that the real origin and cause of the problems psychoanalysis deals with are be found in relation to language.

An important corollary of the fact that speech is an inherently social practice is the fact that it always supposes an answer or response, even if it only meets with silence. This is the case in the patient's 'empty speech', a type of speech that constantly seeks the affirmation of others as a way of attempting to substantialize, to give fullness or wholeness, to the ego. 'Empty speech', says Verhaeghe (2020), 'corresponds to a certain reality about the self image [the ego] and how it is perceived by other people ... [t]he emptiness has to do with an all too full imaginary ... [This] has to be undermined by the analytic work. Being fully identified with oneself leads to ... .empty speech'. Analysts are all too familiar with this situation: the analysand speaks, the analyst experiences the call to respond, to 'seek a reality beyond speech to fill the emptiness' (206, 5). The clinician feels the temptation to 'analyze the subject's behavior in order to find in it what the subject is not saying' (206, 6). Yet, Lacan stresses, even if the analyst were to find something there, they would nonetheless need to return to speech if they were to relay this, whatever it might be, to their analysand. This returns us to Lacan's opposition to forms of psychoanalysis focused on fantasized object relations that are thought to occur at preverbal stages of development, and to his related hostility to the notion that a regressive reappearance of such fantasies might occur in clinical work with adults. By the time any of this material finds its way into the analysis, it does so via speech. 'The preverbal is known only as verbalized in the course of the analysand's speech, and Lacan insists that it is theoretically naïve to ignore the ways in which language is bound to shape the reports of fantasy' (Lee, 1990, p. 34).

What the analysand is asking for in their empty speech is truth (they are making 'an appeal to truth at its very core' (206, 7)). Yet at the same time, they avoid a confrontation with truth, making demands of the analyst and using them as a means of supporting their imaginary identifications. In this case, moments of silence are not moments of introspection, as many analysts seem to think. Even when the analysand prepares their introspection prior to sessions, free association nonetheless has the effect of undoing this pre-emptive defensive maneuver. Free association is 'forced labor of a discourse that leaves no way out' (207, 2); it counters the ego's attempts at affirming itself in its own image. Psychoanalysis is not a matter of (imaginary) introspection; it is a (symbolic) inter-subjective procedure in which the speaking subject realizes their status as divided precisely when and insofar one addresses one's self to the Other.

While it can be qualified as 'work', free association does not make the apprentice in psychoanalysis a 'skilled worker' (207, 3). What is at stake in the cure is work in the sense of what Freud calls *'durcharbeiten'*, or 'working through'. This German term is difficult to translate into French, Lacan adds, quoting the seventeenth century poet Nicolas Boileau (2007) from his *L'Art Poétique* where Boileau states that one should, if necessary, rewrite things twenty times. It illustrates perfectly what precisely *'durcharbeiten'* means (207, 5).[20]

The notion of working through calls to mind the 'triad: frustration, aggressiveness, regression' (207, 6). Lacan vehemently criticizes the then commonplace practice of linking frustration to 'affectivity'. Where does 'this frustration comes from[?]', he asks (207, 6). Not from the non-answer or the silence the analysand receives from their analyst, for an answer would frustrate them even more. Rather, it is the case that frustration is inherent to the analysand's discourse itself. And this is a good thing, for the analysand has to get 'involved here in an ever greater dispossession of himself' (207, 7). In other words, the analysand has to become aware of the imaginary dimension of their experience of themselves (their self-impressions, images, idealizing objectifications, etc.) as it contrasts against their existence as a subject of the symbolic order, who, accordingly, takes on an identity in relation to the desire of the Other. The work of analysis can thus be likened to a deconstruction of the imaginary ego. It is for this reason that Lacan speaks of the subject becoming involved 'in an ever greater dispossession of himself as a being ...

[of] sincere portraits ... of narcissistic embraces' (207, 7). This subject, can, through the process of analysis, recognize that his or her 'being has never been anything more than [their] own construction in the imaginary' (207, 7). In the work of analysis – or for that matter, in a successful example of working through – the analysand undertakes a type of reconstruction '*for another*' in which he or she 'encounters anew the fundamental alienation that made [them] ... construct it [their self-image, their ego] *like another*' (208, 1). Lacan here wishes both to impress upon us the breadth of imaginary alienation and its paranoiac connotations (the ego constructed *like another,* destined to be taken away *by another*) and to suggest that it is precisely through again experiencing (more precisely, *working through*) such frustrations that some distance may open up between the subject and these alienating identifications. There is also an intimation, by virtue of the qualified types of relation to the other (for/like/by) that Lacan has in mind here the famous Hegelian maxim (desire is 'the desire of the Other' (750, 3)), which is to say: analysis affords the analysand the opportunity to recognize how their own desire is Other.

Unlike ego-oriented versions of psychoanalysis which explain the ego as a positive power able to withstand frustration, Lacan defines the ego as 'frustration in its very essence' (208, 2). It is not, to be precise, the frustration *of the analysand's desire* which is in question, for the ego is precisely the imaginary formation in which (the Other's) desire – inclusive of its accompanying enjoyment – has been thoroughly alienated. It is this ego which, in the working through of the cure, needs to undergo frustration.

Aggressiveness, for Lacan, is not some regression to an animal stage. It is rather a reaction of the ego which is trying to hold off any attempt by the analyst to break through the analysand's imaginary constructions. This is what happens in the so-called countertransference – as put forward by that 'naïve analyst' (208, 4), 'the same one' (208, 5), who situates the origin of the patient's problem outside the field of speech and language (this is, as we have seen, the 'causalist' position, ironized in the second epigraph opening this section of Lacan's essay). Again, Lacan refers here to Maurice Bénassy, leaving the author once more unnamed and reproaching him for 'the anxiety of having to think that his patient's freedom may depend on ... his own intervention' (208, 5). What, according to Lacan, Bénassy is afraid of, is the intersubjective play between analysand and analyst in which the former has to realize themselves as the subject of desire for and of the Other. Importantly, however – a point that might easily be overlooked – the analyst is likewise to be located in such a dependent relation, in terms of desire for and of the Other.

Some say that what must be analyzed in a psychoanalytic cure, is simply what happens in the 'here and now' ('the *hic et nunc*') of the exchange between analysand and analyst (208, 6). Of course, the patient's history is very much part of the game, but what must be analyzed is how the analysand *reports* that history, and how it emerges in speech directed toward the analyst. Attending to the 'here and now' has its place in clinical practice, provided that the analyst does not detach the analysand's 'imaginary intention … from the symbolic relation in which it is expressed' (208, 6). That is to say, the analysand's imaginary '*moi*' is useful only insofar as the *je* (the 'I' as the speaking function in terms of which all discourse about the *moi* unfolds) is adequately highlighted. Drawing attention to the discontinuity between the *moi* and the *je* will prove a crucial facet of the analytical work. It is in this way that the subject eventually arrives at the formula Lacan cites: 'I was this only in order to become what I can be' (209, 1). Or, as we might put it: 'I was and am an imaginary ego, a *moi*, but my fate is not to remain this; it is instead to realize, via the speaking function of the *je,* the subject I can come to be'. (This is itself, of course, a reformulation of the Freudian declaration, '*Wo Es war, soll Ich werden*' ['Where It was, I shall become'], which Lacan revisited and reinterpreted multiple times across his teaching.[20]) Analysis can thus be construed as a working through of the fixations of the ego. Hence Lacan's insistence that the analyst's art involves 'suspending the subject's certainties until their final mirages have been consumed' (209, 3).

All of this is to say: the speech of the analysand has to be disconnected from its imaginary contents. The imaginary aspect of meaning-making – of empty speech – engenders illusions; it functions to create effects of wholeness and ego-coherence, to reify both its speaker and their objects. This is the medium of self-narrative, of the stories we tell ourselves via others, stories which, psychoanalytically, are not to be trusted, even when they do seemingly accord with reality, for the simple fact that their over-riding objective is to sustain ego-affirming images. Empty speech has an alienating destination, even if composed of factually true fragments; full speech, by contrast, can be error-ridden, may involve falsities and untruths *en route* to a moment of revelation.[21] The paradox of this situation is that empty speech is often exceedingly full of non-substantive ego-supporting contents (it is full of shit, we might say). So, while empty speech is typically loaded with insubstantial materials, symbolic full speech is often very sparse when it comes to content, being stripped of imaginary trappings. This is an idea that resonates with Roman Jakobson's (1960) concept of phatic communication, with the idea of essentially meaningless exchanges that function simply to maintain a social bond, to keep communicative channels open and effective. This is particularly evident in a paragraph in which Lacan draws on Mallarmé, who, he says:

> compares the common use of language to the exchange of a coin whose obverse and reverse no longer bear any but eroded faces, and which people pass from hand to hand 'in silence'. This metaphor suffices to remind us that speech, even when almost worn out, retains its value as a *tessera* [a ticket, a token of admission] Even if it communicates nothing, discourse represents the existence of communication; even if it denies the obvious, it affirms that speech constitutes truth; even if it is intended to deceive, the discourse speculates on faith in testimony. (209, 5–209, 6)

What are we to conclude from this? Well, Lacan's discussion of the symbolic role of worn-out coins makes it clear that language is not merely a means of conveying imaginary identities. Language, by contrast, is a medium of inter-subjectivity which enables the creation of symbolic relations between people. Identity does not precede the medium – language – that people use in order to communicate. The reverse is rather the case: it is the medium, *language*, that it is primary. It is the fact that a child is addressed with signifiers that give the child the opportunity to imagine themselves as the subject of those signifiers. This is how they will ultimately constitute themselves as a subject, i.e. as a subject of language: not merely as a subject that supposes itself to be *the signified* of all these signifiers (the imaginary position of the ego), but as the subject of *signifiers*, signifiers that refer always to other signifiers, signifiers that they, the subject, will pursue endlessly, in a ceaseless attempt to respond to their lack of being. It is within such moments of speech – moments where the analysand realizes that they have their origin in and are radically alienated by the Other – that they are potentially able to confront their truth. And the reference to that truth is implied in every act of speaking, which is why, 'even if it commu-nicates nothing … it affirms that speech constitutes truth' (209, 6).

More simply put: Lacan is telling us that despite the omnipresence of empty speech and how it constantly consolidates the imaginary functions of the ego, a type of truth is possible via the symbolic function of speech and *full* speech more particularly. To appreciate this distinction it helps to refer to a definition of full speech that Lacan offers in Seminar I: 'Full speech is speech which aims at, which forms, the truth … Full speech is speech which performs' (1988a, p. 107). It is a speech by means of which the speaking subject 'finds himself, afterwards, other than he was before' (p. 107). It is the analyst who bears responsibility for bringing this full speech – the speech of the subject's realization – to light, for hearing 'within the description of an everyday event … a fable addressed as a word to the wise', for drawing attention to how 'a simple slip of the tongue [entails] a highly complex statement' (209, 7). At such moments, the speech of the analysand reveals something Other than the imaginary intentions of the ego; we have here the possibility of the emergence of the subject. The analyst can provoke such breaking points by means of interventions, interruptions or, as Lacan puts it here, 'propitious punctuation[s]' (209, 8), the most dramatic of which is perhaps the scansion involved in the analyst's precipitous ending of a session, an ending which deserves the status of a psychoanalytic intervention.[22] The aim of freeing the ending of sessions from its 'routine framework and employ[ing] it for useful aims of analytical technique' (209, 8), provides an interesting segue way to Lacan's thoughts on regression.

Lacan implies that the principle of the abruptly terminated session applies also to how regression might occur. Both such situations rely upon the efficacy of pre-empting conclusions and other imaginary fixities. Regression is, after all, but 'the bringing into the present in the subject's discourse of the fantasmatic relations discharged by an ego … in the decomposition of its structure' (209, 9). This is a highly original move on Lacan's part, one which highlights that regression remains a vital psychoanalytic concept for him inasmuch as it facilitates the aforementioned 'decomposition' of the ego. This is so despite his attacks in *Seminar II* on analysts who maintain a 'magical' view of regression, seeing it as a real temporal phenomenon, a kind of reversion in which adults 'actually regress, return to the state of a small child' (Lacan, 1988b, p. 103). What Lacan stresses in *Seminar II*, the idea that '[re]gression doesn't exist' (1988b, p. 103) at least *in the sense of a lived return to a younger state,* is anticipated in *Function & Field* in Lacan's declaration that 'regression is not real' (210, 1). Whereas such a temporal experiential regression does not exist, regression is indeed manifested in speech, 'by inflections, turns of phrase' (210, 1), which is to say that it occurs 'on the plane of signification and not on the plane of reality' (1988b, p. 103).[23]

One of the traps many analysts fall into, Lacan continues, is to think that the cure consists not in leading the subject to their truth, but in freeing them from deleterious fantasies and restoring a proper 'contact' with reality (210, 3). The supervision that every young analyst is obliged to undergo demonstrates that the contrary is true. It is not conformity to reality, Lacan adds, that makes supervision thoughtful, but the new perspective – the 'second sight' – it can give to the same 'reality' (210, 3), which is by definition a thoroughly fantasmatic one. For the analyst is always in the 'position of ... second subjectivity' (210, 5), and this is what a supervision should bring about in the one supervised, so Lacan adds, criticizing the worrying connotations of the French term for supervision: *contrôle* [control].

An analyst must be aware of this 'second subjectivity' when they listen to their patients with what is classically referred to as a 'defuse, or even absent-minded, attention' (210, 6), hearing not the manifest content of what the patient says but their hesitations and slips of the tongue. Lacan stresses once again that the analyst certainly should not listen to 'an object beyond the patient's speech' (210, 6). If there is an 'object' the analyst has to attend to in the patient's discourse, it is 'the imaginary relation that links him to the subject qua ego' (211, 2). The analyst must be aware that they will become a key reference point within the analysand's discourse; they will be the *signified* of many of the signifiers that their patients utter. Similarly, they need to be cognizant of how they are being positioned as an imaginary object so as not to be seduced into affirming this imaginary relation between themselves and the ego of the analysand. And the difficulties here lie not solely with the analysand. The analyst has to be vigilant of the temptation to see – that is, to (mis) recognize – in the *moi* of the analysand the projected imaginary contents that stem from the analyst themselves. While this might, to some extent, be impossible to avoid, the analyst's best counter-imaginary strategy is to attend to the *materiality of the signifier*, prioritizing thus the significations (that is, precisely *signifiers*) rather than merely the meanings (*signifieds*) produced by the analysand. The analyst must listen in the way that the Gospels says one should not: 'having ears *in order not to hear*' (211, 2),[24] which is to say: listening in a way that does not fortify the imaginary relationship between analyst and analysand. Such a non-hearing listening facilitates a movement away from the imaginary operation of empty speech 'in which the subject seems to speak in vain about someone who – even if he were a dead ringer for him ... - will never join him in the assumption of his desire' (211, 3).

In the second part of this first section of *Function & Field*, Lacan focuses on what, within the analytical cure, disrupts the patient's imaginary strategy and enables 'full speech' (211, 4). It becomes important to ask here: is the aim and task of a 'talking cure' not 'anamnesis', i.e. making conscious the patient's unconscious traumas? Are these events not the cause of their symptoms, since 'putting the event into words' (211, 7) leads to the removal of such symptoms? And is the speech of the patient only a '*flatus vocis*' (212, 1), that is, a mere sound or series of words without a corresponding object, that needs as such to be assessed in facts rather than in words and speech? Is it not the case that the success of the cure depends on the patient becoming aware of those very facts?

Lacan responds to these questions with a resounding 'no'. What is decisive for him is that the patient has brought these events to the level of speech, verbalized them, mixed them up with earlier verbalizations, and made them comprehensible within the terms of 'their present discourse' (212, 2). It is not the past event as such that matters here, but the way the subject appropriates that past in their present speech. As Jacques-Alain Miller clarifies: 'Lacan considered an analytic session to be a construction of history, history constructed with its meaning by the subject ... The history which is spoken in analysis is a reconstruction of the subject's project' (1996b, p. 28).

Lacan takes up a Heideggerian perspective here. In *Being and Time*, Heidegger (1996) explains that the past of the *Dasein* (his term for 'subject') is not situated behind but *before* them. *Dasein* is not at the origin of their life and world, but is rather *thrown into* a world that existed prior to them. Dasein, therefore, has to take that 'thrownness' (*Geworfenheit*) up as a project ('*Entwurf*') that needs to be realized. Our past, that which we have been (our '*Gewesenheit*'), is lived not as something behind us, but as what we *have to* be, *have to* assume, indeed, as belonging to us. In this sense, our past is located in the time in which we live, and this is not simply the present as such, but the present unfolding always outward toward the future. This is why, for Heidegger, human existence is *ex-sistence*, a mode of existing which 'stands out' in the direction of the future. I am not what I am *now*, I am what I have to be. I always *have to* be what I am, and also what I *was*. I have to take my past upon me as a possibility allowing me to become what I am.[25]

Speaking of the 'ambiguity of hysterical revelation of the past' Lacan notes that this ambiguity occurs not because of an oscillation between imagination and reality nor because 'it is made up with lies', but because it shows us the 'birth of truth in speech' (212, 4). It is this truth through speech that brings the analysand up against 'the reality of what is neither true nor false' (212, 4). What kind of truth does Lacan have in mind here? It is certainly not the truth defined by a proposition's correspondence to reality. Lacan repeatedly places emphasis on the present speech of the analysand as a vehicle of truths of the past: 'it is present speech which bears witness to the truth of ... revelation in current reality' (212, 5–213, 1), 'only speech bears witness in this reality to ... the powers of the past' (213, 1). This begs the question of how we think the relation of past to present psychoanalytically, and Lacan wastes little time in stressing that Freud's idea of the condition of continuity in anamnesis (that is, in respect of memories of the past) is paradigmatically opposed to Henri Bergson's notion of duration.[26] Whereas in a 'Bergsonian myth of a restoration' (213, 2), the authenticity of a single instant relies upon the modulation of all foregoing instances, for Freud one can access and work with memory (one can perform a type of 'psychoanalytic anamnesis' (213, 2)) in and through speech precisely because a type of *full speech* (a speech of revelation) is made possible in the clinical exchange. For Freud then, to clarify, what is operative is not biological memory, some mystical form of intuition, or the 'paramnesia of the symptom' (213, 2), that is, memory confusions or distortions (such as confabulation or déjà vu) associated with the core of the analysand's suffering. It is, by contrast, the register of history, and the subject's relation to their history through the vehicle of speech, which is crucial. This is what Lacan has in mind when he says 'In psychoanalytic anamnesis, what is at stake is not reality, but truth' (213, 2). Commenting on this section of *Function & Field* (on the idea that truth is a function of speech), Lee (1990) remarks:

> [W]hat is important is not so much the historical accuracy of the analysand's memory as the intersubjectively intelligible narration of his past in the form of a tale or even an epic ... The analysand's free association, punctuated by the analyst's replies ... ultimately yields a coherent narrative that has the double effect of constructing the analysand as a subject and of revealing his truth ... As an autobiography of sorts the analysand's storytelling comes to cast the analysand as a subject who has a history ... the psychoanalytic dialogue constructs in narrative a subject 'who has been' in relation to a future which is taken to be the subject's own in the course of the psychoanalysis ... [For all of the above reasons] Lacan is arguing ... that truth is a function of speech, that outside of the use of language there is no sense to be made of the notion of truth, and thus that the ... reality external to the symbolic resources of language is also external to the categories of true and false. In the reality of the psychoanalytic session the only truth that counts is that constituted by the analyand's narration. (pp. 42–43)

We have here a rapid succession of ideas that elaborate upon the subjectivizing effects of speech within the analytic process. Speech is the fulcrum of truth not only inasmuch as it allows the subject to articulate and assume aspects of their own history in a narrativized form attended to and punctuated by the Other. Speech and language, furthermore, provide the medium through which deliberations of truth can occur. Speech allows the subject to situate themselves relative to their future, and here it is again apparent that Lacan is approaching these issues in a Heideggerian way. Truth qualifies the event in which *Dasein* takes upon themselves the *Da* (the 'thereness') of their being, inclusive of their being in the past (the 'thenness' as we might put it), so as to assume the being they will always again *have to* be.

Lacan thus reformulates Heidegger's (1996) idea of *Erschlossenheit* (*Disclosedness*) in his own psychoanalytical terms. Truth is the event of 'full speech', he writes, in which the patient 'reorders past contingencies by conferring on them the sense of necessities to come, such as they are constituted by the scant freedom through which the subject makes them present' (213, 2). Truth emerges when the patient takes upon themselves the true (that is, *symbolic*) condition that their imaginary ego denies. The subjectivity of the analysand, their sense of who they are and how they relate to the world, cannot be accounted for simply in terms of the gestalt effect of their ego. The subject's truth emerges in their attempts to put their life into words. Such a life story, which has its origins in the Other, contains moments of inconsistency and ambiguity, moments where imaginary meaning breaks down. It is the virtue of the subject's encountering such points of breakdown that new future possibilities are opened up. By assuming a subjective stance in which they coincide with an openness to the future (an openness that makes them the subject of a radical, i.e. unfulfillable desire), the speaking subject relates in a new way to what they are and were (their *Gewesenheit*), to 'the sense of necessities to come' (213, 2).

In order to illustrate this, Lacan refers to Freud's (1918/2001) analysis of the Wolf Man and to his own essay on *Logical Time* (161–175). In the latter, Lacan presents what he calls a sophism – in effect a thought experiment – in which three prisoners have had a white or black disk pinned to their backs. These disks have been selected from a set comprised of two black and three white disks. The prisoners, who are prohibited from speaking to one another, can see the disks that their fellow prisoners wear, although they cannot see the disk that has been attached to their own clothing. The prisoner who first correctly deduces the color of the disk that has been affixed to them, and explains how they have arrived at this logical conclusion, will win their freedom. Lacan explains that each of the prisoners is capable, by considering the thought process of the other prisoners, of deducing the color of the disk that they are wearing.[27] Lacan endeavors to show that the truth the prisoners have to deal with is a truth that they must decide upon; it is a matter of anticipating a certainty to come. In other words, there is not only a crucial anticipatory – indeed preemptive – dimension to these proceedings, there is also the fact of the subjective assumption by each participant of a deduced truth, the necessity, in other words, of a precipitative identification that will in turn effect how the whole scenario unfolds. Similarly, in the psychoanalytic cure, the subject assumes 'his history, insofar as it is constituted by speech addressed to the other' (213, 6). Herein, Lacan adds, lies 'the basis of the new method Freud calls psychoanalysis' (213, 6).[28]

This is not to say that there are no 'psychophysiological discontinuities' in hysteria and neurosis, but to stress that the psychoanalytical method should not rely on them (213, 7–214, 1). Lacan repeats his earlier insistence that the means of psychoanalysis are exclusively 'those of speech' (214, 3). Its domain is the 'concrete discourse qua field of the subject's transindividual reality' (214, 3), which is to say that speech facilitates the inter-subjective field in which they can constitute themselves (precisely as the subject of the desire of the Other). This implies that the unconscious is not a direct object of inquiry. It is, by contrast, a 'third term' (214, 7), something 'transindividual, which is not at the subject's disposal in reestablishing the continuity of his conscious discourse' (214, 8). This is Lacan's way of responding to the paradox of unconscious thought as advanced by Freud (in *The Interpretation of Dreams*, for example, Freud (1900/2001) maintains that 'dreams are nothing other than a particular form of thinking' (pp. 506–507, n2)). How, though, can thinking be unconscious? Lacan argues that it is a *language* that provides the support of thinking, rather than consciousness. The unconscious can be conceived as a type of thinking – enabled by the processes of language – which is 'not at the subject's disposal' (214, 8).

This is why the unconscious can be thought of as chapters of the subject's history, chapters that are 'marked by a blank or occupied by a lie', which is to say, 'censored chapter[s]' (215, 3). The truth of such lost or redacted chapters can be retrieved – and here, Lacan very deliberately uses descriptive terminology drawn from the domain of literary production – in:

- bodily monuments/inscriptions (hysterical symptoms which manifest the structure of language and can be deciphered);
- archival documents pertaining to the subject's history (such as childhood memories);
- semantic evolution (the particularity of the subject's own vocabulary, the idiosyncrasy of their stock of words and acceptations);
- the symbolic density of oral and literary traditions, of oft-rehearsed myths, legends and popular narratives (which provide a vehicle for expressing the subject's history);
- traces (indeed, *editorial* traces, we might add) which are preserved by virtue of the distortions necessitated by censorship and by the addition of adulterated (that is, euphemized, banalized) chapters into one's history to cover over what has been hidden.

Given the above conceptualization, we can appreciate how for Lacan the 'distinctiveness of the psychoanalytic domain ... reveals the reality of discourse in its autonomy' (215, 2). The above overview of the unconscious cannot – perhaps obviously – be reduced to any understanding that would identify it with instinctual urges or drives and/or developmental stages. It is for this reason – as Muller & Richardson (1982) emphasize – that Lacan consistently stresses the primacy of the symbolic over the biological, and insists that 'What we teach the subject to recognize as his unconscious is his history' (217, 3). Putting to one side what he clearly views as the problematic theory of psychosexual stages/development, Lacan advances that 'every fixation at a supposed instinctual stage is above all a historical stigma' (217, 3).

Back though to Lacan's catalog of the various formations of the unconscious. Clearly, there is much here that recalls Freud, as Lacan himself readily admits ('what I have just said is hardly original, even in its verve' (215, 5)). Wilden's (1968) commentary on this section helpfully illuminates the Freudian background of Lacan's concerns:

> One recognizes the metaphor of the ancient city undergoing excavation through various layers: that of the somatic compliance of the historical symptom, which may exhibit the condensation and displacement to be found in language and which 'joins in the conversation', as Freud put it; that of Freud's view that resonances of unconscious meanings and linguistic relationships from a mythical earlier time are exhibited in the language of dreams; that of double inscription. Moreover, we are reminded of Freud's constant recourse to the myth and to the fairy tale as exhibiting universal structures or as serving as representatives in the subject's discourse ... as well as to the personal or individual myth of the subject ... And lastly, there is the instance of 'secondary revision' and of the *Enstellungen* ('distortions') in the dream and in the symptom, where the subject, unbeknownst to himself, seeks to 'make it all make better sense' – notably after the topographical regression to perception in the dream, the fundamental meaning being finally restored only by putting into words of the 'images' (the thing presentations) and their assumption by the subject's discourse in the dream text, where the dialectical working through of associations enables the subject to provide himself (unconsciously at first) with the exegesis of his own dream (or symptom).
>
> (Wilden, 1968, pp. 108–109)

This commentary astutely notes the implicit factor of secondary revision in Lacan's listing of various formations of the unconscious. It likewise highlights the importance of topographical regression as it occurs in dreams (Lacan had alluded to this earlier, but it is not explicitly evident in his list).

Novice analysts will realize that many of the key metaphors Freud introduces – Lacan cites the example of negation – quickly 'lose their metaphorical dimension' (216, 1) in the domain of clinical practice. The conceptual apparatus of psychoanalysis is not, in other words, *merely* metaphorical, even though to practice clinical psychoanalysis is to operate 'in metaphor's own realm' (216, 1). Lacan reminds his readers that metaphor is itself 'a synonym for the symbolic displacement brought into play in the symptom' (216, 1). In other words, it is not simply the case that bringing the concept of metaphor to psychoanalysis helps us to better understand the phenomena of psychical life. A more radical thesis is being affirmed here: the underlying basis of psychical operations (such as the formation of symptoms) is itself linguistic. We might put it this way: the symptom is no less metaphoric than the linguistic devices that Freud utilizes to teach us about what he observes in the clinic. The clinical practice of psychoanalysis – to refer back to the phrase used above – again 'reveals the reality of discourse in its autonomy' (215, 2).

And this is precisely what a popular psychoanalytic writer like Otto Fenichel – a well-known summarizer of Freud's work – has not seen. Fenichel (1946) approaches the history of the patient to 'the supposedly organic stages of individual development', where he would have been better served by 'searching for the particular events of a subject's history' (216, 2). This distinction is tantamount to that between an account of 'the supposed laws of history' (which, as Lacan points out, vary for every historical period, depending on the values of the scholars tasked with identifying them) and 'authentic historical research' (216, 2). Attention to the laws of history might have some attraction – it enables us to pinpoint the ideals of a given historical period – but 'their role in scientific progress is rather slight' (216, 4), indeed, such abstract and speculative laws 'are worth as little for directing research into the recent past as they are from making any reasonable presumptions about tomorrow's events' (216, 3). The same holds for the alleged usefulness of 'organic stages of individual development' (216, 2). Confusing the laws of history (or the generalizing assumptions of stages of psychological development) for an attention to precise historical moments (or particular events of a subject's history) amounts to bad history for Lacan, who goes on to remind us that psychoanalysis and history 'are both sciences of the particular' dealing with facts that might seem 'purely accidental or even factitious' (216, 5).

Lacan's comment that we need to distinguish between 'primary and secondary functions of historicization' (216, 4) is deserving of further comment. We can do this by referring back to the idea of secondary revision, that is, to an awareness of what conscious (or ego-led) narrativization does to the experience of a dream. The re-arrangement of the dream's elements, the filling in of gaps, the selection of only certain components in the re-telling of the dream, all of these considerations, along with the general imposition of considerations of narrative intelligibility, exercise a significant reworking of that material (Freud, 1900/2001). This is true also for the primary historicization – which Lacan also refers to as 'primal' historicization (216, 6), referring even at one point to 'the constitutive subjectivity of primal historicization' (238, 2) – and secondary historization. We can think of this as the original ('primal') experience as it was lived by the subject and how it is historically reconstructed in the subject's autobiography. Hence Lacan's comment that 'Events are engendered in a primal historicization ... history is already being made on the stage where it will be played out once it has been written down, both in one's heart of hearts and outside' (216, 6). Documented history is always effectively secondary historicization; it is always what was *said* to have happened. History immediately plays out within a scene of interpretation, representation and language, and within the inter-subjective dimension that such a scene implies.[29]

Lacan extends his conceptualization by way of a historical example, referring to the battle of Faubourg Saint-Antoine which occurred on the 2nd of July 1652. On this date, a series of rebels, members of the revolutionary movement called *La Fronde*, overcame royalist forces and took control of the city. The Parliamentary cause that they supported proved victorious; the Royal Court lost. While this victory was not long-lasting – royalists retook the city later that same year – it proved, in retrospect, to be of considerable historical significance, certainly inasmuch as it proved a key point of inspiration for the storming of the Bastille on 14 July 1789. Some, as Lacan avers, even retrospectively enlisted this revolt 'in the struggle for the proletariat's political ascension' (217, 1), which is to say that they interpreted the battle in light of the principles of dialectical materialism. All of this tells us that primary historicization can be overwritten, afforded very different – indeed, diametrically opposed – meanings by a series of successive historical eras. Such ascribed meanings can be so divergent that, to all intents and purposes 'it is not at all the same historical event' they refer to, for such recordings 'do not leave behind the same sort of memory in men's minds' (216, 7). There are interesting implications for trauma here. The overwriting of one period of history by another can return to an early crucial event (such as the battle of Faubourg Saint-Antoine) 'its traumatic value' (216, 8), allowing, furthermore, for a 'progressive and authentic effacement' (216, 8–217, 1) of differing interpretations and meanings of the event. Lacan's suggestion here – which adheres to Freud's conceptualization of *nachträglichkeit* (deferred action/après-coup) – is that historical changes can retroactively make new traumas of the old. More than this, the historical and psychical effects of repression amount to 'one of the liveliest forms of memory' (217, 1).

Lacan takes the opportunity to remark on the necessity of distinguishing between 'the technique of deciphering the unconscious' on the one hand, and 'the theory of ... drives' (217, 2) on the other. These are two facets of psychoanalytic conceptualization that have been routinely conflated in a way, which for Lacan, is hugely problematic, because doing so makes an adequate historicization of the analysand virtually impossible. To superimpose patterns of drive behavior, or stages of 'instinctual development' on the life of an analysand, obstructs our ability to bring into focus the crucial moments of change in their history. As Lacan states: 'What we teach the subject to recognize as his unconscious is his history ... we help him complete the current historicization of the facts that have already determined ... the historical 'turning points' in his existence' (217, 3).

As opposed to linear or stage-theory approaches to the history of the subject, Lacan gives us to understand that the traumas they have lived through *were being interpreted even while they were being experienced*, and are, in this sense, involved in later traumatic events and how they are interpreted. This is also the case in respect of the so-called 'instinctual stages' (217, 5). Lacan takes the example of the anal stage, indicating that there, the child is engaged in an intersubjective field in which they 'register victories and defeats' (217, 5). Lacan's perspective offers an insight into the installation of the 'anal' structuration of the child's body. The child confronts a series of prohibitions regarding any anal activities that exceed necessary biological excretory functions. The child can thus constitute a 'self' – an ego – precisely by denying such prohibitions. It is only after a long oedipal struggle that the child manages, out of love for those who have prohibited such anal activities, to do what he has been asked. This is their way of 'turning ... excremental expulsions into aggressions ... retentions into seductions, and [the] movement of release into symbols' (217, 5). With emphasizing italics, Lacan adds: this release into symbols '*is not fundamentally different* from the subjectivity of the analyst' (217, 5) when they try to understand their analysands. The analyst, too, is inclined to give themselves the position of an imaginary ego mastering the patient's problem by referring it to 'some supposed instinctual maturation', to some cause in the sphere of 'ontogenesis' (217, 6), or to any other fixed cause outside the intersubjective play (i.e. the field of language and speech). So, the work of analysis concerns as much the analyst's own imaginary tricks and ruses as the analysand's.

This is why psychoanalysis must not fall into the trap of 'analogical thinking' (218, 2), of explaining cultural phenomena by referring to ostensibly analogous natural phenomena. 'Analogy is not the same ... as metaphor' stresses Lacan, emphasizing also that it was 'by deliberately avoiding analogy that Freud opened up the path appropriate to the interpretation of dreams', a path which relied on '[a]nalytical symbolism' (218, 2). An analogical comparison – like analogical symbolism – relies on one person or thing corresponding to another in a stable and consistent manner. Such a one-to-one correspondence is not what Freud has in mind with dream symbolism, which entails a far more diversified and complex set of significations that are, as a result, more difficult to interpret. The symbolism of dreams needs to be approached by the work of the free association, not by being interpreted as a series of analogs. Lacan understands the term 'symbolism' analytically, in a strictly Lévi-Straussian sense, which acknowledges the radical difference between culture and nature. Culture takes place within the symbolic field of signifiers, whose functioning cannot be reduced to natural laws or to a system of correspondences between signifiers and objects.

Psychoanalytic theory cannot rely on conceptualizations of a typical natural development that leads the libidinal being from an uncertain and unstable so-called 'pre-genital' (217, 5) phase into a certain and stable 'genital' phase, enabling them in this way to maintain a mature relationship with their basic object of desire – the achievement, in other words, of an apparent type of 'genital love' (218, 4).[30] Analytical theories that make this claim consider the goal of the cure to be of a moral nature. Psychoanalysis needs a discourse and a practice that surpasses this kind of morality.

Lacan speaks critically of 'the poverty of the terms within which we try to contain a subjective problem' (218, 6), stressing how such a vocabulary – presumably that of proponents of 'psychoanalytic normalization' (218, 4) and stage theories of maturation – 'leave a great deal to be desired' (218, 6). For Lacan, the very idea of a maturational timetable is anathema, and contrary to Freud's (1900/2001) insistence that the unconscious knows no distinction between infantile wishes and those of the adult. The relation of the subject to their object of desire is never simply straightforward or direct; it certainly does not follow a pre-established series of steps; nor does it trace the trajectory of a triumphal ascension to a fulfilling object of genital harmony.

In a footnote, Lacan refers to Pascal's famous wager, that is, the idea that a rational person should live as though God exists because only a finite loss will be incurred if in fact He does not whereas a believer stands to receive infinite gains if He does exist (266, f. 14). In Lacan's interpretation, this wager provides a formulation of the way in which libidinal being constitutes itself as a subject of desire (as a subject of language/signifier). It also echoes the idea of an anticipatory form of temporality which necessarily involves the subjective act of making a wager, which Lacan had dramatized in his *Logical Time* essay. Certain truth-effects accrue to such a mode of temporality; there are some truths that are only truths due to the fact that they were anticipated, pre-empted by a subjective act of wagering. These ideas concerning the role of precipitous subjective gestures and/or identifications and desires clearly run counter to sequential stage theories of development and related notions of maturational periods.

The libidinal relation of the subject to its object is complex, moreover, because 'Logos' (218, 6) is involved. This is a characteristic move on Lacan's part, introducing a complex philosophical term into clinical discourse. Logos refers both to the divine Word that in its Grace created all that is, and to the order of the signifier which provides the medium – that of the symbolic order – that enables us to live and pursue our libidinal life. A 'better appreciation of the functions of the Logos' (218, 6) will help save us from the conceptual and clinical dead-ends of post-Freudian psychoanalysis.

A more lucid spokesperson regards the relation of the subject to their object of desire is to be found in the figure of François La Rochefoucauld, and Lacan accordingly cites one of the celebrated French author's maxims: 'There are people who would never have fallen in love but for hearing love discussed' (219, 1). This assertion helps us recognize what 'love owes to the symbol' (219, 1). Human love, like desire, proceeds along symbolic terrain and is never merely natural or instinctual. This idea – that love is not to be reduced to the level of instinct – is illustrated by a further reference to Freud's (1918/2001) analysis of Sergei Pankejeff (the 'Wolf Man'), whose subjective conflicts in love are in effect 'only a question of the vicissitudes of subjectivity' (219, 2). 'Perfect love is the fruit not of nature but of grace'; it is an 'intersubjective agreement' (219, 3) that is rooted in the field of signifiers (219, 3).

'But what, then, is this subject? ... Haven't we already learned ... from Monsieur de La Palice [i.e. Mister Nobody] that everything experienced by the individual is subjective?'[31](219, 4). Lacan's response to this commonplace assumption is unequivocal: 'The subject goes beyond what is experienced 'subjectively' by the individual' (219, 5). The subject exceeds the confines of the ego, stretching as it does beyond such imaginary parameters, going 'exactly as far as the truth [he/she] is able to attain', the truth here being understood as the truth of one's history – that is, as unconscious truths – 'not all contained in [their] script' (219, 5). The subject's unconscious is thus attained in – in effect *is* – the Other's discourse.

The subject occurs at the point where the libidinal being finds its support and condition in language, in the signifiers of the Other. This is how the analysand confronts their truth, a truth which is located beyond conscious experience (and beyond the remit of the imaginary). Psychoanalysis is never a simply 'a two-person relation' (220, 2). If that were the case, the experience would be a basically imaginary and not a profoundly symbolic one. With this assertion, Lacan marks the transition to the second section of *Function & Field*.

II Symbol and Language as structure and limit of the psychoanalytic field

Having focused on speech in the first section of his essay, Lacan now turns his attention to the field of language. He leaves the first epigraph for this section – a quote from the Gospel of John (8:25) – untranslated. It is Jesus's answer to the question posed to him by the Pharisees: 'Who are you?'. As Muller & Richardson (1982) point out:

> the Gospel text admits of several translations, including 'What I have told you all along' ... 'Why do I talk to you at all' ... 'What I have told you from the outset' ... Lacan may have read the translation from the Vulgate, 'I am the Beginning who speaks to you,' now seen as grammatically impossible. (p. 111)

Lacan's focus is not on the content of Jesus's expression, but on his speech *as such*, on the 'material' that his identity is made of: signifiers. It is in the field of the symbolic that the subject, and the truth of their desire, might be realized. Lacan accordingly advances the thesis that, in psychoanalysis, one should re-main focused on the materiality of the signifier. The second epigraph also draws attention to language and the role of signifiers: 'Do crossword puzzles'

(220, 4), which is to say: take up exercises in playing with language on the level of its mere superficiality.

Lacan begins this section by invoking the idea of psychoanalysis as a science of the particular. Psychoanalysis is about that which is not reducible to general patterns such as those offered 'genetic psychology' (220, 3). The particular in this context, he qualifies, is not about the individual's abilities and characteristics (such as the analysand's 'ability to retain things' or 'which parts of [their] body are sensitive' (221, 1)). He refers, sarcastically, to the 'young analyst[s]-in-training' who considered 'sniffing each other' as an aspect of the transference relation (221, 3) and who thought 'being smelled' by their analysands would be important in their eventual qualification as analysts.[32] Grasping the particularity in questions requires an adequate understanding of what the experience of psychoanalysis is. Such an understanding is vital if psychoanalysis is to avoid being reduced to a series of technical procedures. This particularity of the subject comes to the fore in the materiality of the discourse of the analysand as it is performed before the Other, or in the clinical context, before the analyst.

This is why it remains important to go directly back to Freud's oeuvre, avoiding interpretations of Freud's work which relegate the crucial linguistic sensibilities of his work to a secondary status. Freud's (1900/2001) *The Interpretation of Dreams* for instance, tells us that dreams are structured as a sentence or, more exactly, as a rebus. This text foregrounds the irreducible rhetorical dimension of dreams which pertains both to how dreams are composed by the dreamwork, and how they are conveyed through speech. Dreams are rhetorical productions that utilize a variety of linguistic devices (such as ellipses, pleonasm, hypebaton, syllepsis, regression, repetition and apposition) to a wider variety of effects 'ostentatious or demonstrative, dissimulating or persuasive, retaliatory or seductive' (222, 1).[33]

The dream is a work of desire, Lacan states ('as a rule … the expression of a desire must always be sought in a dream' (222, 2)) thereby affirming Freud, before adding that this desire must also be located in the inter-subjective field of the analytic cure. The desire at work in the dream may also be the desire to contradict Freud's (or the analyst's) thesis that in dreams desire is at work. Yet, this desire, too, has its full place and function in the inter-subjective play between patient and analyst. This perfectly illustrates the thesis that a subject's desire finds its meaning in the Other's desire, not simply in the sense that the Other possesses a much-desired object or attribute, but because our first 'object(ive) is to be recognized' (222, 2) by the Other.

The analyst's job requires a reading of the analysand's desire which is always already performed as a text. Such a text is marked by all kinds of rhetorical tricks and ruses; it is addressed to the Other, and it constitutes as such an inter-subjective scene. It is, accordingly, to be 'interpreted as a provocation, a latent avowal … by its relation to the analytical discourse' (222, 4). The bungled actions that Freud (1901/2001) so astutely analyzes in *The*

Psychopathology of Every Day Life are likewise to be grasped as linguistic, as 'successful, even 'well-phrased,' [instances of] discourse' (222, 5). The predominance of the rhetorical, the linguistic and the symbolic in Freud's early work is apparent also in his discussion of apparently randomly selected numbers. Whereas Freud appeals in such situations to 'unknown [unconscious] thought process', this is in fact a result of 'the total confidence he [Freud] placed in symbols' (222, 6). The unconscious at work in such examples is thus itself considered to be set in motion by means of the signifying chain, that is, via the effects of insistence, combination, repetition and symbolic efficacy that the symbolic order enables. As Lacan puts it a few lines later: 'the experience of the numerical association will immediately show … .[that] the combinatory power that orders its equivocations … [is] the very mainspring of the unconscious' (223, 2).[34]

Symptoms are also linguistic. They are structured as overdetermined signifiers. A symptom, after all, is 'constituted by a double meaning' (222, 7). It is the symbolization of a conflict, and it 'can be entirely resolved in an analysis of language' (223, 1). Lacan's account here is complex, so it helps perhaps to consider as a case in point a symptomatic behavior from Freud's (1909b/2001) case of Ernst Lanzer (the 'Rat Man'). On a summer holiday, Lanzer was struck with a sudden mania for slimming. He started exercising to the point of dangerous excess as a result of the idea that he was too fat. It did not take Freud long, via a series of word associations, to notice that the German word for fat ['*dick*'] corresponded with the name of the English cousin of Ernst's much loved Gisela. Gisela has openly expressed much affection for this Dick, and Lanzer was intensely jealous of him, hence Freud's initial interpretation: 'Our patient … had wanted to kill this Dick; he had been far more jealous of him and enraged with him than he could admit to himself, and that was why he had imposed on himself this course of slimming by way of punishment' (Freud, 1909b/2001, p. 188). This example is less than straightforward, however, because the symptomatic behavior in question can be read in multiple ways, both as acting out a desire to effectively erase *dick*/Dick and – here is the overtly obsessional component – as *a mode of self-punishment* for having had such jealous and furious thoughts in the first place. The example serves thus to illustrate the Freudian directive as voiced by Lacan, namely that the analyst needs to 'follow the ascending ramifications of the symbolic lineage in the text of the patient's free associations' (223, 1). It demonstrates also how 'a symptom is … structured like a language' (223, 1), which is why it can be treated by speech.[35]

Lacan praises Freud's (1905b/2001) *Jokes and Their Relation to the Unconscious* (as 'the most unchallengeable of…[Freud's] works' (223, 6)) noting especially how Freud's analysis of wit and witticism 'demonstrate [the unconscious] in all its subtlety' (223, 6). Lacan's own role as a translator of Freud should be noted here, especially in respect of the less than obvious distinction between wit and witticism. Whereas previously Freud's German '*Witz*' had been translated into French as '*mot d'esprit*', that is, as the capacity for wittiness, Lacan preferred 'trait d'esprit' which incurs rather a sense of the 'flash of wit' (Quinodoz, 2004). This translation foregrounds the temporal moment – an instance, a flash, a disruptive intrusion – which characterizes the opening of the unconscious. Lacan is clearly attentive to Freud's distinction between: (1) jokes which depend on the *materiality of the* signifier (that is, actual words and how they are verbally expressed) and which are classed as instances of wit [*l'esprit*], and (2) those which are reliant on *the thought contained with the joke itself*, and which do not depend on verbal expression, that is, the witticism [*pointe*]. Lacan is particularly enthused by the expressiveness of jokes 'in which language's creative activity unveils its absolute gratuitousness' and their ability to 'symbolize a truth' even if it is one that 'does not say its last word' (223, 6). Lacan takes this opportunity to stress two of his own theoretical contributions to psychoanalysis. The first concerns his distinction between the individual and the subject (between the imaginary identifications of the *moi* and the symbolic utterances of the *je*). In a successful joke, we see how the individual's intent – the meaning they had imagined – is upended by 'the subject's find' (224, 3), that is by the unexpected factor of the joke made possible by its linguistic dimension (the double entendre, the pun, unanticipated implication, etc.). This would not have been possible unless – and here is the second of Lacan's contributions – there was 'something foreign to me [my ego] in my [symbolic] find for me to take pleasure in' (224, 3). Lacan is here pointing to the Otherness in the speech of a joke, hence his declaration that 'some of it [the speech of the joke] must remain foreign for this find [discovery] to hit home' (224, 3). This never fully assimilable foreignness – ultimately that of language itself – tells us that the parameters of the subject exceed that of the ego. This foreignness, moreover, should emphatically not be viewed in the parameters of a dual ego–other (that is, imaginary) relation, but must be understood as entailing a three-part structure. This is something Freud had already grasped in his reference to a 'joke's third person' (224, 3). Such a third person is always presupposed in the telling of a joke; the efficacy of a joke is never, after all, reducible to a two-person exchange (even in cases where 'I don't get it' the necessary implication is that some Other does, that the joke could be explained to me). Freud demonstrates an awareness of this three-person structure – and thereby, by implication, of 'the Other's locus' – throughout *Jokes and Their Relation to the Unconscious* (1905b/2001). Two examples will suffice. In a chapter of the book discussing the purpose of jokes, Freud remarks: '[A] joke calls for three people: in addition to the one who makes the joke, there must be a second who is taken as the object … and a third in whom the joke's aim of producing pleasure is fulfilled' (Freud, 1905a/2001, p. 100). In a subsequent section of the book devoted to considering jokes as a social process, Freud extends this observation when differentiating between the telling of jokes and the effects of the comic:

> The comic process is content with two persons: the self and the person who is the object; a third person may come into it, but is not

essential. Joking as a *play* with one's own words and thoughts is to begin with a person as its object. But … if it has succeeded in making play and nonsense safe from the protests of reason, it demands another person to whom it can communicate its result … this person in the case of jokes does not correspond to the person who is the object, but to the *third* person, the 'other'. (p. 144)

The making of a joke exemplifies Lacan's thesis that (unconscious) truth is only to be found in the field of language, most typically – and most dramatically – in the intersubjective exchange of speech.

There is much we can tell about the analysis of the subject from the analysis of jokes. This point can be made – appropriately enough – via Lacan's use of a double meaning or, in terms reminiscent of Freud, a switch-word. Fink's translation preserves the French word *esprit* alongside his own chosen interpretation of its meaning (i.e. mind) in the following sentence: 'The mind [*esprit*] that lives as an exile in the creation whose invisible support he is, knows that he is at every instant the master able of annihilating it' (224, 1). *Esprit* can be translated as mind, spirit, joke or wit, and Fink may have ensured a degree of continuity here by opting instead here for wit. Had he done so, the sentence would convey a sense of how wit is the hidden support underlying the meaning given to a string of signifiers, a meaning which it is capable of upending by introducing a sudden and unexpected added meaning, which is then laughed away. This, after all, is how the joke works and how it illustrates the primacy of the signifier over the signified (how language works proceeding from the materiality of the signifier and not from the 'ideality' of the signified or the meaning). And yet, Fink's choice, of opting for 'mind' instead of 'wit', and the switch-effect of moving between registers of meaning, nicely conveys Lacan's over-arching point: the subject is to be analyzed in the same way as the joke and its wit. The subject – like wit – is the 'support' ('*soutient*') of a chain of signifiers that remain repressed by the signified, by the meaning, i.e. by the imaginary ego.[36] That subject can only be revealed at the moment when the predominance of the meaning/signified – itself supported and kept in place by the imaginary ego – is disrupted and the 'naked' signifier suddenly suggests an unexpected, repressed, unconscious meaning. In the fleeting emergence of that 'naked' signifier, the subject – itself a flash, a pulse that quickly vanishes – is momentarily revealed. As in the case of the joke, however, this revelation does not last and is repressed again almost immediately. It depends, moreover, on the subject as to whether they are willing to take up the more disruptive signification opened up by the joke. This is an ethical opportunity, for subjective change might result from taking seriously what one (as a subject) said but did not mean (as an ego). For Freud, only the dreamer authorizes an interpretation of their dream, and the same holds for the degree to which the subject assumes the unconscious signification and impact of a joke. Lacan refers to Freud to make the point: 'A joke [*esprit*] in fact entails such a sub-jective conditionality … a joke is only what I accept as such' (224, 2).

This kind of acceptance lies at the heart of a psychoanalytic treatment. During the cure, the analysand has to decide whether to accept this Other truth that disturbs the comfort of their imaginary identity. They have the ethical opportunity of realizing that their 'I' is an Other: not the other of the imaginary image of the self, but the symbolic Other, the Other as materialized in language that endlessly defers their desired identity from one signifier to another. Like the joke, the subject 'is always about something else' (224, 2); it always supposes the Other. And just as the joke disappears once the subject's truth is explained, the truth of the subject needs to be repeatedly regained in the act of speaking.

All of this relates back to the overarching problem that Lacan is addressing: the utter disregard, within the predominant schools psychoanalysis, for serious studies of language or symbolism. Such disregard threatens to set psycho-analysis on an altogether different tack, ensuring 'nothing less than a change of object' (224, 5). This problem, of thinking of communication at 'the most undifferentiated level' (224, 5), persists in psychoanalysis today. Many clin-icians are inclined to understand the most profound instances of commu-nication as occurring in the expression of affects or bodily reactions, or in instances of countertransference or projective identification.[37] For Lacan, speech is never to be superseded by other communicative means. It is not the case that speech might simply run its course, exhaust itself, and require the supplementation of other channels of communication. Speech, in a significant sense, is endless ('speech [cannot] exhaust the meaning of speech' (224, 6)): it is irreducible to other modes of expression, and other such modes do not allow for a meta-perspective on speech itself.

Lacan makes a nice dialectic move in revisiting the famous Biblical declaration 'In the beginning was the Word' (English Standard Version Bible, 2001, John. 1:1). The point, he suggests, is not simply a reversal of a reversal, that is, to dispute Goethe's preferred formulation 'In the beginning was the act' (225, 1) which, put in the mouth of his character Faust, was obviously intended to replace the Biblical proverb. Lacan's preference is for the latter: 'it was', he affirms, 'the Word that was in the beginning' (225, 1), certainly so in the sense of all that the notion of the Word – as the func-tionality of the signifier and the symbolic order – entails. And yet Word and action are not so easily separable. The Word 'was in the beginning, and we live in its creation, but it is … action that continues this creation by con-stantly renewing it' (225, 1). It benefits us to consult the record of Lacan's spoken presentation in respect of this facet of his argument. Not only does it affirms the importance of reading Word and action together; it stresses also the role of the Other, connecting thus back to this topic as it was fore-grounded in the discussion of Freud's book on jokes:

Setting off from the action of the Word ... seizing it in the original and absolute position of the 'In the beginning was the Word [*le Verbe*]' ... of the Fourth Gospel, with which Faust's 'In the beginning was the action' cannot be in contradiction, since this action of the *Verbe* is coextensive with it and renews its creation every day ... [This is to go] beyond the phenomenology of the alter ego in Imaginary alienation, to the problem of the mediation of the Other.

(Lacan, 1956, p. 203)[38]

This attention to how action and Word are coextensive requires that analysts consider the hitherto underestimated and under-theorized *agency of the signifier* in clinical work; the title of Lacan's 1957 écrit, *The Instance of the Letter*, underscores precisely this imperative.

In the second section of part II of *Function & Field*, Lacan draws on sources within structuralism and anthropology to develop a distinctive psychoanalytic account of why and law is underpinned by language ('the law of man' effectively being 'the law of language' (225, 3)). Lacan stresses that human culture in its entirety, reaching back to so-called 'pre-historical' societies, necessarily rests upon the structure of language – and the associated activities of speech – which underpin the functioning of law. He begins by reflecting upon an anthropological insight drawn from the work of Maurice Leenhardt (1947), namely the idea that for certain cultures (such as that of the Pacific Argonauts) 'gifts, the act of giving them and the objects given, their transmutation into signs, and even their fabrication, were [all] ... closely intertwined ... .[and interwined] with speech' (225, 3).[39] We need to register the primacy of gift-giving in such cultures and the role that such gift-giving has in uniting diverse parts of a community via the making of a symbolic bond. More than this, we need also to recognize the lack of conceptual differentiation between gift as an object, as an act, as a symbol and as a means of forging alliances. Wilden (1968) provides an instructive sketch of the background to Lacan's thinking here, summarizing the relevant section of Leenhardt's work that Lacan took inspiration from:

Leenhardt deals with the Melanesian concepts *no* and *ewekë*, in the Houailou and Lifou languages, respectively translated by the natives themselves as parole and later, after missionaries introduced them to the New Testament, by *verbe*. The native words cover a vast range of concepts including 'thought,' 'act,' 'action,' and 'discourse,' all of which are fundamentally related to the myth, to the structure of society, and to the being of the native himself.

(Wilden, p. 120)

Wilden (1968) also notes the response of Lévi-Strauss to Leenhardt's findings: 'It is evident from this that the conception of the Word as *verbe*, as power and action, certainly represents a universal trait of human thought' (Lévi-Strauss, cited in Wilden, 1968, pp. 121–122). What had until now seemed like a series of abrupt historical juxtapositions – the move from Freud's joke book to the Biblical insistence on the ontological primacy of the Word on to a consideration of the cultural life of the pacific Argonauts – now starts to cohere. Lacan is impressing upon us the primacy of the symbolic in the establishment of human and social and cultural life. Lacan's ambitious sweep of cultural examples intends to demonstrate that Freud's discovery 'was that of the field of effects, in man's nature, of his relations to the symbolic order and the fact that their meaning goes all the way back to the most radical symbolization in being' (227, 5).

How Lacan conceives of the symbolic order will develop in the subsequent years of his teaching. It is important though to stress the interconnection of law and language in how the symbolic order operates, particularly so that we might anticipate a conceptual error, namely, that of assuming that the symbolic order can be equated with the contents of language or culture (that is, with signifieds), or – drawing on contemporary terminology – with that which is socially constructed. *The symbolic order as a type of operating system is essentially content-less*; it has no essential subject matter, it possesses no materials. The same, incidentally, is true of the unconscious approached via Lévi-Strauss's instructive suggestion that 'the unconscious is always empty ... it is as much a stranger to images as is the stomach to the food which passes through it' (1963, pp. 224–225).[40] This content-less nature of the symbolic order is nicely stressed by Muller & Richardson (1982), who likewise call attention to how the operation of the symbolic order encompasses more than language in its verbal and written forms:

> the symbolic order, conceived ... as 'law,' governs not only the order
> of language, but the logic of mathematical combination, and indeed,
> the whole pattern of social relatedness that emerges under the guise of
> marriage ties and kinship relationships, superimposing [here they cite
> Lacan] 'the kingdom of culture on that of ... nature.'
>
> (Muller & Richardson, 1982, p. 77)

The symbolic order produces a range of structuring laws by virtue of how it works, which is precisely on the basis of combinatorial logics (such as grammar, and more specifically, the operations of metaphor and metonymy). Eleven years after *Function & Field*, in *Seminar XI* Lacan will still be stressing this point, emphasizing that the priority for psychoanalysis lies with 'the combinatorial operation, functioning spontaneously ... in a presubjective way – it is this linguistic structure that gives its status to the unconscious' (Lacan, 1977, pp. 20–21). More clearly yet:

[S]tructuralism … [shows] that it is at the level of matrimonial alliance, as opposed to natural generation … at the level therefore of the signifier – that the fundamental exchanges take place … it is there that we find once again that the most elementary structures of social functioning are inscribed in the terms of a combinatory. (1977, p. 150)

Back though to Lacan's engagement with Leenhardt. Lacan asks: 'Is it with these gifts, or with the passwords that give them their salutary nonmeaning, that language begins along with law?' (225, 4) Is it, in other words, by means of gift-giving – i.e. the capacity to abstract things from their primary use-value and to utilize them as 'words [signifiers] of recognition' (225, 3) – that properly symbolic and law-instantiating behaviors, and more importantly yet, *language*, really begin? Initially, the answer appears to be a tentative yes, because gifts seem always already to function as rudimentary symbols. This is made evident by the fact that objects of symbolic exchange are often practically useless (vases made to remain empty, shields too heavy to be carried, etc.). Symbolic value here then clearly outweighs practical value. Significantly also, we need bear in mind that 'symbol means pact', that such gifts are 'first and foremost signifiers of the pact' (225, 4). For these reasons, we are led to the conclusion that 'neutralization by means of the signifier' (225, 6), that is, the establishment of pacts, laws and social relations as made possible by symbolization, is the underlying basis of language itself. Yet if this were the case then the nature of animal symbolism would not be radically different from human language. Lacan refers here to an ethological observation: sea swallows pass fish to one another 'from beak to beak' (225, 6), an act which can be seen as effectively turning the captured item of food into a type of gift. Lacan immediately adds that he does 'not shrink from seeking the origins of the symbolic behavior outside the human sphere' (225, 6), suggesting thus that this is a line of speculation that is possibly worthy of consideration.

Lacan breaks off at this point and launches into an excoriating attack on Jules Masserman, a psychoanalytic author who had already proclaimed such a thesis (the idea that symbolic behavior originated outside of the human sphere), although in a way that Lacan is radically opposed to.[41] Lacan sarcastically reports how Masserman 'reproduced neurosis ex-pe-ri-men-tal-ly' (226, 2) in a dog, by putting the animal in a setting in which their reactions to controlled stimuli could be empirically observed. Such experimental procedures were meant to eliminate the 'extensive ruminations' (226, 2) generated by philosophers in their discussions of the origins of language, so Masserman explains, supposing thus that there is a direct 'road … from signal to symbol' (226, 4). The symbol, in this line of argument, is considered a signal, and man's behavior – as it occurs within the context of a psychoanalytic cure (for Masserman at least) – can be traced back to such signals.

Lacan's exasperation at these ideas virtually rises off of the page. Masserman's ideas are based on a fundamental misconception regards how language works.

Despite the appearance that language operates in a predominantly referential way, by constantly pointing to, or naming, things in the world (things accordingly understood as *referents*), the functioning of language is, in an important sense, autonomous of this world of objects. The autonomous character of this order is crucial here, for, as Muller & Richardson (1982) remind us, this is what distinguishes language as a system of signifiers 'from the set of signals that are evident in the animal kingdom and that can be simulated in conditioning experiments' (p. 76). What behaviorist approaches such as Masserman's do not see, Lacan explains, is that understanding a word must be seen as the result of 'particular effects of ... element[s] of language' (227, 3), effects which, moreover, entail a split between the materiality of speech and the contents of that speech (the split between signifier and signified). Given that words – or more specifically, signifiers – function as the result of a differential interplay of elements, they cannot, as Masserman apparently believes, be conceptualized as 'idea-symbol[s]' (226, 5).[42] Masserman has not grasped that people relate to the world (themselves included) only via the mediation of language, i.e. the mediation of a differential system of signifiers that refer first of all to other signifiers and only subsequently produce the effects of signifieds (meanings).[43]

Lacan now returns to his reflections upon the 'symbolic object' (228, 2) that he had questioned as an element in the archaic culture of gift-giving. Is the symbolic order, and language itself, founded in this transformation of an object into a gift ... ? Are sea swallows capable of symbolism? No, says Lacan, there is 'something else' that 'completes the symbol, making language of it' (228, 4). What then is it that makes a prospective symbol (an object of exchange, a gift, for example) effective *as a symbol*, or, more accurately, *as a unit of language*? It is not the fact that we are dealing with sound, with verbal exclamations, for it is 'in its vanishing being in which the symbol finds ... .permanence' (228, 4). This seems somewhat enigmatic, and it is as such worthwhile tracing Lacan's argument in a methodical way.

What effectively makes a word – indeed, a signifier – operate in a properly linguistic manner is *not* simply the fact that it has become disconnected from any immediate relation to the signified. This signifying element also has to *signify* this very disconnection; it needs to instantiate an absence: 'the word ... . [is] a presence made absence' (228 4). A gift becomes properly symbolic when 'absence itself comes to be named' (228, 5). The point is worth reiterating: it is not 'the sonorous quality of its matter' (228, 4) that makes a word a linguistic element – the fact, in other words, that it has a proper materiality disconnected from its *signified* – but that it *names that disconnection* and proceeds from that very naming. This deserves more by way of elaboration, but let us note at this point, before continuing, that Lacan agrees with the anthropologists Mauss, Malinowski and Leenhardt that language is a gift of sorts, but he understands this gift not in the functionalistic way they do (i.e. as *directly* supporting the processes of social recognition). Lacan by contrast reads the gift of language in a structuralist way, that is as Lévi-Strauss does (i.e. in the terms of an autonomously functioning structure which, by means of this functioning, makes social recognition possible in the first place).[44]

Returning then to the question of 'a presence made absence' (228, 5) which marks the true beginning of language, Lacan turns to the famous *fort/da* game discussed by Freud (1920/2001) in *Beyond the Pleasure Principle*. Recall, there, how a little child, in a series of acts which join signifiers and actions, throws away a small object (a cotton reel), saying '*fort*' ['gone'] before retrieving it, uttering the word '*da*' ['there']. In this way, the child not only symbolizes the coming and going of the mother, but also symbolizes the very fact of *symbolization itself* (228, 5). In this way 'from this articulated couple of presence and absence ... a language's world of meaning is born' (228, 5).

Lacan's arguments concerning the vacillations of absence and presence in the making of language are both counter-intuitive and under-developed at this point, yet, undeterred, he throws another example into the mix, citing the '*koua* mantics of China' (228, 5). He is referring here to the origin of Chinese writing: eight characters, each of which consists of three bars (trigrams) and which can be distinguished from the others according to how their respective bars are broken up (Figure 4.1).[45]

These characters constitute a break with the physical reality of objects; they operate in a non-representational manner. They are not merely substitutes or replacements for items in the world, a fact which is evident given that it is their arrangement in differing combinations which produces meaning rather than the prospect of any one-to-one correspondence with objects. The quality that sets signifiers apart from objects in the world – the fact of their 'signifierness' – is precisely *their ability to engender an absence by virtue of their presence*. They are definitively *not* what they signify (hence the idea of engendering an absence), and yet they do signify something (a presence) and they thus make meaning possible. It is the very *how* of this break with reality – the fact of their minimal combinatorial differences – which proves to be the crucial distinguishing element of each such character. This is how they function to signify meaning: only by virtue of such relations and *differences*. It is this that enables them to function as an operational differential system through which everything, in principle, can be signified. This holds for language as such: a finite set of letters or differentiated sounds can be arranged in an infinite set of ways to produce a non-ending series of significations. In the depiction of the eight Chinese characters included below, we see the elementary components that enable a naming of the entire cosmos. In fact, it is on the basis of these eight characters that the cosmos becomes a well-ordered symbolic system, as is the case in the ancient Chinese text, the *I Ching* (*Book of Changes*), which is based on this elementary matrix.

It helps, in grasping these ideas pertaining to signifierness (the 'presence made of absence' (228, 5) that makes language work), to identify and explore one of the most important philosophical resources that Lacan is drawing on. The key here lies in grasping Lacan's conjunction of Freud and Hegel, or

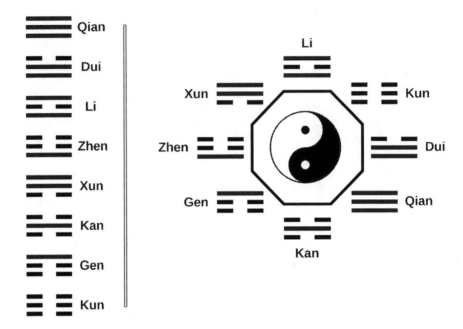

Figure 4.1 Bagua Trigram. Image sourced from Wikipedia Commons.

Freud and Alexandre Kojève's (1969) reading of Hegel, to be more specific. We have already seen how Freud, for Lacan, intuited the interplay of presence and absence within the operation of language (in the *fort/da* game); now we need to factor in Hegel, and Hegel's account of *absence in language* into this picture. If we have understood the basics of the structuralist account of language as a system, we know that

> what distinguishes mere symbols from words is that, while both are material objects, each of my words is an absence as well as a material presence. More specifically, each of my words is what it is – namely a word and as such an element in my language – because of its preexistent relations with all other possible words of my language ... 'mouse' is what it is because of the particular ways in which it resembles and yet differs from 'house' ... both phonologically and semantically, and because of the particular syntactical context ... [T]hese linguistic relations are not present in my words, although my words are what they are because of these absent but effective relations.
>
> (Lee, 1990, p. 52)

To this structuralist understanding, which highlights how absence/presence operates in respect of signifiers both in relation to one another and in relation to broader rules of syntax, we must now add, again with the help of Lee, an additional addition Hegelian twist:

> [W]hat Lacan finds in [Kojève's reading of] Hegel ... is essentially the claim that the absences that transform symbols into elements of language constitute what are ordinarily thought of as *concepts* ... Where[as] Kojève's Hegel clearly takes the concept or word to 'realize' or preserve the vanished empirical past of the thing and thus sees the 'word-concept' as constituted by the absence of the past, Lacan grafts onto this reading his essentially structuralist, differential view of language. What results, then, is a rather complex theory of language, according to which the word is constituted by a double absence: that of the thing's past (Hegel-Kojève) and that of the system of language (Saussure). Going somewhat beyond Kojève's claim that the thing's past is 'is 'eternally' preserved in the Word-Concept,' Lacan asserts the fundamental priority of the language or conceptual system – the symbolic to 'the world of things.'
>
> (Lee, 1990, p. 53)

We better understand now why Lacan was so sure in advancing that 'it was ... the Word that was in the beginning' (225, 1). Why so? Well, it is the 'nothingness' of words – of 'concepts' as Lacan calls them here, as a result of his use of Hegel – that 'engender things' (228, 6) in the first place. And yet the feature of *preservation* – of a type of symbolic immortality – is crucial also. In the word 'three', for example, any actual instantiation of three-ness is denied and negated, yet at the same time this signifier, certainly as a conceptual entity, becomes immune to the mortality affecting all material examples of three-ness. Concepts, 'in preserving the duration of what passes away', succeed thus in 'engender[ing] things' (228, 6). 'It is the world of words that creates the world of things' (229, 1), reiterates Lacan, adding to this a phrase which he renders in the original Greek, which means: 'an eternal possession'. This phrase derives, as Wilden (1968) tells us, from Thucydides: 'My history has been composed to be an everlasting possession, not the showpiece of an hour' (Thucydides, cited in Wilden, 1968, p. 125). So, to restate the point, it is words – or more appropriately perhaps, signifiers – that abstract things from their inaccessible singularity of ephemeral, temporal existence, providing them the status of firmness and constancy. And it is words, too, that make the man: 'Man thus speaks, but it is because the symbol has made him man' (229, 2).

Lacan might be accused at this point of playing somewhat fast and loose with his underlying conceptual resources. He seems here to blur the distinction between word (signifier) and concept (signified).[46] Although it is true that he has welded together structuralist ideas concerning the differential operation of the signifier with Hegelian notions of the word-concept in a highly original way, it is nonetheless clear – and his subsequent work will affirm this[47] – that it is the *signifier* and not the notion of the word-concept (or the *signified*) to which he accords over-riding importance. Lacan is using philosophical ideas unfaithfully, bending them to his own purpose. And we can see to what end: utilizing the Hegelian notion of the word-concept allows him to stress the everlasting factor of the word, despite that ultimately he is most interested in the symbolic efficacy of the *signifier*. If we were to mount a defense of Lacan – which we cannot do in any detail here – we could do so by pointing out that the word-concept (and, subsequently, the dimension of the signified) has not been forgotten by Lacan. It remains an important part of his conceptual vocabulary, even though the role it plays is itself secondary to – an outcome of – the primacy of the operations of the signifier. Concepts, and perhaps more importantly yet, broader conceptual systems evinced by cultural word-views, are of crucial importance. They most certainly do exert an influence on culture, even though they themselves are, in the final analysis only made possible by the arrangements – or structuring effects – of the signifier/ symbolic order/Other.

Lacan now resumes his anthropological speculations. Without mentioning him by name, Lacan puts forward Lévi-Strauss's structuralist thinking as a retort to various of the ideas of Maurice Leenhardt discussed earlier. As we have seen, anthropologists such as Lévi-Strauss and Bronislaw Malinowski had argued that cultural objects are never simply 'what they are', but have to be approached as elements in a system of symbolic gifts. Yet, for Lacan, picking up where he had left off a few paragraphs ago, it is not the gift as such, but the operations of language – 'the whole logic of combinations' (229, 2) – which serve as a necessary condition of possibility for the laws that structure the giving of gifts. Consequently – and this allows us to clarify Lacan's position – it is not primarily *gift-giving* but *language* that 'constitute[s] a community' and 'subject[s it]' to the rules of matrimonial alliance; language 'determining [in this way] the direction in which the exchange of women takes place' (229, 2). Here, Lacan fully embraces Lévi-Strauss' (1963) thesis, as articulated in the latter's *Structural Anthropology*, concerning the primacy of the symbolic order and language in structuring human cultures. Hence Lacan quotes the motto – a ŠiRonga proverb – from the *Elementary Structures of Kinship*: 'A relative by marriage is an elephant's hip' (Lévi-Strauss, 1969, p. 1). For Lévi-Strauss (1969) the structure of elementary kinship systems is essentially linguistic. It is a language that provides the grammar of this structure; in this language/structure one finds the 'logic of combinations; thus the law of numbers – that is the most highly purified of all symbols – [which] prove[s] to be immanent to the original symbolism' (229, 2). Elementary kinship relations set the parameters for who a given man might take for a wife, and for how children relate to their relatives. The fact that such kinship relations are structured by laws means that, in the choice of matrimonial partners, one is not as free as one might suppose.

What underlies the unconscious law governing elementary – and also more complex – kinship relations is precisely the Oedipus complex, which, 'covers the whole field of our experience' and 'mark[s] the limits' that psychoanalysis 'assigns to subjectivity' (229, 3). Lacan now introduces the notion of the primordial Law, which 'in regulating marriage ties, superimposes the reign of culture over the reign of nature', noting also that '[t]he prohibition of incest is merely the subjective pivot of that Law' (229, 4). In order to understand this notion of the primordial Law, we need both to build upon the structuralist ideas introduced above – highlighting the crucial place of law within symbolic systems of exchange – and then take one further step in stressing the disjunction between nature and culture.

For Lacan, following Lévi-Strauss, the law is present whenever a rudimentary form of symbolic activity is present, whenever – to indulge briefly in more technical terms – a type of combinatorial logic is in operation. In more straightforward terms: the law is an irreducible condition of the symbolic order (of the Other), in the same way, that grammar is an irreducible condition of language. In this sense, the law is immanent in all structured forms of social exchange and is constantly reinscribed in even the most rudimentary instances of communicative interaction. This holds for the reciprocal social roles we take on in interactions with one another and, as we have seen, for kinship systems and structures of social hierarchy. Our various and innumerable symbolic exchanges are constantly structuring the fabric of social relations which, in turn, define our own symbolic identities within them. It is worth reiterating that such complex systems of laws (and their associated social norms) are presubjective; they exhibit an agency that is prior to – more primary than – psychological individuality. That the insistence of such combinatory rules continues over generations demonstrates this agency of the symbolic order over that of its singular subjects. All of this is crucial to grasp is understanding Lacan's assertion that the law is linguistic, or more accurately yet, as he puts it: 'The primordial Law ... reveals itself clearly enough to be identical to a language order' (229, 4–229, 5)

Yet there is a further aspect to Lacan's conceptualization of law. Despite the importance of the multiple social/cultural re-inscriptions of the law that we have just described, the primordial Law – like the taboo against incest – is not reducible to either nature nor culture alone. It exists, rather, as an outcome of their disunity, as a product of the non-reconciliability of these two domains. This is what makes the primordial Law properly *primordial* and not merely an aggregation of innumerable reiterations of given social rules. We might put it this way: the primordial Law is founded in a system that takes the ultimate incompatibility of nature and culture, their incommensurability – the fact that they never fully harmonize or align – as a productive principle. Shepherdson helpfully elaborates upon this idea, namely, the non-reducibility of Law to either nature or culture, in respect of the incest taboo:

[T]he incest taboo presents us with a peculiar contradiction: on the one hand it is a prohibition, a cultural institution that imposes family relations and kinships structures upon what would otherwise be the state of nature; on the other hand, however, this law, because of its universality, is also defined as something natural, since it cannot be ascribed to a particular social group or located in a single historical period. Lévi-Strauss ... stressed the paradox ... of the incest taboo ... [of which he said:] 'It constitutes a rule ... but a rule which, alone among all the social rules, possesses at the same time a universal character' ... .Derrida has stressed that this impasse should not be reduced to a mere contradiction ... It is not a question of eliminating ambiguity by determining, once and for all, whether this law is 'cultural' or 'natural' – whether it is 'really' a human invention (a symbolic law), or a biological principle that insures genetic distribution (a natural mechanism). The scandalous or paradoxical character of the incest prohibition is not an ambiguity to be eliminated, but must be taken rather as the actual positive content of the concept itself: it suggests that ... the incest taboo must be situated prior to the division between nature and culture.

(Shepherdson, 2008, p. 19)

Two points should be noted about the disjunction represented by this incompatibility between nature and culture. Such a disjunctive relation is, firstly, an instantiation of the Lacanian real. It is, secondly, a productive disjunction, one which is at work in every instance of signification. As we have seen: words/signifiers do not refer primordially to whatever it is they signify. This makes the break with nature the productive hallmark of every signifier. And it is this linguistic law underlying culture – that is, the constitutive break with nature – which institutes man's two forbidden 'natural' 'objects' in patrilineal contexts: his mother and sisters. We should bear in mind here that for Lacan it is not so much the case that these are two desired types of 'natural' objects that then must be prohibited by an act of culture. This would be an over-simplistic way of understanding the relationship between nature and culture, one in which culture domesticates or 'gentrifies' nature, in which the two might be effectively partitioned by an act of culture itself. For Lacan, the act of prohibition is itself a fundamental part of what makes such objects desirable in the first place. Culture, or the symbolic order, is always already there in the case of speaking subjects, even in the most primal of states. This complicates any neat compartmentalization of nature and culture because culture is already at work within the desire for ostensibly 'natural' objects. This again points to the necessity of seeing the nature/culture relation not only as an instantiation of the Lacanian real but as a productive and indeed generative incompatibility that allows for no resolution. As we have seen above in relation to language, the factor of an ongoing non-reconcilability/impossibility also drives the process of deferral and substitution (signifiers need to refer to other signifiers because of their inability to primordially signify reality itself). It is in this sense that we can say that it is the non-reconcilability of culture and nature that constitutes the heart of the (cultural) family. For the family is in the end not based on the natural relation among its members, but must always be defined in relation to just such a process of deferral, that is to a cultural alliance *with another family* and the substitutions and relationships thus made possible. We have here the basic elements of Lacan's structuralist interpretation of the Oedipus complex.

This structuralist re-thinking of the Oedipus complex necessitates in turn a re-thinking of the relation to the father, indeed, of the role and symbolic function of the father as such. The paternal function must be re-formulated from a position that foregrounds the primacy of language. The father involved in the Oedipus complex – and, consequently in the formation of both the subject's identity and the law that governs society – is a symbolic father, a signifier: the *name* of the father. And, adds Lacan, in a memorable line: 'It is in the name of the father that we must recognize the basis of the symbolic function which since the dawn of historical time, has identified his person with the figure of the law' (230, 5). This important new concept, which Lacan will revisit and elaborate upon many times in the years to come, amounts to a type of privileged signifier which grounds and stabilizes the symbolic order and confers authority on those who act in its name. The clinical value of this concept soon becomes apparent because 'it allows us to clearly distinguish [in any given subject] ... the unconscious effects of this [paternal] function from the narcissistic relations, or even real relations, that the subject has with the image ... who embodies this function' (230, 5). In short, the analyst's grasp of a case is increased by being able to differentiate, in the analysand's relation to figures of paternity and/or authority, how they relate to: the symbolic father function, the imaginary father (occurring within the realm of imaginary identifications), and the figure of the actual flesh-and-blood father.

Lacan is essentially offering his own solution to the question he broached several pages ago in querying how language might underpin the operation of law. It is language, and the symbolic order more generally, particularly *insofar as it enables the paternal operations of the Name-of-the-Father*, that makes the law. It is thus the Word says Lacan – invoking here a poetic phrase by François Rabelais (1990) – that perpetuates the movement of a great debt, a debt which is inviolable, absolute, priceless, and that marks everything humans exchange with one another. That debt is the name of the distance between things as they are symbolized and as they are in their everyday materiality, a distance which, as we have seen, proves to be the productive principle of the symbolic system. In Polynesian archaic cultures, this distance is incorporated in the 'sacred *hau* or the omnipresent *mana*', which, for Lévi-Strauss, indicates the 'zero-symbol', the symbol indicating the symbolic nature of all things constituting a culture (231, 2).[48]

The concept of the zero-symbol (such as *mana*) deserves more by way of description than Lacan allows for in his text. Wilden (1968) again proves helpful here, and it is worthwhile quoting him at length:

Concepts like that of mana devolve from what Lévi-Strauss conceives of as 'overabundance of signifier' in relation to the actual signifieds (that is the universe, the cosmos) which are available to human 'symbolic thought.' Thus a concept like mana seeks to fulfil the function of representing all [encompassed by] this 'floating signifier,' and consequently all the antinomies and contradictions involved – since mana may mean almost anything. Mauss's celebrated *Essai sur le don* [*The Gift*] depends upon the notion of the *hau* or mana as the *raison d'être* of the symbolic exchange (whose prime importance lies in the act or transmission of mana or *hau* rather than any profit or advantage), and Lévi-Strauss seeks to interpret this mysterious anthropological entity in scientific terms as something like an algebraic symbol, representing an 'indeterminate value of significa-tion,' in the same way as the zero-phoneme is one whose function is simply to be opposed to all other phonemes, without entailing any phonetic or differential value in itself. Just as the function of the zero-phoneme [a concept developed by Roman Jakobson] is also to exist in opposition to the absence of phonemes, mana is viewed by Lévi-Strauss as a significative symbol empty of meaning in itself, but therefore capable of taking on any meaning required. The function of mana is therefore to fill a gap between signifier and signified at whatever level a lack of adequation between them is revealed. For the native, mana is simply [here quoting Lévi-Strauss] 'the subjective [reflex/response] … to a totality which he cannot perceive.' Mana is a category of thought rather than a category of the real [that is, of the actual world]; it fulfills for the native the role of explanation that modern science fulfils for us. On this view, like the zero-phoneme, mana is pure form without specific content, pure symbol, a symbol with the value of zero.

(Wilden, 1968, pp. 127–128)

The notion of the zero-signifier points to the function of the 'non-meaning-bearing', 'purified' symbol emptied of all prospective contents or references to the world. It indexes the 'symbolicity' of the signifier, or the quality of 'sig-nifierness', by which we wish to stress that the structured relations between signifiers in a signifying network necessarily produce significations exceeding a literal or actual set of referents. Such a system of significations requires a type of null token, a signifier (precisely such as *mana*) which is necessarily meaningless and which signifies the ongoing role of signification, of signifierness. What Wilden also draws attention to here is that this the zero-symbol can become a reference-point or, better yet perhaps, an empty placeholder for a prospective explanation that is held in abeyance (as in the tendency to defer difficult ex-planations to signifiers such 'science' or 'God'). We can discern here then the origins of Lacan's subsequent concept of the master signifier, which comes to function as an anchoring-point (or, in the terms of Lacan's Seminar III, as a *point de capiton* or quilting point) so as to ground meaning and value precisely – if paradoxically – because of the nothingess it stands for.[49] Mladen Dolar speaks of this operation of the master signifier as 'a pure positivization of a void' (1999, p. 87).

It is on this basis that some religious cultures – Catholicism being perhaps the most notable case in point – are able to consider everything to be subjected to something such as The Last Judgment. The latter can be read as a means of implementing the zero-symbol – that symbol of symbolicity, the signifier marking everything with negativity, with the fact *of its disconnection from the mere physical/material actuality of the world*. We appreciate then the extent of the reach of the signifier, and Lacan's insistence that:

> Symbols ... envelop the life of man with a network so total that they ... engender him 'by bone and flesh' before he comes into the world; so total that they ... [shape] his destiny; so total that they provide the words that will make him faithful or renegade, the law of the acts that will follow him to the very place where he is not yet and beyond his death; and so total that through him his end finds its meaning in the last judgment. (231, 3)

Even if one does not acknowledge cultural or religious ideas such as a Last Judgment, one can nonetheless recognize the function of the zero-symbol in what Heidegger (1996) calls being-towards-death. As already mentioned, according to Heidegger, human existence – *Dasein* – is a project (*Entwurf*) inherently oriented to the future. The human being 'is' their 'having to be' (both what he or she is and was). And this goes also for the moment of their dying: even then, he or she is to be their dying. This means that their orientation to the future goes hand in hand with their radically finite condition: even while dying, one is living in the primordial future tense. Lacan reads this combination of future tense and finitude in a distinctive way which draws on the inspiration of Lévi-Strauss even as it highlights the role of desire. Finitude is thus realized in the order of the signifier as it denies – or negates – actual/material entities, i.e. the notion that the symbolic order implies the 'death' of the things as they are (following here the Hegelian idea that 'the word is the death of the thing'). Human existence, realizing itself within the realm of the signifier, is thus also marked by desire, indeed, human existence is to be considered as the movement *of desire* that 'preserve[s] his part in the interferences and pulsations that the cycles of language cause to converge on him' (231, 4). We might put it this way: the subject as lack of being *(manqué-à-être'*, 'want-to-be') searches for who they are and for the satisfaction of their desires. As a result, they invest in a succession of signifiers and thus become caught in an endless process of being deferred from one signifier to another. It is in this sense that human beings live life as desired.

Desire, furthermore, requires recognition, to be obtained either in an imaginary way, as is for instance the case in the 'struggle for prestige', or in a symbolic capacity, via the exchanges of speech. We can expand upon this by referring back to the difference between the imaginary strategies of empty speech and the symbolic dimension of the full speech. To reiterate: the former is an ego-serving mode of speech in which the speaker thinks of themselves as the owner of their story; it is a type of speech that appeals to the imaginary others for their recognition. It is only in full speech, by contrast, that the speaker comes to hear – often with accompanying effects of denial, surprise or realization – that they are the subject of a story that originates in the Other of language. In full speech, the patient realizes that they are not the same as their imaginary image, and, furthermore, that they are the subject of a chain of signifiers that constitutes them as lacking, as desiring. The aim of psycho-analysis is to facilitate full speech, to allow the patient's desire to be spoken. It is only by entering into speech – and, ultimately, through the enunciations of a full speech – that the analysand can adequately explore their symbolic conflicts and be separated from their imaginary fixations. This is what allows them, in transitory moments of the opening of the unconscious, to assume their status as subjects of desire. In the psychoanalytic cure then, a great deal comes down to problems occurring in the way the analysand, tries, by means of speech, to assume their position as the subject of language. We need to be aware here of the difference between the subject's *vocalizations of speech* and how they are located in relative to *the structure of language*, a point Lacan underlines when he stresses that 'the problem is that of the relations between speech and language' (231, 7).

This opposition between speech and language perhaps comes as something of a surprise, since much of what Lacan has said up until this point has em-phasized the conjoined importance of speech *and* language. The distinction that now comes to the fore is the difference between language as a *fixed structure* and speech as a *creative function*. Dunand (1996) elaborates upon this difference, noting that 'To Lacan, speech is distinct from language essentially because it has meaning to a subject; it is a revelation of meaning, and beyond that, a revelation of being' (1996, p. 106). In the relation between speech and language, three distinct paradoxes, or subjective situations, can be identified.

1   We see in psychosis, the 'negative freedom' of a type of speech which 'has given up trying to gain recognition' (231, 9). This non-recognition-seeking speech occurs alongside the 'singular formation of a delusion' (231, 9) which is brought about, in turn, by the process in which the subject is objectified by language. This objectifying language no longer possesses dialectical nuance. All it affords the subject is a type of stuckness – hence Lacan's reference to 'the unconscious in petrified forms' (232, 1) – which permits for no possibility of a working through of the forms of suffering the subject is experiencing. Miller (1996b) glosses this paradox of madness:

in madness we see an absence of speech instead of the creative function of speech. We find language only as a fixed form without creativity or dialectic ... [T]he madman [is] someone who doesn't recognize the Other, who exercises an unthinkable, negative freedom not to recognize any Other ... the Other speaks directly to the subject instead of being symbolic ... instead of receiving the symbolic order from the linguistic Other, you receive something in the real and so you hear what the Other is saying in your head (Miller, 1996b, p. 34).

2 Moving now to the domain of neurosis, Lacan considers symptoms, inhibitions and anxiety (conjuring up the title of Freud's (1926a/2001) famous book), stating that we see here how 'speech is driven out of the concrete discourse that orders consciousness' (232, 4). This speech nonetheless finds expression either in bodily symptoms ('symbol[s] written in the sand of the flesh' (232, 5)) as is the case in hysteria, or in the form of the images that characterize phobia or obsessional neurosis. The symptom as it occurs in hysterical, obsessional or phobic form, is 'fully functioning speech' (232, 6) in the sense that it is inherently addressed to the Other (232, 6). And it is by 'deciphering the speech' of those symptoms 'that Freud rediscovered the first language of symbols' (232, 7).

3 The subject may, furthermore, lose the creative function of their own singular speech as a result of the objectifications of discourse. We live in a culture 'where everything has already been said, where the creative function of speech is reduced, [where only] objective discourse remains', a situation in which 'a wall of structure [is] opposed to speech' (Miller, 1996b, p. 35). This, maintains Lacan, 'is the most profound alienation of the subject in our scientific civilization': it is this alienation 'that we encounter first when the subject begins to talk to us about himself' (233, 1), that is, at the beginning of a psychoanalytic cure. Lacan stresses that, for the analyst, it is a matter of leaving such objectifications behind – the analyst here is called upon to champion the potentiality of creative speech over existing discursive structures. The attention to scientific objectifications is particularly note-worthy here because scientific discourse is one of the ways the patient supports their imaginary strategies. One needs only consider how often patients make use of the diagnostic categories of the DSM (2013) as a way of understanding their difficulties in a way that leaves questions of their own desire and subjectivity untouched.

For Lacan, the objectifications of scientific discourse are paradigmatic in the constitution of 'modern man' (233, 2) and he provides two apt illustrations of what he has in mind. He invokes, firstly, the Hegelian concept of the *Beautiful Soul* – that self-understanding of the modern bourgeois subject who supposes that, in ethics, all is fine when one has done one's duty, not acknowledging that ethics requires action and, furthermore, that they will need to dirty their hands.[50] The 'dialectical impasse of the beautiful soul' (233, 3) resides in the fact that such a soul fails to recognize that their 'very reason for being' lies in the disorder he or she 'denounces in the world' (233, 3).[51] Lacan refers, by way of a second example, to a verse by the fifteenth century French poet François Villon, who, in a famous poem, uses the expression 'it is I' ('*ce suis-je*') instead of 'it's me' ('*c'est moi*') (233, 2).[52] The switch from 'it is I' to 'it's me' summarizes the transition in self-understanding that modern individuals have made from being *strictly symbolic subjects* (proceeding, that is, *from a basis in the Other* in order to talk about oneself: *ce suis-je*) to foregrounding the imaginary ego (proceeding *from oneself* in order to talk about everything else, supposing thus that one's relation to the world has its starting point in himself: *c'est moi*).

Such ego-sustaining empty speech amounts to 'a wall of language' (233, 6) which blocks the process of the full speech. Lacan makes reference here to the many 'precautions against verbalism' (233, 6) that can be evinced in popular culture and in innumerable examples of scientific research. This distrust of the verbal likewise instantiates a wall (of language) which gives the impression – as do all walls – that there is something *on the other side*. So while psychoanalysis necessarily involves empty speech – it being, after all, the 'talking cure' – it endeavors to disrupt the illusions of such ego-substantializing talk and draw attention to *what is realized within speech itself*. The aim of psychoanalysis is to punctuate moments of the full speech, to highlight those instances of disjunction, slippage or overdetermination in the analysand's speaking which indicate that they are the lacking/desiring subject of the signifier, of the Other.[53]

Madness, Lacan continues, is not a matter of the body, a matter of phrenology, for instance, as Hegel already understood in his critique of 'the philosophy of the skull' (234, 3). It is a matter of meaning,[52] which Lacan underscores with reference to a Blaise Pascal: 'Men are so necessarily mad that it would be another twist of madness not to be mad' (234, 3). None of this is to imply that a person is so *entirely* subjected to the symbolic order that they are unable to intervene within it. On the contrary, human beings are equipped with a 'creative subjectivity', and are able thus to 'renew the never-exhausted power of symbols', to introduce new impulses into the symbolic, or support it in an active way (234, 5). 'Psychoanalysis has played a role in the direction of modern subjectivity' (235, 1), says Lacan, even though it could have done a better job of this, had it not been seduced by the 'objectification of our experience' and by the 'experimental method' as practiced in behaviorism (235, 4). It is surprising, he avers, that psychoanalysts, 'as practitioners of the symbolic function' (235, 5), have neglected to elaborate upon and extend this functionality. Had they done so, psychoanalysis might well have been at the center of a new order of sciences that was by then taking shape under the influence of the rethinking of anthropology inaugurated by Lévi-Strauss.

That new discipline – and structuralism more generally – resists the ten-dency to reduce science to positivism and takes up again the tradition of 'true science' which is as old as Plato's *Theaetetus*. It is today's 'conjectural sciences' that discover 'once again the old-age notion of science' (235, 7). Lacan em-phasizes that linguistics, with its own particular 'form of mathematization', should play a guiding role here, as is already the case in the new anthropology established by Lévi-Strauss. This is a mathematization of phonemes, of the elementary components of language. Lacan again refers to Freud's *'fort/da'* observations to illustrate the compatibility of linguistic and psychoanalytic theory. Such a 'general theory of the symbol' constitutes an excellent basis for the 'sciences of man' now acknowledged as 'sciences of subjectivity' (236, 4). Crucial here is an awareness of 'a twofold movement in the subject' (236, 5), which is to say that human beings make their actions into objects, speaking about them, symbolizing them, and that this symbolizing activity has, in turn, a further 'knock-on' effect on subjectivity itself. It helps here to make re-ference to the clinic. The words that I, as analysand, speak in describing a significant event in my life can have an unintended subjective and transfor-mative impact upon me. Such words, spoken in the first moment with little regard for how they might be heard, have the capacity, in the second moment, to rebound, to affect me, particularly so once I am aware of how the Other may have heard something else in what I said. Full speech requires precisely this twofold movement of the symbolic which, importantly, both involves the declarative dimension of the speech act and adds something to it:

> [T]he 'twofold movement' of the symbolic … is not just a question of how a form of speech performs an act, but of how this act itself is reintegrated by the subject. There is a subjective after-effect to the speech act, the prospect whereby a subjective 'truth change' can be effected by virtue of it having been uttered. This is not just an issue of what I *do* by means of saying something, but of what is *done to me* by my saying – I can after all be surprised by virtue of what is thus done, by what I have committed myself to – of what subjective 'truth change' has been instantiated. That is to say, the perlocutionary effect of a speech act contains a reflexive impact, so much so that what I enact in saying provides the basis for a different order of subjective truth … certain symbolic utterances themselves function as acts necessary for transforming the dispositions of the speaking subject.
>
> (Hook, 2018, pp. 78–79)

The more challenging examples that Lacan provides of this twofold movement in the symbolic are of a greater macro-sociological and cultural significance. The use of mathematical symbolization, for example, not only, in the first movement, objectifies facets of reality – rendering it in certain forms, con-ceptualizing it in certain ways – it also, in the second, allows for symbolic computations and operations which ensure that this reality can be acted upon, treated and re-arranged in very different ways to what had hitherto been the case. Similarly, using Marxist terminology not only allows one to label various facets of reality in a distinctive way (processes of production, for example, being viewed as capitalist exploitation), it provides also a means of identification and belonging that in turn serves as a condition of possibility for involvement in a general strike.

Having drawn our attention to how this twofold movement has the capacity to 'forge a new reality' or bring about revolutionary change (via the efficacy of 'a symbol in action') (236, 9), Lacan now makes the case that this level of engagement – an attention to *the agency of the signifier* – is the domain of the conjectural sciences. This, indeed, is how the conjectural sciences, as opposed to the exact sciences, work. Whereas the former are about truth the latter are about exactitude. Both nonetheless have their own forms of 'rigor' (237, 1). Neither enables direct access to reality; both are experimental in the sense that they apply an '*experimentum mentis*' (a mental experiment) to reality. So, even though experimental science is rightly to be credited with exactitude – which it derives from mathematics – its 'relation to nature is nonetheless problematic' (237, 1) in the sense of being mediated, non-direct. It is for this reason that Lacan maintains that experimental science 'is not so much defined by the quantity to which it is ... applied, as by the measurement it introduces into reality' (237, 5).

It is worth reiterating that the conjectural science of subjectivity – propelled and enabled, as we have seen, by the twofold movement of the symbolic – also utilizes mathematics. Mathematics, like any symbolic or signifying system allows for a double treatment of reality; it does not simply name or represent that reality, it changes it – or, more significantly for psychoanalysis – the subject's view and relation to that reality. Lacan returns to his essay on logical time in which, as already described, the logical reasoning of the subject involves a pressurized temporal dimension, their conclusion not being possible without the factor of pre-emptive anticipation. The truth here then is not strictly a matter of correspondence with reality (for Lacan, even modern 'exact sciences' have broken with such a paradigm), but a matter of subjective decision, of 'certainty anticipated by the subject' as mediated *via means of logical/ symbolic processes* (237, 10). Two vital implications regards subjective truth for psychoanalytic practice should be noted here. First, the fact that the subject only knows through signifiers – which are always, as we have seen, disconnected from their apparent signifieds – means they can only access reality – and *themselves* – via the mediation of the symbolic (that is via the function and field of language, via the Other). Moreover, such truth entails the anticipatory and pre-emptive temporality of subjective decisions. In short, when it comes to subjective truth, the subject has to make a decision both by mediating reality via the tools of the symbolic and by taking on, as one's own, the truth decided upon.

Lacan applies this thinking to the 'historian's technique' (238, 2). In speaking about their past, the analysand does not have to remember the 'lived reaction' of the original experience. More important is the point at which they anticipated something as an event to come, as a future, as an otherness that makes of them a particular type of subject. Unlike Carl Gustav Jung, adds Lacan, Freud understood the 'progressive dimension' implied in 'psycho-analytic regression' (238, 3).

Lacan indicates several disciplines from which psychoanalysis can benefit. Linguistics, for example, provides the crucial distinction between the diachronic and the synchronic. The 'sister sciences' that Freud mentioned in *The Question of Lay Analysis* (1926b/2001) as to be taught in an 'ideal Department of Psychoanalysis' (p. 246), would likewise prove a crucial resource, as would the 'liberal arts' taught in the medieval university such as 'rhetoric, dialectic, … grammar, and poetics' (238, 7). All these disciplinary contributions provide 'scientific foundations' (239, 3) for psychoanalytical theory and practice.

III   The resonances of interpretation and the time of the subject in
psychoanalytic technique

The third section of Lacan's essay is about psychoanalytic technique and how this technique needs to be brought back to its foundations in speech and language. The epigraphs he selects are once again deserving of comment. The first quote, draw from Antoine Tudal's poem, *Paris in the Year 2000*, makes reference to the idea that a wall exists between every person and the world (Tudal's reference to a wall, incidentally, entails a wonderful verbal ambiguity – 'wall' (le mur) in French sounds very much like l'amour ('love')).[53] This returns us to Lacan's notion of the wall of language and Lacan's associated directive that analysis takes place through speech and not via some other inaccessible subjective realm of the analysand's experience. The second quote, the epigraph to T.S. Eliot's *The Wasteland*, stems from Petronius's *Satyricon*. In the myth from which these lines are drawn, Sibyl was subjected to a terrible punishment by her lover Apollo, after she had embarked on a failed love affair. Her response to the children who saw her undergoing this punishment expressed her ultimate desire. The quote reflects Lacan's thinking on the 'death instinct' (241, 4) as the ultimate form of desire, as a drive to escape the field of language and speech which is, of course, indispensable if the desire is to exist at all.

Psychoanalysis, unlike a form of psychology such as behaviorism, cannot be based on something that is thought to occur beyond language and speech. This is worth reiterating because the technique of interpretation has, in particular, been distanced 'from its core' (239, 6) which is to be found in 'the inter-subjectivity of speech' (240, 4). This distancing is linked to a 'deviation in psychoanalytic practice', and indeed, to 'the new aims to which psychoanalytic theory has become receptive' (239, 6). Lacan does not explain exactly what these new aims are, perhaps because he is confident that his audience knows that the therapeutic goals associated with of behaviorist therapies and ego psychology – such as adaptation to more positive behaviors or correcting oneself in the direction of a psychic maturity – are most assuredly not the aims of a psychoanalytic cure.

According to Lacan, the problems psychoanalysis has with 'symbolic interpretation' (211, 4) go back to a misunderstanding concerning what was assumed to be Freud's directive style as a clinician. The case studies Freud published give the impression that he all too directly explained to his patients what was wrong with them – as if a type of pedagogical diagnosis on the part of the doctor would be enough to heal the patient. The prospect of such an 'unseemly indoctrination' (239, 7) stimulates the idea that 'a complete objectification' of mental disease or diagnosis might be possible (240, 3). Such an approach appears, moreover, to show Freud neglecting both the transferential relation with his analysands and the resistances of those analysands. It is as if Freud himself was guilty of a 'misrecognition of the subject', of ignoring 'the intersubjectivity of speech' (240, 4). Such errors, for Lacan, are ingrained within psychotherapeutic approaches that focus on 'the analysis of the resistances' (240, 4). A shortcoming of a directive style of psychotherapy is that it neglects the patient's own responsibility in coming to grips with and working through their problems. Infinitely preferable is an approach that foregrounds how the analysand is the subject of language and speech, to emphasize, via a variety of clinical techniques, how they are the subject of the desire of the Other.

Lacan takes up the defense of Freud who, according to him, 'understood perfectly well the seductive scope of this game in the imaginary' (240, 6). This is what the analyst has to analyze in the first place: how, in the intersubjective relation of the cure, the analysand uses the figure of the analyst as a means of maintaining their imaginary ego so as to deny the real nature of their problem. The problem, at least in the case of the clinic of neurosis, concerns the barred or 'non-whole' nature of the analysand's subjectivity, the fact that as *manqué-à-être*, they essentially *are* unfulfilled desire. This is what underlies the transference. The analysand constantly attempts to use the analyst's reactions so as to maintain their own imaginary strategies, as a means of bolstering their own ideal-ego identifications.

Lacan notices, for example, that during his analysis of Ernst Lanzer Freud (1909b/2001) pays particular attention to the pleasure Lanzer exhibits while relating the cruel memory of the torturing technique in which a rat burrows into the anus of the unfortunate victim. Lacan here cites Freud, who noted of Lanzer's expression while describing this horrific form of torture: 'His face … reflected horror at a *jouissance* of which he was unaware' (240, 6).[54] Lacan writes: 'The effect in the present of his repeating this narrative did not escape Freud, no more than did the fact that he identified his analyst with the 'cruel captain' who forced his narrative to become etched in the subject's memory' (240, 6). Lacan concludes that Freud's relation to his patients is not marked by 'indoctrination' but rather by the 'symbolic gift of speech' (240, 8). Freud does not 'misrecogniz[e] the resistance', but 'uses it as a propitious predisposition for setting in motion the resonances of speech' (241, 2). This is why Freud 'changes tack abruptly', in order to prevent the analysand from 'seducing the analyst by slipping beyond his reach' (241, 2). This is to say that the analyst must be aware at which level they are located in the intersubjective play opened up by the patient's speech, imaginary or symbolic. The crucial point here is that the analyst should be less concerned with the resistances of the analysand and how they should be interpreted than with attending to the signifiers set in play by the analysand's speech. Hence Lacan's directive that analysis 'consists in playing on the multiple staves that speech constitutes in the registers of language' (241, 3).

'These principles are nothing but the dialectics of self-consciousness, as it is realized from Socrates to Hegel' (241, 7), states Lacan. In psychoanalysis, the patient's questions come down to the enigma: 'Who am I?' According to Socrates, 'know thyself' ('γνωθι σεαυτον', '*gnoothi seauton*', as inscribed above the entrance of the Delphi Oracle), was the central task of human thought, and he invented the dialectical mode of dialogue in order to respond to this imperative. For Hegel, in a comparable way, the logic of history is, at basis, the dialectical progression of consciousness, of a search for a 'self', even though, crucially, this self has to be repeatedly alienated in the process of recognizing the otherness that is inherent to it. Freud's discovery must be seen as a further step in this tradition. The search for the 'self' – or more aptly, for the *subject* – remains of paramount importance, yet it is not to be found in *self-consciousness*, as Hegel put it, but instead in 'decentering [the subject] from self-consciousness' (241, 8), in separating the subject – even if only momentarily, in flashes of wit, lapses of speech, bungled acts – from the imaginary ego.

Lacan refers to Hegel's 'ironic assumption that all that is rational is real' which precipitates 'the scientific judgment that all that is real is rational' (241, 8).[55] Lacan notes this philosophical maxim principally to highlight the distinctiveness of Freud's discovery of the subject of the unconscious. This discovery, whilst still relying on the tools of rationality so valued by Hegel, nonetheless parts ways with Hegel inasmuch as it fundamentally *decenters* the subject from the 'self-consciousness, to which ... [they were] confined by Hegel's reconstruction of the phenomenology of mind' (241, 8). In more straightforward terms: the more Freud uses rationality to pursue an investigation of the subject, the more he is obliged to put consciousness to one side and look elsewhere, to the role of the unconscious. So, Freud and Lacan alike may well agree with Hegel's idea that all of reality is capable of being expressed in rational categories ('the rational is real'), but the idea that rationality underlies the very nature of the world and of consciousness ('the real is rational') needs to be supplemented for the simple reason that consciousness is not the only game in town.

Lacan nonetheless abides by a central Hegelian idea, namely Hegel's insight according to which the self has to recognize itself in its otherness. Lacan, however, radicalizes this assertion. The Other in which the subject comes to recognize themselves remains obstinate to consciousness and has to be understood via the notion of the unconscious (hence Lacan's assertion that 'the unconscious is the Other's discourse' (436, 4)). Ultimately then – and here we are blending Hegelian and Lacanian conceptualizations – the self (or the ego) is an 'object' of sorts which resists the dialectic process, whether that be understood in terms of Hegel's ideal of self-consciousness or the Lacanian aim of the 'dialecticization' of imaginary demands that is necessary in order if the subject is to realize its desire.[56] This 'object' of self or ego might – via the work of analysis – realize itself as the subject of the unconscious.[57] More succinctly put: human 'identity' – i.e. the imaginary ego – is 'realized as disjunctive of the subject' of the unconscious (242, 2). This is why Lacan refutes 'any reference to totality in the individual' (242, 3), similarly rejecting any suggestion that treatment should appeal to the lived experience of the subject fully present to him or herself. Psychoanalysis relegates such an imaginary ideal 'to the status of mirages' (242, 3).

We should not skip too quickly over Lacan's reference to Hegel's 'insistence on the fundamental identity of the particular and the universal' (242, 2). This philosophical notion has a direct bearing on how Lacan thinks about the role of language, psychoanalytically. Language, after all, permits for an infinite variety of singular (or particular) articulations, in its enunciative/spoken dimension, even while its broader structural dimensions (most significantly, the processes of metonymy and metaphor) are inherently universal.[58] This also tells us why *speech* and not just language is crucial for Lacan: it the particularity of language in its enunciative dimension (that is, as *parole*) as it disrupts the universality of language (as *langue*) that brings desire to the fore.

The reference to Hegel is significant also in understanding the ideal of 'so-called analytic neutrality' which maintains that the analyst must hold themselves at some distance from their patients (242, 5). Lacan's meaning here is not evident, although Wilden (1968) adds an insightful comment which plays off Hegel's idea of the cunning of reason. Hegel, for Lacan, says Wilden, 'is always sure that Truth will be found again in ... [a] final accounting, because it is always already there' (p. 140). Subsequently, if the analyst could be equally sure that this Truth will be found again, they would be able to be neutral in a much more effective way.[59] Analytical neutrality is best served, in short, by allowing the Other to be heard.

Lacan once again mentions Socrates, in order to underscore the active mode of intervention needed in an analytic cure. Like Socrates's maieutic method which allows a slave to discover a geometrical truth, the analyst must help their patient to discover the truth, although not in the sense of simply taking up and repeating the discourse – or universal truths – of the master. By way of differentiation Lacan stresses both 'the unresolved enigma of the analyst' – a reference to the analyst's role in inculcating the desire of the analysand and thereby keeping the work of analysis on track – and the singularity of the analysand's 'relation to truth' (242, 5). The latter of course contrasts to the perfect, unchanging concepts or ideals which exist in Plato's Realm of Forms, which the Socractic master directs their interlocutor toward. Lacan draws a contrast between 'the reminiscence Plato was led to presume to exist in any advent of the idea' and 'Kierkegaardian repetition', which Muller & Richardson (1982) describe as follows:

> the Platonic *skopia*, a vision of the whole as well as underlying pattern, provides a model for Lacan, but with the following corrective: whereas Plato's vision is grounded in the recollection of eternal essences and Kierkegaard's in the repetition anticipated in an eternal future, Lacan places himself in-between and thereby accents here the temporality and historicity of the subject and of truth. (p. 117)

As opposed then to the Socratic teacher 'whose mission is universal' the goal of analyst's is to restore to their analysand's the 'sovereign freedom displayed by Humpty Dumpty, when he reminds Alice that he is, after all, master of the signifier, even if he is not master of the signified form from which his being derived its shape' (242, 6). To avoid a misunderstanding: the idea is not simply to foreground Humpty Dumpty's famous insistence 'When I use a word … it means just what I chose it to mean – neither more nor less' (Carroll, 1923, p. 246), but to stress also the subsequent lines of the dialogue:

> 'The question is,' said Alice, 'whether you *can* make words mean so many different things.'
>
> 'The question is,' said Humpty Dumpty, 'which is to be master – that's all'.
>
> (Carroll, 1923, p. 246)

It is *the signifier* as master, as we might put it (by way of answer to Humpty Dumpty), or an attention to speech within the domain of the Other, this is what analysis is concerned with. This is the *'primary language'* that Lacan foregrounds: the 'language of [the patient's] desire … in which – beyond what he tells us of himself – he is already speaking to us unbeknown to himself, first and foremost, in the symbols of his symptom' (243, 1). It is this, language, which despite maintaining a 'universal character' is nonetheless 'absolutely particular to the subject' (243, 2). Freud was the 'Champollion' who deciphered this language.[60]

Lacan sees this confirmed in what Ernest Jones (1918) has to say about symbolism. Symptoms must be read in reference to this primary language (the language of the patient's desire), and the analyst can 'play with the power of symbols by evoking them in a calculated fashion in the semantic resonances of [the patient's] remarks' (243, 6). For beneath the semantic level of language (of the meaning), there is the symbolic level (of the signifier); only the 'interferences' between signifiers give access to repressed meanings (244, 3). A familiarity with literary texts can be very helpful in reading symptoms in this way, says Lacan, noting that Freud had already pointed this out.

Lacan wastes little time in attacking another psychoanalytic theory of interpretation which, in contrast to his own, does not proceed from the primacy of the signifier. He refers to the notion of 'wording' which he links to the work of the psychoanalyst Ernst Kris, whom he accordingly critiques for maintaining that the analysis of symptoms should involve tracing symptoms back to an origin outside of language. Kris's erroneous approach endeavors also to explore how such symptoms might have taken the shape of words if their symptomatic form had not won out. This is the background to the confusion between need and demand in Kris's work. The fact that these terms might be used interchangeably, says Lacan, 'amounts to a radical ignorance of the *summoning* characteristic of speech' (245, 1). Whereas needs have a biological basis, demands are essentially *demands for love* that arise in the context of an intersubjective condition, a condition that is necessarily mediated by language. A demand is to be situated in the context of the speech, which is radically different from 'wording' or any other associated reference to pre- or non-linguistic domains. Conceptualizing demand as an instance of the summoning dimension of speech, Lacan insists that speech, in its symbolizing function, 'tends toward nothing less than a transformation of the subject to whom it is addressed by means of the link it establishes with the speaker – namely, by bringing about a signifying effect' (245, 2).

Language is thus not to be understood as a series of signals, just as words are not to be understood as renderings or translations of an extra-linguistic reality. So disconnected have analysts become from speech that Lacan laments 'we find ourselves in search of a gesture, a grimace, a posture adopted, a face made, a movement, a shudder' (245, 5). Not only is it imperative to forego attempts at reading any type of body language or meaning, it is also crucial to 'definitively dispel the mistaken notion of 'language as signs'' (245, 3). Lacan demonstrates the shortcomings of such an approach by means of reference to Karl von Frisch's (1956, 1993) research on the 'wagging dance' of bees (245, 7). Such communicative acts in bees cannot be considered an example of language for the simple reason that we see there a 'fixed correlation between its signs and the reality they signify' (245, 9). In language this correlation is broken and 'signs take on their value from their relations to each other' (246, 1). Signifiers relate first and foremost to other signifiers, and the same goes for signifieds[61] – Lacan here holds with the principles of structural linguistics as elaborated by Ferdinand de Saussure and Roman Jacobson. A further crucial difference between the communicative acts of bees and human language concerns the fact that in the latter, a subject is involved; spoken instances of language involve the subject as the addressee. This addressee function invests the subject 'with a new reality, as for example, when a subject seals his fate as a married man by saying 'You are my wife'' (246, 3). Hence the paradox of communication offered to Lacan by one of his 'most acute auditors': 'the sender receives his own message back from the receiver in an inverted form' (246, 5).[62]

In calling someone my wife, for example, I receive my own message back from them, from their subjective position (that is, 'in an inverted form'), that is, I am implied in my message, not merely as the speaking subject/agent but as the object for (or of) the person who receives my statement. It is precisely this position as the object in the discourse of the Other – I being that object which the Other speaks of – that the subject needs to assume, take up and identify with (i.e. I thus become the subject via the Other). It is the act of speaking in relation to the Other that constitutes me as simultaneously both subject and object.

This is also why 'speech always subjectively includes its own reply' (246, 5), a remark which serves as a suitable axiom for psychoanalytic practice. How so? Well, the fact that the patient addresses their demand to an analyst presupposes that the analyst has an answer to their demand. As Lacan elaborates, applying a quote from Pascal: 'Thou wouldst not seek Me, if thou hadst not found Me' (246, 5). This idea (that speech includes its own reply) also sheds light on what Lacan refers to as 'the paranoiac refusal of recognition' (246, 5). It is in the form of a 'negative verbalization that the unavowable feeling eventually emerges in a persecutory 'interpretation'' (246, 5). In other words: their persecutory 'interpretations' of the world are the return-effect of the paranoiac's own 'negative verbalizations' (246, 5). This helps us understand something about paranoia more generally. The paranoiac feels persecuted by the Other, i.e. by the fact that they (the paranoiac) are who/what they think they are only via reference to the Other. What the paranoiac cannot abide is that that they are profoundly emersed in the signifiers of the Other, signifiers that they use to speak of and understand themselves; the Other is thus always already a constitutive element that makes them what they are.[63]

In moments when we assume that another 'speaks the same language' like us, we have not in fact encountered 'the discourse of everyman' (246, 6). What unites us with that person is not simply the factor of a shared language but rather the fact that we each have 'a particular way of speaking' (246, 6). This is the 'antinomy immanent in the relations between speech and language' says Lacan, adding that '[t]he more functional language becomes, the less suited it is to speech, and when it becomes overly characteristic of me alone, it loses its function as language' (246, 7). Speech – particularly in the sense of full speech – is the act in which the libidinal being assumes their singular position as the subject of the Other, i.e. of language. Importantly, however, the subject is not a totalizing encapsulation of language; the subject is what *lacks* in language, which is why their relation to a given language is absolutely singular and distinctive.

For these reasons, language is not approached by psychoanalysis in the same way that it is by many disciplines within the human sciences. According to psychoanalysis, the language – indeed, the speech – in play between the analysand and the analyst (or between the ego and subject dimensions of the analysand themselves), cannot be adequately understood via insights into the *general functioning* of language. This leads to a series of criticisms on the limitations of communication theory. Many theories of communication (Lacan speaks of 'the economics of long-distance communication' (247, 3)), focus on what is redundant in communication, redundant that is, in terms of information conveyed. In prioritizing the information exchanged in instances of communication, such theories neglect how the subject is involved in the language exchange. This is a serious omission for 'the function of language in speech is not to inform but to evoke' (247, 5). It is by looking to a response from the Other that one constitutes one's own answers and identifications: 'What constitutes me as a subject is my question' (247, 6). That is to say: I lose myself, i.e. my imaginary ego; I, as an ego, am not who I think I am; I need to take up my position as a subject in the field of the Other, needing to constitute myself in relation to these signifiers and as a question in relation to the desire of the Other. Lacan emphasizes the implications this has for the historicity of the subject:

> What is realized in my history is neither the past definite as what was, since it is no more, nor even the perfect as what has been in what I am, but the future anterior as what I will have been, given that I am in the process of becoming (247, 7).

Speaking, in a context – like that of psychoanalysis – in which the dimension of the Other is consistently stressed within my speech means that I am forced to realize myself as something Other than the imaginary ego that I suppose I am. This realization of the subject – the grasping of a shifting Otherness to their subjectivity that exceeds their ego's sense of itself – pertains to the different times of the subject, to the temporality of the subject as he or she is located in the past, the present and the future. The subject's Otherness unsettles, firstly, the dimension of the *past definite tense*, which is to say, the determining temporality of what was, is now considered to be over, complete and locked in place (the dimension, in other words, of *what one has always been*). The subject's Otherness unsettles, secondly, the dimension of the *present perfect tense*, exercising thus an unsettling influence upon the ego's ideas of what had occurred previously and continues still in the present (the aspect, in short, of 'what has been in what I am' (247, 7)). Third, the *future perfect* (or anterior) *tense* – in which one looks toward a future event which is nonetheless punctuated by a definitive end point (the end of the analysis, the end of one's life, for example) – is likewise affected. The disruptive effects of Otherness on the ego mean that the subject here is invited to assume the existential contingencies of 'what I will have been' – a 'will have been' which, of course, implies a definitive end-point – whilst simultaneously assuming the potential futurity of being 'in the process of becoming' (247, 7).

While there is a good deal more that could be said in respect of Lacan's notion of the future perfect tense as it applies to psychoanalytic treatment and theorization let us simply note here that, as Wang (2019) insists, Lacan's conceptualization of the future anterior should not be reduced to Freud's notion of *nachträglichkeit*:

> what has been deferred in the future anterior is not the realization of meaning, as Freud's *nachträglichkeit* implies, but the very closure of meaning since the subject leaps into an unknown future when the moment of symbolic determination has become the past. While *nachträglichkeit* offers a temporal loop that contains the future in the past, Lacan's future anterior aims at an openness of being in the unpredictable future. (Wang, 2019, p. 209)[64]

Forrester (1990) adds a wry comment that develops a little further the possible impact of the type of opening discussed above:

> So the analyst is not so very different from the fortune-teller, except that he is always dealing in hypotheticals. He says: 'It is *as if* you were the mother, and, on that basis, you expect to have two children by the time you are thirty-two.' Whereas the fortune-teller says: 'You *will* have two children by the time you are thirty-two'. ... this invoking of the hypothetical reveals something crucial to Freud's epistemological stance. The aim of psychoanalysis is to undo such identifications. In this sense, its aim is to *un*write the future, which the neurotic lives as already written, structured by the words and deeds of those he or she has identified with ... For Freud, such a future is a blank page, with invisible writing on it. (1990, p. 95)

In light of all of this, it is abundantly clear that for Lacan the subject cannot be thought in the terms of stimulus/reaction theory. A response is not a reaction; it is not an answer. Unlike a mere reaction, a response is constitutive of the subject. Paying attention to the issue of response, and to the response of patients, leads us to consider the question of 'the analyst's *responsibility*' (248, 1), a responsibility that comes into play every time they intervene in their patient's discourse. A crucial implication – and here Lacan approvingly cites the work of Edward Glover (1931) – is that a 'bad' response/interpretation on the part of the analyst – i.e. one which does not open the patient's demand into a question regards their underlying desire – simply maintains the patient in their neurotic position.

Lacan then broaches the issue of the materiality of language. Language, he says, is 'not immaterial. It is a subtle body, but body it is' (248, 3). Indeed, words come to be caught up in the body images that captivate the subject ('they may 'knock up' the hysteric' (248, 3) for example). Words, can, furthermore, 'suffer symbolic lesions and accomplish imaginary acts whose victim is the subject' (248, 4). Lacan refers here to a specific scene within Freud's (1918/2001) Wolf Man case as an example. As a child, the Wolf Man had urinated on the floor after seeing Grusha, an employee of his family, down on her knees scrubbing. Grusha, who he had come to associate with yellow stripes, had responded, perhaps jokingly, with a threat of castration. As Freud notes, this link – between castration and the Grusha scene – was then affirmed in an ingenious dream that pivoted on a particular signifier:

> 'I had a dream,' he said, of a man tearing off the wings of an *Espe.*'
> '*Espe?*' I asked; 'what do you mean by that?' 'You know; that insect with yellow stripes on its body, that stings.' I could now put him right: 'So what you mean is a *Wespe* [wasp].' 'It is called a *Wespe*? I really thought it was called an *Espe.*' (Like so many people, he used his difficulties with a foreign language as a screen for his symptomatic acts.) 'But *Espe*, why, that's myself: S.P.' (which were his initials). The *Espe* was of course a mutilated *Wespe*. The dream said clearly that he was avenging himself on Grusha for her threat of castration. (Freud, 1918/2001, p. 94)

It was in this way, says Lacan, that the Wolf Man 'carried out the symbolic punishment to which he himself was subjected by Grusha, the wasp' (248, 4). Lacan offers several further examples – including, interestingly, a paper on silence and verbalization by Robert Fleiss (1949), the son of Freud's former friend and correspondent – to substantiate his claim that 'one's discourse as a whole may become eroticized, following the displacements of erogeneity in the body image, momentarily determined by the analytic relationship' (248, 6).

Freud's interpretations, Lacan continues, are sometimes wrong ('not only factually, but also psychologically, inexact' (249, 6)), but they nonetheless point to the patient's truth. Psychoanalytically then, it is not the facts as such that count, but the way the patient relates to them or, more precisely, *the way the subject constitutes themselves in the intersubjective event of reporting the events of which they speak*. It is not a matter then of looking at the affective content or for causes behind the resistances that come to the fore in the analytic process. It is the process itself – i.e. the dialectics (as Lacan sometimes calls it) of the intersubjective language exchange – that most matters. In that exchange, the psychoanalytic method tries first of all to 'to determine where … [the patient's] ego is situated' (205, 4), to locate the imaginary identity that the analysand's symptom and/or demands hold in place. This will reveal the ways in which the analysand uses the analyst's reactions so as to sustain their ego; a maneuver that helps them maintain the belief that they are not marked by lack or desire. An imperative of analytical treatment comes to the fore here. We need to figure out 'through whom and for whom the subject asks ... [*his/her*] *question*' (250, 4). If we do not have an answer to this question we misconstrue 'the desire that must be recognized there and the object to whom this desire is addressed' (250, 4). Lacan's schematization of desire involves not merely the subject and the fantasized object of desire, but adds the reference-point of the Other from whose standpoint a prospective object of desire is deemed desirable in the first place. The effect of such an addition is like that of moving from a two to a three-dimensional depiction: it causes us to ask for whom – for what Other – a particular scene of desire is being staged. It is in terms of this Other standpoint that we can differentiate the respective performances of the hysteric and the obsessional.

Lacan's Latin phrase '*Trahit sua quemque voluptas*' (250, 6) ('To each his own *jouissance*' or 'Everyone is led by their own pleasure (or passion)' (Fink, 2006, p. 791)), suggests that there are characteristic relations to *jouissance* that characterize the positions of the hysteric and the obsessional. The hysteric 'identifies with the spectacle' and the obsessional 'puts on a show' (250, 6). This reference to the register of the performative yields two clinically informative descriptions. We have, firstly, the hysteric who literally 'acts out', that is, who enacts in a variety of ('external') relationships that of which they complain (that is 'internal' psychical ailments). In evocative language, Lacan describes how the hysteric captivates the 'object [of desire] in a subtle intrigue' and does so 'in the third person' (250, 5), such that 'the subject enjoys the object who incarnates her question' (250, 5). There are multiple implications here. Not only can the hysteric identify with both feminine and masculine positions, potentially positioning themselves thus as both the object and subject of desire (hence both the famous question 'Am I a man or am I a woman?' and the triangular love relationships in which the hysteric so often finds themselves). Their acting out also involves 'enjoying the object who incarnates her question' (250, 5), which is to say they enjoy making the Other – from whom existential and subjective questions arise – lack, and do so as way of denying their own lack. The associated clinical imperative that Lacan offers is a type of relocation: the analyst needs to get the hysteric to recognize 'where their action is situated' (250, 6).

The obsessional, secondly, drags the objects of desire 'into the cage of [his/her] narcissism' (250, 5), lest the reverberating questions of desire and lack emitting from such objects prove too disconcerting. Assimilating prospective objects of the Other's desire into their repetitive rituals, ruminations, procrastinations and neurotic vacillations, works – or so the obsessional hopes – to maintain their imaginary wholeness, to keep lack at bay. Such a strategy of lack domestication is likewise facilitated by acting as if one is dead (hence the reference to 'the multiplied alibi of deadly figures' (250, 5)), that is, by not acting, by being frozen, by insisting that – and living as if – one is *not* subject to

117

desire (one recalls here Lacan's idea that the obsessional's desire is a desire for an impossible desire). Ambivalence has its part to play here; the obsessional plays 'ambiguous homage … [to] the master who cannot be seen' (250, 5). The analyst's task is to be recognized in the figure of the spectator who has been consigned to invisibility, and to whom the obsessional may in fact be 'united by the meditation of death (250, 7). We might understand this by noting that the obsessional's attempts at petrification affect both themselves and the analyst. They are stuck in perpetual prevarication (the position of waiting for the master to die) even as they put on a show of doing the work of analysis, routinely consigning the interventions of the analyst – in other words, the lack/desire of the Other – to irrelevance. It is by stressing the inconsistencies in the Otherness of the obsessional's speech, by facilitating instances of full speech through punctuation and scansion, thereby touching upon moments of their Other desires, that the treatment of the obsessional might proceed. What is required, in clinical work with hysterics and obsessionals alike, is intervention at a specific juncture: 'It is therefore always in the relation between the subject's *ego* and his discourse's *I* that you must understand the meaning of the discourse if you are to unalienate the subject' (250, 8).

Note that to 'unalienate', here, does not mean that the subject must be brought back to some kind of authentic 'self'. On the contrary, and somewhat paradoxically, 'unalienating the subject' aims precisely at a subject *assuming* their alienated condition, i.e. at preventing their denial of this alienated state by means of imaginary strategies. This means that, as Lacan puts it, 'the subject's ego is [not] identical to the presence that is speaking to you' (250, 9). As such, Lacan's approach is contrary to theories and perspectives which entail 'an objectifying cast of mind' (251, 1), which, in Lacan's terms, 'slide from the ego defined as the perception-consciousness system … to the ego conceived of as the correlate of an absolute reality' (251, 1). Such a regression, in theory, amounts to a return to as pre-Freudian form of psychologistic thought, one which erroneously takes the ego as tantamount to a type of psychical reality-function. It is just such a prioritization of the ego (as perception-consciousness system, as reality function) that Lacan has in mind when speaking of the 'the system of the subject's objectifications' (251, 1) which he identifies in a range of psychological theories. Such ideas have taken root within psychoanalysis itself – ego psychology being the prime suspect here – in a way that means that analysts 'became involved in a sort of psychological orthopedics' (251, 2), a project whose moral, corrective and normalizing implications appall Lacan.

Michael Balint's definition of psychoanalysis as 'two-body psychology' is also critiqued here, not only because 'speech is excluded from a search for lived experience' (251, 4), but because analysis here is reduced to 'the relation of two bodies … in which the analyst teaches the subject to apprehend himself as an object' (251, 3). The approach of such a two-body psychology leads to a state in which 'the intrasubjective topography … become[s] entified' (251, 5), that is, turned into objects.

118

The play between ego, id and superego, for example – concepts which Lacan feels have become objectified, treated as intrapsychic entities rather than being understood as operations within the symbolic domain – should be approached as occurring within the exchanges between subject and other/Other. Most schools of psychoanalysis do not prioritize this dimension of the linguistic subject /Other exchange, preferring instead to focus on *intra*-subjective dynamics. The result of this is precisely a form of objectification in which the patient is required to adapt themselves to their supposed ego, or worse yet, to the ego of the analyst. Hence the idea, to which Lacan takes such exception, that an 'analysis of resistances' (252, 3) should come first in the psychoanalytic cure. The presumption here, of course, is that the analyst's ego provides the grounding in reality, and the bench-mark, against which such resistances can be measured and or corrected.

Lacan develops his argument via reference to Freud's Dora case. Freud, he says, made errors in his handling of the treatment: he forced her to accept interpretations that betrayed *his* rather than her hidden wishes and he became overly focused on analyzing her resistances. In this way, Freud 'presents us with a rough idea of the intersubjective complicity that an 'analysis of resistances' … might have perpetuated between them' (252, 3). Lacan offers a critical remark here on counter-transference, a term whose correct application he says, cannot be extended *beyond its use in highlighting reasons for clinical errors* (errors, which the analyst 'immediately pays the price for … in the form of a negative transference' (252, 1)). So while Lacan does not reject the term out of hand, it is true to say that from his perspective the crucial technical concept – and clinical reality – is, by contrast, *transference*. Both partners in the psychoanalytic treatment need to analyze the transference – the transference, more specifically, as it is made operative in the dialectical interchange of their relationship as it occurs via the Other of language – in order to realize themselves as subjects of desire.

One possible reason that analysts have lost interest in language and the materiality of the signifier is that they have come to doubt that the capacity to heal via words can be scientifically justified or validated. For Lacan, the primacy of speech and language in analytic treatments is not only perfectly defensible; it is also in line with 'mediations of scientific discourse' (253, 3) in disciplines such as linguistics and anthropology. In a series of dense paragraphs, Lacan warns once more that psychoanalysis has nothing to seek 'beyond the wall of language' (254, 2). That the analysand believes that there is some important truth existing beyond language goes hand-in-hand with their assumption that 'truth is already there in us [analysts], that we [analysts] know it in advance', a problematic assumption that elevates analysts to a position of mastery over the analysand. Lacan sounds a cautionary note here: 'This is also why … [the analysand] is so open to our objectifying interventions' (254, 2).

Lacan now launches into a series of scathing comments directed at Maurice Bénassy, and more specifically at Bénassy's (1953) article 'Théorie des instincts'. As we have seen, Bénassy had already been the (unnamed) recipient of Lacan's scorn earlier on.[65] It is worth noting here that Bénassy's 'Théorie des instincts' served as the principal theoretical report for the 15th Conference of French-Speaking Psychoanalysts, which was held in Paris in 1952.[66] Lacan's 'Function & Field' was the principal theoretical report for the follow-up event. Given this context and the fact that delegates typically reflected on the previous year's principal report, it would have been abundantly clear who Lacan was referring to. The words that Lacan implicitly attributes to Bénassy ('It is high time we put an end to the fraud that tends to perpetrate the belief that anything real whatsoever takes place during treatment' (254, 6)), do not appear to be from a written text. The sentence seems rather to have been conveyed to Lacan by a colleague reporting on Bénassy's presentation of this material.[67] Lacan's retort is contemptuous, largely no doubt due to the fact that Bénassy had begun utilizing several of Lacan's concepts ('[his] debt to me can be recognized by his use of the term 'real'' (254, 6)), without adequately understanding them or locating them in the broader theoretical context from which they had originated.[68]

Lacan pivots from Bénassy to draw attention to his own achievements ('those elementary registers ... the symbolic, the imaginary and the real [represent] ... a distinction never previously made in psychoanalysis' (255, 2)), going on to discuss '[r]eality in analytic experience' alongside his notion of the real. Analytic reality often remains 'veiled in negative forms' (255, 3), he says, stressing that two seemingly opposed stances on the part of the analyst (that of active intervention and of abstention) are both 'element[s] of reality in analysis' (255, 4). Lacan is particularly concerned with the 'junction between the symbolic and the real' in clinical work, a junction which is marked by negativity 'insofar as it is pure ... detached from any particular motive' (255, 5). There are multiple ways of interpreting Lacan here. He seems to be stressing how dissonance between the symbolic and real ('this negativity') might underlie moments of psychoanalytic efficacy, might indeed underlie the possibility of a psychoanalytic act. And yet he seems also to suggest that in such provocative instances of negativity (where symbolic and real are experienced as non-aligned or dissonant), the subject might 'find anew its measure' (255, 6). There might be many creative ways – such as the analyst's 'refusal to respond' (255, 4), their 'non-action' (255, 5) or for that matter, their active intervention – that produce such productive negativities, where, instead of relying on what might be expected, the patient experiences themselves as *a subject finding itself anew*.

Differently put, we might say that it is at the moment of *'parole pleine'* ['full speech], that the real is to be located. It is at precisely this moment that the subject recognizes themselves in the caesura, in the punctuation of their discourse – there, where their discourse confronts its own finitude or lack. This punctuation is provoked by the intervention of the analyst. Given the importance of this idea of punctuation, Lacan dwells 'for a moment on time's impact on technique' (255, 7), emphasizing again 'the symbolic and the real [as

they] come together' (255, 7). 'Time', he says, 'plays a role in analytic technique in several ways' (255, 8).

The first of these concerns the unforeseeable length of an analysis. We
cannot predict in advance how long a subject's *time for understanding* (the
second moment of the analysis's logical time) will last (255, 11). Lacan sounds
a cautionary note here, warning us that 'setting a time limit to ... analysis' can
mean that the subject 'finds himself alienated from himself' (256, 1). The
analyst's setting of a 'due date' can result in the patient situating their truth *in
the authority of the analyst,* and this weight of authority – which retains the
mirage of the patient's original imaginary ego – will set the analysis off 'on an
aberrant path' (256, 1). Lacan illustrates this by once again referring to Freud's
(1918/2001) case of the Wolf Man. Freud's action there, of setting a pre-
determined time limit to the work, assured that the Wolf Man was left alienated from his own truth. Despite all of Freud's efforts, the Wolf Man did not
succeed in integrating his recollection of the primordial scene into his history.
And, what is worse, the alienation ended up in paranoia.

Lacan's second point in respect of the temporality of analysis concerns the
'function of time in analytic technique ... the length of sessions' (257, 3). He
devotes several pages to this topic, clearly intent on defending his innovation
of the variable-length session. Lacan starts with the suggestion that maintaining
an inflexible standard with regard to the length of sessions is somewhat 'obsessive' (257, 5). He also suggests that the reluctance of analysts to broach this
topic has much to do with the extent to which 'it would entail questioning the
analyst's function' (257, 5). However, before elaborating further on obsessional neurosis (which he will do in due course), Lacan develops a general
reflection on the historicity of time. For time as we know it – time as objectively measurable – is an invention of modernity, a notion Koyré (1953)
had asserted with the idea of 'the universe of precision' (257, 6). Lacan goes so
far as to provide a date for the beginning of this distinctively new and modern
relation to temporality, referring to the invention, by Christiaan Huygens, of
the first clock in 1659. In psychoanalysis, however, we need to understand
time – and the time of the unconscious – very differently.

Lacan offers a series of interesting characterizations of the function of the
analyst, remarking how the analyst 'play[s] a recording role' (258, 2), acting
not only as a witness but as the 'trustee of the record of [the patient's] discourse
... [as] keeper of its testament ... [as] a scribe' (258, 2). Interestingly, 'it is the
analyst above all who punctuates ... [the] dialectic [of the progress of the
treatment]' (258, 4). The punctuation performed by the variable ending of
sessions – which has the potential to change, renew or upset meaning – is
contrasted to the routine application of a standard length sessions. The 'in-
difference' of the latter, that is, of fixed timing 'interrupts the subject's moments of haste', which 'can be fatal to the conclusion toward which his
discourse was rushing headlong' (258, 7).

Lacan now returns to the argument that fixed-length sessions run the risk of installing an obsessional attitude in the analyst. The insistence on rigidly adhering to a set time allows the analyst to secretly connive with their patients. Waiting is a typically obsessional attitude, one which risks maintaining the patient in an imaginary position. Lacan elaborates upon this by referring to Hegel's master/slave dialectic. The obsessional, like the slave, is afraid of risking their lives in a confrontation with the other (which is why they have become a slave in the first place). 'The slave slips away when faced with the risk of death, when the opportunity to acquire mastery is offered ... in a struggle for pure prestige' (259, 1). The slave thus spends their life waiting for the death of the master. They bide their time, accepting that they will work for the master 'and give up *jouissance* in the meantime' (259, 1), and wait. In this way, the obsessional essentially plays dead. 'This' says Lacan, 'is the intersubjective reason for both the doubt and procrastination that are obsessive character traits' (259, 2).

Obsessional neurosis is thus afforded a Hegelian reading: the obsessional 'is in the anticipated moment of the master's death ... he identifies with the master as dead and is thus already dead himself' (259, 3). This is the obsessional's way of constituting themselves as the imaginary answer to the Other's lack/desire.[69] The obsessional lives a life of postponement, forever delaying the time in which they will actually get around to living. In the analytic cure, such patients will use the fixed ending of sessions as a defense, precisely as a way of forestalling an ending. They sidestep also the assumption of subjectivity that the prospect of such an ending – and the prospect of their own finitude – enables. They bypass the crucial subjectivizing *moment of understanding*, attempting instead to seduce the analyst by constantly putting their good intentions and hard work on display, showing wherever possible that they are 'working through' (259, 5) their problems.

By way of supporting his arguments in favor of the variable-length session, Lacan recalls an incident from his own practice. Had he not implemented variable sessions with one particular analysand, so he tells us, he would have 'still been listening to his speculations on Dostoyevsky's artistry' (259, 10). Yet, he insists: 'I am not here to defend this procedure, but to show that it has a precise dialectical meaning in analytical technique' (260 1). The variable-length session is not, in other words, a technical procedure to be dogmatically applied, but a device that should be considered in view of its *various potential punctuating uses* apropos temporality, interpretation and the role of (non) meaning within sessions. Nonetheless, this procedure is affirmed by reference to 'the traditional ascesis of certain Far Eastern schools', more precisely 'the technique known as Zen' (260, 2). The variable session is, furthermore, infinitely preferable to 'the so-called analysis of resistances' insofar as it 'does not in itself entail any danger of alienating the subject' (260, 3). It 'shatters discourse only in order to bring forth speech' (260, 4).

Lacan returns to the conceit of the wall of language. We are, he says, 'up against the wall of language ... on the same side of the wall as the patient, and it is off this wall ... that we shall try to respond to the echo of his speech' (260, 5). There is, moreover, 'nothing that is anything but outer darkness to us beyond this wall' (260, 6). This does not at all imply that the analyst 'thoroughly masters the situation' (260, 6). The futility of such an agenda is writ large, especially when considering the prospect of the 'negative therapeutic reaction' which, according to Freud (1920/2001), is rooted in the death drive.

Freud's enigmatic notion of the 'death instinct' as Lacan describes it – deliberately emphasizing the paradoxical nature of the concept – cannot be discounted. Both ego psychology and those, like Wilhelm Reich, who sought 'an ineffable organic expression beyond speech' are in error in denying this 'culminating point of Freud's doctrine' (260, 9). At this late point in his essay, Lacan introduces a twist, claiming that he can demonstrate 'the profound relationship uniting the notion of the death instinct to the problems of speech', insisting, moreover that there is 'a rigorous logic' underlying 'this joining of forces' (260, 10).

The 'relation of polar opposites' evident in the notion of a 'death instinct' should not surprise us; it lies at 'the very heart of phenomena that people associate with life' (261, 1). Lacan remarks that the French anatomist Xavier Bichat, at the very beginning of modern biology, conceptualized life as 'the set of forces that resists death', an idea which was confirmed by the American physiologist W. B. Cannon's articulation of the idea of homeostasis (261, 1).[70] There is a relation of congruence, says Lacan, between 'the contrasting terms of the death instinct ... [and] the phenomena of repetition' (261, 2). It is pertinent that Freud himself related the death drive to the term 'automatism'. And yet from the standpoint of psychoanalysis, avers Lacan, the death drive should not be understood from a biological perspective. We should, instead, focus on the broader *resonance* of the words and concepts rather than remaining fixated on the first or most obvious meanings.[71] It is in this sense that Lacan speaks of 'the poetics of Freud's work' (261, 4), an example of which is the use Freud makes of ancient sources, extrapolating as he does, from the pre-Socratic philosopher Empedocles' ideas about 'the two principles governing the alteration of all life' (261, 5) so as to develop the idea of the death drive. In Freud's conceptualization of the death drive, we can hear the echoes of Empedocles who claimed that the universe is governed by an unending fight between love and hate. Lacan grants himself a similar poetic license, in this case to extrapolate beyond the biological parameters of Freud's own conceptualization of the death drive.

Lacan's challenging evocations of the death drive become somewhat more defined – and certainly more theoretically grounded – once he refers to Heidegger's notion of *being-towards-death*: 'the death instinct essentially expresses the limit of the subject's historical function' (261, 7). The subject is the subject of language, of history, of a story; and the sense of this story is made possible by its finite condition, by the fact that it ends. A sentence only attains a semblance of meaning retrospectively once it has been completed. Similarly, analysands realize themselves as subjects of the desire of the Other only due to the punctuation of the analyst's interpretation. That punctuation redoubles the limit which makes the subject's history/story possible. In that sense 'this limit is present at every instant in what is finished in this history' (262, 1). Lacan takes this opportunity to add a further note on the nature of temporality in the psychoanalytic cure and in respect of the relationship between repetition and the death drive.

> [T]he past in its real form ... is not the physical past whose existence is abolished, nor the epic past as it has become perfected in the work of memory, nor the historical past in which man finds the guarantor of his future, but rather the past which manifests in an inverted form in repetition. (262, 2)

In a single sentence, Lacan deftly weaves together the themes of the real, the nature of the past in the psychoanalytic cure, and the Freudian motif of repetition as they apply to the death drive, which, in turn, is posed an unending yet endlessly productive relation to finitude.

In the struggle between love and hate as described by Empedocles ('the universal conflict of *Philia*, love and *Neikos*, strife' (262, 3)), the subject finds their partner in death. For it is death – and the limits, the sense of finitude accompanying it – that brings everything to the level of the symbolic. We might say then that it is the Hegelian force of the negative as realized in *the signifier* – that is, precisely the process of symbolization (the changing of everything into signifiers) – that goes some way to 'master[ing our] ... dereliction' just as it simultaneously 'raises [our] ... desire to a second power' (262, 6).

Lacan refers back to Freud's description of the *fort/da* game. By using the signifiers *fort* and *da,* the child negates the comings and goings of his mother. As Lacan puts it: 'his action destroys the object that it causes to appear and disappear by *bringing about* its absence and presence in advance' (262, 6). What we should note here is not only that the child's object was destroyed – the mother's absence and presence being mediated and transformed by means of signifying terms – but that *the child itself* is also affected by this process. Via the use of signifiers and symbolic operations, the child is made into an object, an object *within language*, which is to say a *symbolic* and therefore also a crucially *absent* object, an object, which, by virtue of its absence, is at play within the field of desire. This is why Lacan is careful to stress that the child does not simply 'master his deprivation by assuming it' (262, 6), that the use of signifiers (which 'destroy ... the object') 'raises his desire to a second power' (262, 6). This action 'negativizes the force field of desire in order to become its own object to itself' (262, 6). The child has thus constituted themselves in reference to these signifiers (*fort/da*) and to signifiers in general – and in reference to the world of the Other, realizing themselves simultaneously as object and subject of desire. The child – it is worth stressing this point – thus plays a crucial role, in their use of such signifiers in ushering in their own status as a subject of language, of the Other, and of the interplay of desire in relation to the Other. As Lacan puts it: '*Fort!/Da!* It is already when quite alone that the desire of the human child becomes the desire of another ... whose object of desire is henceforth his own affliction' (262, 7).

Playing on Hegel's famous phrase Lacan reminds us that it is the symbol which 'first manifests itself as the killing of the thing', extending this idea to stress that this death 'results in the endless perpetuation of the subject's desire' (262, 9). It helps here to bear in mind the Hegelian logic according to which symbols come to substitute for actual entities in a way that ensures that such objects are once symbolically preserved and yet necessarily replaced, 'negated' even. This preservative/negativization process is how desire is made eternal, ensured as essentially unsatisfiable.[72] It is, moreover, on this basis, of signifiers killing things and the endless perpetuation of desire that results, that humans are effectively 'born into the life of history' (263, 1). Lacan evinces a particular interest in burials ('the first symbol in which we recognize humanity ... is the burial' (262, 10–263, 1)). Burial rites at once underscore the undeniable fact of mortality while enabling a form of symbolic life (be it via commemoration, the marking of a legacy) that reaches beyond the parameters of biological life. It is via symbolic functions – language, the use of signifiers, speech, writing – that human beings are able to transfer their lives and culture to subsequent generations. An example from antiquity is summoned to drive the point home: 'Empedocles, by throwing himself into Mount Etna, leaves forever present in the memory of men the symbolic act of his being-toward-death' (263, 2).

In a difficult paragraph, in which he once again refers to Hegel's master-slave dialectic, Lacan describes human freedom as 'circumscribed within ... [a] constitutive triangle' (263, 3). Each point of this triangle involves a subjective position (a 'figure of death' (263, 4)). The first position concerns the re-nunciation the master imposes on the other's desire 'by threatening to kill the other in order to enjoy the fruits of the other's serfdom' (263, 3). The second involves the slave subjecting themselves to the desire of the other (which is the position of the speaking subject more generally, given that they are the subject of the desire of the Other). The third position is the most radical, entailing as it does 'the suicidal abnegation of the vanquished party that deprives the master of his victory and leaves him to his inhuman solitude' (263, 3). In this position, desire coincides with the death drive. And, as Lacan stresses, the death drive here is be viewed 'not ... [as] a perversion of instinct, but rather a desperate affirmation of life' (263, 4). Lacan presents us with an account of the 'pure desire' resulting from the coincidence of desire and the death drive.[73]

Lacan now takes up two questions that, by this point in his paper, have become inevitable: 'what was before ... speech in the subject[?]' and 'what was prior to the birth of symbols[?]' (263, 6). This may seem surprising given that the entire thrust of *Function & Field* has been to stress the necessity of fore-grounding speech and language and to dissuade us from attempting to 'reach behind' language for anything ostensibly more fundamental. Then again, these questions have come to the fore as Lacan discusses variations on the theme of death (being-toward-death, the death instinct, the notion of a death wish, etc.), and they are thus approached with reference to finitude and mortality rather than in the register of the psychological. And, indeed, it is death that Lacan provides by way of an answer to these questions. The twist that Lacan adds is that death – which presumably always in some way exceeds the grasp of language – is also that 'from which ... existence derives all the meaning it has' (262, 6). At the very moment that we find an apparent outside of language – some 'real' which language can never domesticate or adequate symbolize of convey – we also stumble upon a point of symbolic density, a type of generative impossibility from which a variety of attempts at signification proliferate. Lacan then, as early as 1953 is already utilizing the concept of the real to great effect,[74] stressing that what seems to be definitively outside of language (death itself, the necessary limit imposed by mortality) is also importantly within language – is even inherent to it – in the sense that it is death which more than anything else confers meaning and prompts attempts at symbolization. We have then a situation in which a condition of impossibility (death as a limit beyond which language cannot reach) is simultaneously also a condition of possibility (a limit-point against which all meaning might be measured and ascertained). We should stay close to Lacan's wording here though. Not only does he assert that 'mortal meaning reveals in speech a center that is outside of language', he stresses also that this 'manifests a structure' (263, 7). The structure in question – the topological form of the torus (Figure 4.2) – 'differs from the spatialization of the circumference or sphere' (263, 7) because it defies the binary opposition of a mutually exclusive inside/outside categorization. After all, a torus' 'peripheral exteriority and central exteriority constitute but one single region' (264, 2). This is an ingenious move. It ensures that what had seemed definitely outside of the structure, i.e. the space in the middle of the donut-shaped formation of the torus (or, the externality to language as represented by death) remains an essential part, an 'inside of', that selfsame structure (death as apparent externality which is nonetheless an ultimate reference-point of meaning for language).

We have seen how Lacan has theorized the coincidence of desire and death drive. He now returns to the question of desire, using the figure of the torus as a way of elaborating his thinking. We can locate desire on the surface of the torus, a surface which we can think of as the field of language, a veritably universe of signifiers. This surface is continuous, but is nonetheless marked by a central void. This topological formation provides an elegant means of formalizing the nature of desire. This void has a structuring and defining influence on the workings of the subject's desire just as it does on this subject's being-towards-death. As Lacan puts it: the schema (of the torus) represents

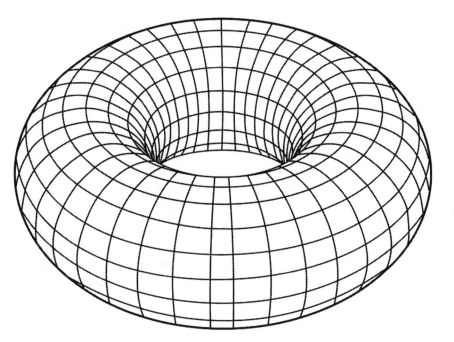

Figure 4.2 Torus. Image sourced from Wikipedia Commons.

'the endless circularity of the dialectical process that occurs when the subject achieves his solitude ... [in] immediate desire or in the full assumption of his being-toward-death' (264, 3). This dialectical process, moreover, is not merely individual – and here, appropriately enough, Lacan takes up the theme of endings, of the termination of an analysis – but pertains to 'all those it involves in a human undertaking' (264, 4). Put differently: there is no line that effectively divides the individual from culture, the subject from language, or the unconscious from the symbolic. This is why the analyst must be trained in the symbolic order – that is, in the art, literature and visual culture of their era – for their place will be at the center of 'an ongoing enterprise of Babel' where they will need to 'function as an interpreter in the strife of languages' (264, 5).

Lacan builds to his dénouement with a rhetorical flourish which contains a rich layering of biblical, literary and philosophical allusions:

> Psychoanalytic experience had rediscovered in man the imperative of the Word as the law that has shaped him in his image. It exploits the poetic function of language to give his desire its symbolic mediation ... it is through this gift that all reality has come to man and through its ongoing action that he sustains reality. (264, 8–265, 1)

Once we grasp the extent and vitality of language – which, importantly, is inclusive of the symbolic worlds of culture, religion and philosophy made possible precisely by language (that is, by the signifier, the symbolic order, the Other) – then we understand that the Freudian imperative of privileging language and speech by no means narrows the domain of psychoanalysis. Quite the contrary, an appreciation of the breadth of the function and field of language and speech widens our appreciation of the wealth of human experience that the signifier makes possible. Hence Lacan's ontological prioritization of language and speech, the latter indeed being 'the gift' through which 'all reality has come', 'its ongoing action' being that which 'sustains reality' (265, 1).

Lacan offers an extended quotation from the ancient Sanskrit text, *Brihadaranyaka Upanishad*. The relevant section of this text – probably suggested to Lacan by T.S. Eliot's *The Waste Land* – recounts how Prajapati, the god of thunder rumbles three times, each such rumbling being heard and understood differently by groups of his disciplines. The first of these groups, the Devas, respond to Prajapati's '*Da*' and the accompanying question 'Did you hear me?' by affirming that they have received the imperative '*Damyata*, master yourselves'. A second group confirms to him that they have received his message '*Datta*, give'. Those known as the Asuras tell him 'Thou hast said to us: *Dayadhvam*, be merciful' (265, 4–265, 6). Of course, what Prajapati says in each instance is exactly the same: '*Da!*' (a vocalization which of course recalls Freud's grandson's *fort/da* game). Prajapati's response to the three sacred ideals of speech as they are heard and echoed back to him (that the powers above 'are governed by the laws of speech' (265, 4), that 'men recognize each other by the gift of speech' (265, 5), that 'the powers below resound to the invocation of speech' (265, 6)) is the same: 'You have heard me' (265, 8). The '*Da da da*' that corresponds to each of these ideals of 'Submission, gift, grace' (265, 7) seems a perfect way to end Lacan's 1953 manifesto, representing, as it does, the coincidence of wisdom ('what the divine voice conveys' (265, 7)) and nonsense (as nicely evoked in the monosyllabic sounds of baby-speech). It would be hard to find a more resonant example of the Lacanian idea that the materiality of speech and the associated the multivalence of the signifier must, in a psychoanalytic treatment, eclipse the imaginary fixity of meaning

Notes

1 This statement was part of Lacan's presentation, *Opening to the Seminar,* delivered in Caracas, Venezuela on 12 July 1980.

2 Although *Function & Field* is often referred to simply as the *Rome Discourse*, this is in fact a problematic conflation. The remarks that Lacan delivered in person on 26 September 1953 (the *Rome Discourse*) represented only a few of the broader themes given far more elaborate treatment within *Function & Field*. A record of Lacan's spoken address in

Rome appears as 'Discours de Jacques Lacan (26 Sept. 1953)' in the journal *La Psychanalyse* (Lacan, 1956) alongside a transcription of the contributions of those present and Lacan's corresponding responses

3 Lacan's *Overture to the Seminar*, the opening text of *Seminar I*, bears the date of 18 November 1953.

4 To understand Lacan's theory of the subject, the term subject should be read in its original meaning of *subiectum* (what Aristotle called *hypokeimenon*). In Aristotle's logic, this term refers to the bearer of attributes. In medieval times, it refers to the ontological bearer of creation in its entirety (that is, to God). In modernity, the term subject refers not to the bearer of the universe, but to *bearing a relation to that universe*. This particular notion of the subject is most notably developed in the seventeenth century as the Cartesian *cogito* and its qualities and dimensions have been heavily discussed ever since. Lacan's theory of the subject must be read as participating in an inquiry that has lasted for more than three centuries. Hence the highly philosophical dimension of the Lacanian oeuvre.

5 'Perverse' should be understood here in the precise sense of being disconnected from biological needs.

6 This is the basic shared insight of both Ferdinand de Saussure and Roman Jakobson's linguistic theories and of Lévi-Strauss' structuralist anthropology: it is the break between nature and culture which is the 'motor' of culture as symbolic system (Zafiropoulos, 2010).

7 This is the background of Lacan's famous advice to analysts: 'Don't try to understand' (394, 7).

8 As we see in the insistence of so many patients today to identify with a diagnosis drawn from the *Diagnostic & Statistical Manual of the* American Psychiatric Association (2013).

9 At the end of *Function & Field*, Lacan will define this surface as topological, and more precisely yet as that of the topological figure of the torus which he offers in opposition to the "two-dimensionality of a zone" (264, 2) which characterizes the imaginary.

10 Lacan's L-Schema, as discussed in *Seminar on* "The Purloined Letter" (40, 2) provides a useful way of mapping this 'dance' of a psychoanalytic treatment.

11 For a more detailed historical account of the underlying conflicts leading up to the secession of key members from the *Société Psychanalytique de Paris* and the subsequent establishment of *Société Française de Psychanalyse*, see Roudinesco (1990).

12 While Lacan will draw inspiration from a wide range of thinkers and influences in *Function & Field*, the names Claude Lévi-Strauss and Martin Heidegger stand out as of particular importance in guiding Lacan's reconceptualization of the foundations of psychoanalysis.

13 The poem is entitled *With Bernard de Mandeville*.

14 The notion of the symbolic order is derived from Lévi-Strauss's (1969) *Elementary Structures of Kinship* (1969). Lévi-Strauss uses the term to refer to "the many different codes which constitute human societies—from social identities and kinship relations to cooking and feasting rituals and religious observances—in short, all cultural practices and inscriptions" (Clark, 2004). Such attention to the underlying structures organizing and giving coherence to a wide variety of cultural practices can be understood, in Lacanian terms, as an approach to culture from the perspective of the primacy of the signifier.

15 Lee provides a helpful qualification here. A relentless attention to the *phenomenological* dimension of the lived experience of countertransference stood in sharp contrast to "Lacan's new emphasis n the ways in which countertransference manifests itself in the analyst's contribution to the analytical dialogue and thus in the analyand's own speech as well. Lacan's point here is simply that it is the effects of the countertransference on the analytical dialogue (rather than the quality of the analyst's lived experience of

countertransference) that are of central importance to psychoanalytic practice and theory" (Lee, 1990, p. 34).

16 On July 8th of the same year (1953), in a lecture entitled "Le symbolique, l'imaginaire et le reel", Lacan introduced his conceptualization of the three registers to the newly created *Société Française de Psychanalyse*. This lecture is contained in its entirety in the short book *Des Noms-du-Père* (Lacan, 2005). At the end of the lecture, Lacan declared that he would say more about these concepts in his lecture in Rome, i.e. in what would become *Function & Field*.

17 Lacan states: "The theory interests us because it shows that all science called psychological must be affected by the ideals of the society in which it is produced ... [From a certain theoretical perspective human beings are] mechanical animals that [are being everywhere produced] ... by the procedure of *feedback* ... Let us indicate this subjective lack [in the objective determinations of the mechanical animal's behavior] by a small c, a symbol to which you can give all the translations that seem to fit. This *factor* escapes our cares as well as our criticism, and yet the subject enjoys it and it guarantees social coherence. But if the effect of the symbolic discordance which we call mental disease, succeeds in breaking this factor, then it would be our task to restore it" (Lacan, 1952, pp. 103–108 [MDK's translation]).

18 Marie Bonaparte, psychoanalyst, author and descendent of Napoleon Bonaparte, used her wealth to support the psychoanalytic movement. As Roudinesco (1993) shows, Lacan was vociferously opposed to Bonaparte's influence on psychoanalysis.

19 See the Moland and D'Haricault (1856) edition of *Le Livre de l'Enternelle Consolacion*, p. 165.

20 See particularly the discussion in *The Freudian Thing* in which Lacan refers to "*Wo Es war, soll Ich warden*" as Freud's "last will and testament" (347, 1). In *Instance of the Letter* stresses the formula (435, 6) before going on to offer the following rearticulation: "It is by touching ... on man's relation to the signifier ... that one changes the course of his history by modifying the moorings of his being" (438, 3). A more developed version appears in *The Subversion of the Subject*: "Where it was just now, where it was for a short while, between an extinction that is still glowing and an opening that stumbles, I can come into being by disappearing from my statement" (678, 5).

21 One interesting implication of this is that the truth-potential of full speech may have little to do with the empirical truth-value of its contents. It's truth-potential concerns more fundamentally *how it brings about a realization of the subject*, how it makes apparent – however fleetingly – a truth of desire. For a more developed analysis of full speech, see Hook (2018).

22 The context for the foregoing description was Lacan's technical innovation of the variable-length session. Instead of sessions of a fixed 50 or 60 minutes, as ordered by the *International Psychoanalytic Association*, Lacan altered the length of his sessions, often providing sessions of considerably shorter length. His reasoning was that "a propitious punctuation" – or ending – "gives meaning to the subject's discourse" (209, 8). This was a challenging assertion for the newly established *Société Française de Psychanalyse*, of which Lacan was, of course, a leading member. It was largely because of Lacan's variable sessions that the *International Psychoanalytic Association* would refuse him official approval for the new *Société*.

23 To clarify, regression certainly does occur for Lacan, but he argues that it needs to be understood – following a strict reading of Freud's use of the term in his *Interpretation of Dreams* (1900/2001) – in a *topographical* rather than a temporal sense. As Evans (1996) helps qualify, regression for Lacan is not to be understood in the instinctual sense, as a resurgence of a prior state, but in the sense of a *reduction of the symbolic to the imaginary*.

24 "He who has ears to hear, let them hear" (English Standard Version Bible, 2001, Mark 4:9). Fink (2006) notes that the French phrase *pour one point entendre* "means both in order not to hear and in order to not understand" (p. 786). Both meanings pertain to the imaginary dimensions of the ego.

25 It is worth consulting Heidegger's own formulations in *Being and Time* by way of comparison:

> Taking over thrownness, however, is possible only in such a way that the futural Dasein can *be* its own most 'as-it-already-was' – that is to say, its 'been' ... Only in so far as Dasein *is* as an "I-*am*-as-having-been", can Dasein come towards itself futurally in such a way that it comes *back*. As authentically futural, Dasein *is* authentically as "*having been*" [*gewesen*]. Anticipation of one's uttermost and own most possibility [death] is coming back understandingly to one's ownmost "been". Only insofar as it is futural can Dasein *be* authentically as having been. The character of "having been" [*Gewesenheit*] arises, in a certain way, from the future (Heidegger, 1996, p. 373).

26 A key reference-point here is Bergson's (1978) *Time and Free Will, An Essay on the Immediate Data of Consciousness*.

27 "That is to say, he annuls the *times of understanding* in favor of the *moments of concluding*" (Lacan, 213, 4). See the commentary on *Logical Time and the Assertion of Anticipated Certainty* by Dominiek Hoens (Chapter 1 of this volume).

28 The jibe that Lacan adds here in remarking that Freud's new method originated in 1895 and not 1904 is once again aimed at Maurice Bénassy ("an authority who ... appeared on that day to know nothing of Freud except the titles of his works" (213, 6)). Freud in fact mentions the term for the first time in 1896, in his paper 'Further Remarks on the Neuro-Psychoses of Defense'.

29 For a fascinating account of how Lacan's distinction between primary and secondary historicization has been taken up within the realm of history itself, see François Regnault's (1967) article, 'La pensée du prince'. In an insightful commentary on this article, where he cites Regnault directly, Yousef Nishat-Botero offers the following:

> secondary historiciziation portrays ... ready made [that is, symbolically mediated] history according to an imaginary narrative, which, like the subject qua ego, is characterized by distortions and organized according to supposed laws of history or development ... primary historicization undoes secondary historicization. In contrast to secondary historicization, primary historicization interrupts imaginary distortions to analyze the censored parts of history, to substitute for the "contorting historicization of conscious discourse, true history – the true history which, by leading this discourse back to its alleged origins, is the only one able to rid the stitched-up narrative of its distortions, hems and hitches". Hence, like full speech, primary historicization is not found in narratives of "progress, of the ideal, and of hopes and expectations" but in narratives of fragmentation and disintegration that disrupt imaginary identifications and create spaces where the failure to symbolize events becomes manifest ... the analyst ... must undo secondary historicization, to move from the 'acting out' of symptoms to full speech's opening of a 'subject space' in history (2018, pp. 32–33).

There is much that is of value here, including the idea that secondary historicization effectively *imaginarizes* primal (or primary) historicization and the suggestion that a parallel exists between full speech and the irreducibility or fragmentary nature of primary historicization. In respect of the latter, it becomes clear that there is clinical value in narratives of fragmentation, in the *failure* to symbolize, in the undoing of secondary historicization.

30 Lacan's target in this respect is largely Maurice Bouvet (1972), who coined the terms "pregenital" and "genital love".

31 Fink leaves "Monsieur de La Palice" untranslated. This is the French way of saying 'Mister Nobody'. It's use here suggests that what is being said is so obvious that it barely need to be stated.

32 Fink (2006) directs our attention here to Lacan's (2021) *Seminar IV*.

33 The long list of rhetorical devices that Lacan lists here are helpfully defined by Muller & Richardson (1982) and illustrated by Fink (2004).

34 This idea will be taken up again in the Postface to Lacan's *Seminar on "The Purloined Letter"*.

35 Strictly speaking, this example might be seen as more an instance of an obsessional thought than a hysterical symptom, although Freud notes in a footnote to this discussion that "Names … are not nearly so frequently … employed in obsessional neurosis as in hysteria for the purpose of establishing a connection between unconscious thoughts … and symptoms" (1909/2001, p. 188).

36 Lacan's well known definition of the subject, as provided in *Seminar XI*, nicely de-prioritizes the subject even in defining it: "a signifier represents a subject for another signifier" (Lacan, 1977, p. 207)

37 For a clinical Lacanian critique of such notions (countertransference and projective identification), see Fink's (2011) *Fundamentals of Psychoanalytic Technique*.

38 We have relied on Wilden's (1968, p. 118) translation of this passage.

39 The work of Maurice Leenhardt that Lacan refers to is: *Do Kamo. Person and Myth in the Polynesian World* (Leenhardt, 1979). Lacan's mention of "pacific Argonauts" (225, 2) refers to Malinowski's (2002) *The Argonauts of the Western Pacific*.

40 The following account should be required reading for anyone grappling with Lacan's notion of the unconscious (as structured like a language), indeed, Lévi-Strauss's description of how the unconscious should be approached sounds like it could have been penned by Lacan himself:

> The unconscious ceases to be the ineffable refuge of in-dividual particularities, the depository of a unique history … The unconscious can be reduced to a term by which we designate a function: the symbolic function, a specifically human function, no doubt, but which is exercised in all men according to the same laws; which is in fact reduced to the ensemble of these laws … The unconscious is always empty, or, more precisely, it is as much a stranger to images as is the stomach to the food which passes through it. An organ of a specific function, the unconscious limits itself to the imposition of structural laws … on unarticulated elements that come from elsewhere: pulsions [drives], emotions, representations, memories … [all of this is organized] according to the laws of the unconscious [which makes it] … a discourse. The vocabulary is less important than the structure (Lévi-Strauss, 1963, pp. 224–225).

41 Lacan refers here to: Jules Masserman's (1944) article (mistakenly spelling the author's name with a double n), "Language, behavior and dynamic psychiatry".

42 In a long parenthesis (227, 4–228, 1) referring to Masserman's work (characterized as a "monument of naïveté" (227, 5)), Lacan writes: "I would prefer to have the raccoon I mentioned earlier sitting in the armchair to which, according to the author, Freud's shyness confined the analyst by placing him behind the couch" (227, 6). The humor of this indictment stems from the fact that one of the test subjects of Masserman's experiment was a raccoon. Since Masserman is not able to understand signs he hears as composed of both signifier and signified, he is, for Lacan, as incompetent when it comes to directing a psychoanalytic treatment as a raccoon would be. Lacan extends his insult to say that thanks to the poet Jacques Prévert, even "the raccoon, at least, has definitely

entered the poetic bestiary and partakes as such, in its essence, of the symbol's eminent function" (228, 1). This is a reference to Prévert's poem *Inventaire* which Lacan cites directly.

43 Much of this critique is conveyed more clearly in Lacan's subsequent écrit, *The Freudian Thing*, where he insist of signifiers that "each element takes on its precise usage ... by being different from the others" (345, 2), before going on to conclude that "the signifier *is not a signification of anything* ... which confirms that Language is never [about] signal[s], but always dialectical movement" (Lacan, cited in Wilden, 1968 p. 122).

44 It helps, in grasping the structuralist underpinnings of Lévi-Strauss's anthropology, to note the qualification he himself made of his work. He studied not "how men think in myths, but how myths operate in men's minds without their being aware ... as if the thinking process were taking place in the myths ... and their interrelations" (Lévi-Strauss, 1983, p. 12).

45 Lacan, who studied Chinese in the early forties and had a degree at the Paris *Ecole des Langues Orientales*, might well have read Zenker's (1932) *Histoire de la Philosophie Chinoise*.

46 A similar, and indeed related problem pertains to how Lacan uses the notion of the symbol in *Function & Field*, as Verhaeghe (2020) points out: "the idea of symbol evokes a more or less stable relationship with a more or less traditional signification – e.g. the symbol 'heart' for love". In other words, to use the idea of the symbol is still – as is the case in relying on the Hegelian notion of the word-concept – to keep in place the role of the signified in an understanding of the workings and efficacy of language. Lacan will move definitely away from any such suggestion in his subsequent teaching, hence his frequent descriptive recourse to 'the signifier'.

47 See particularly the algorithm of linguistics that he offers in *Instance of the Letter* (414, 8), which, in revising Saussure's original conceptualization of the sign, definitively prioritizes the signifier over the signified.

48 For more on the notions of *hau* and mana see Mauss (2002) *The Gift: The Form and Reason for Exchange in Archaic Society*. For the notion of zero-symbol, see Lévi-Strauss (1987), *Introduction to the Work of Marcel Mauss*.

49 Gunkel (2014) nicely defines the concept of the master signifier as follows:

> [B]ecause signifiers refer only to other signifiers, this produces a seemingly endless chain of references ... [T]his seemingly infinite sequence of referral can be fixed or anchored only through the intervention of a ... 'nodal point' ... which 'quilts' them, stops their sliding and fixes their meanings ... this nodal point ... in the series of signifiers is the 'master signifier' – a signifier that, although essentially no different from any other signifier, is situated in such a way that it masters the entire sequence of referral by providing a kind of final ... guarantee of meaning. It is able to do this ... not because it possesses some special significance ... but simply because it is able to halt the process of referral by the empty gesture of referring only to itself. This 'reflective' signifier is nothing more than a kind of cul-de-sac in the chain of equivalences ... .'beneath' the alleged unity of the field of meaning, there is only a ... self-referential, performative gesture (pp. 190–191).

50 See Hegel's (2001) *Philosophy of Right*.

51 This is also the sense of the quote from Lichtenberg in Lacan's endnote 21 (231, 9).

52 See for instance Lacan's *Presentation on Psychical Causality* in *Écrits*, where he states that "madness is experienced entirely within the register of meaning" (135, 5).

53 For detailed commentary on Lacan's use of this poem, see Allouch (2009) and Dor (1992).

54 Or, as the sentence is rendered in the *Standard Edition*: "I could only interpret it as one of horror at pleasure of his own of which he himself was unaware" (Freud, 1909b, p. 167). Notice how Fink, in using the word *jouissance*, gives a Lacanian translation of Freud's sentence.

55 It helps to provide a brief outline of Hegel's assertion (which, in its original formulation, in *Elements of the Philosophy of Right* states: "What is rational is real; And what is real is rational" (1991, p. 20). For Hegel a dualistic division between appearance and reality is not ultimately tenable. Contesting the Kantian division between noumena and phenomena, Hegel asserts, by contrast, that what we perceive simply *is* what is. What appears to us, moreover, is always subject to reason – it is amenable to rational investigation. Hegel takes this is one step further however to advance that what appears to us essentially *is* reason. Reason is the way and how of the world. Rationality, accordingly, underlies the arrangement not just of the world, but of history and consciousness. In this sense "the real is rational". Importantly also, all of reality is rational for Hegel insofar as it yields to rational investigation – an unknowable reality, something which is not amenable to rational investigation, not being strictly conceivable. This implies then that all that is rational – treated with rationality, made intelligible via rationality – is also real.

56 Hegel had already developed the idea that the self has to find themselves in an 'object'. The slave, for example, recognizes themselves in the master; in a progressive stage of the dialectical logic, it becomes apparent that they are the point of recognition that effectively makes the master, a master. We see a similar dialectical progression evinced in the master, who finds their identity in the slave, upon whom they have become reliant. (These are, of course, the terms of the struggle for recognition dramatized in Hegel's famous master-slave dialectic). In Hegel's work recognition results in a subject appropriating the object; in Lacan, by contrast, the subject recognizes in the object its own radical alienation, its divided condition.

57 We should bear in mind here Wilden's (1968) assertion that "the Hegelian subject is not and cannot be the equivalent of the Freudian subject" (p. 306). So, while it is true that Lacan uses the Hegelian master-slave dialectic "he does not accept it as a valid premise for the analytical dialectic" (p. 306). Lacan in fact attempts to show us "the impossibility of the final reconciliation of … [Hegel's] Phenomenology … Given the Freudian notion of the discovery of difference and the 'lost object', reconciliation … is psychologicaly impossible either for the individual in relation to himself or in relation to the group to which he is linked by identificatory ties … The subject-object relationship of the Imaginary order precludes anything but a phantasmatic 'return to unity'" (p. 307).

58 Muller and Richardson (1982) interpret this reference to Hegel differently, applying it to Lacan's understanding of the subject: "It is because of Freud's insistence that the self has this 'other' center, i.e. the unconscious, that the subject warrants this Hegelian description of an 'identity' of the particular (i.e. consciousness) and the universal (i.e. the unconscious). It is this 'identity' of the particular and universal (of consciousness and the unconscious) … that enters the psychoanalytic dialogue" (1982, p. 83). They do go on to add a further comment, which goes some way to bridging our own interpretation of Lacan's use of Hegel (concerning the identity of the particular and universal) and their own: "The unconscious as discourse of the [O]ther provides the locus for the identity of the particular (in terms of the subject's desire as expressed in his own signifying chains of metaphor and metonym) with the universal (in terms of the transindividual structure of language)" (Muller & Richardson, 1982, p. 116).

59 This insight, says Wilden (1968), is echoed elsewhere in *Écrits*, in Lacan's article *Psychoanalysis and it Teaching*, where Lacan says: "The analyst leaves room for this Other beyond the other by the neutrality with which he makes himself … neither the one nor

the other of the two who are there; and if he remains silent, it is in order to let this Other speak" (366, 5).

60 Jean-François Champollion (1790–1832) was the first to decipher the Egyptian hieroglyphs on the Rosetta Stone.

61 Just as signifiers work on a differential basis – that is, on the basis of their difference from other similar signifiers ('cat' is to be differentiated from 'fat', 'mat', 'rat', etc.) so signifieds also refer to and take on value by being differentiated by other signifieds.

62 According to Borch-Jacobsen (1991) this is "a formula suggested by his friend Lévi-Strauss" (p. 143).

63 This accounts also for Lacan's emphasis on the paranoiac quality of knowledge, as described both in his account of the mirror stage and also in *Presentation on Psychical Causality* and *Aggressiveness in Psychoanalysis*.

64 Wang (2019) refers to Weber (1991), who usefully observes: In invoking the future anterior, Lacan troubles the perfected closure of the always-already-having-been by inscribing it in the inconclusive futurity of what will-always-already-having-been, a "time" which can never be entirely remembered, since it will never have fully taken place. It is an irreducible remainder or remnant that will continually prevent the subject from ever becoming entirely self-identical.

65 Lacan had – as discussed earlier – already disdainfully remarked on "the misadventure of Freud's theory of the instincts when revised by an author somewhat less than alert to what Freud explicitly stated to be its mythical content" (205, 4).

66 We are indebted to Dany Nobus for much of the contextualizing historical information regards Lacan's relation to Bénassy discussed in this section.

67 Nobus speculates that the person who shared this comment with Lacan was either Serge Leclaire or Wladimir Granoff.

68 Any doubts as to the caustic quality of Lacan's remarks are quickly laid to rest in the lines that follow. As Dany Nobus points out, Lacan's mention of "the dog's oral vice mentioned in the Scriptures" (255, 1) plays on *Proverbs 26:11*, in which it is stated: "As a dog returns to his vomit, so a fool repeats his folly". Lacan's sarcastic remark here pokes fun at Bénassy for not only lapping up his own vomit [the lamentably poor 'Théorie des instincts'], but for having lapped up the vomit of others, in this case, Marie Bonaparte's, 1934 book *Introduction à la Théorie des Instincts* (Dany Nobus, personal communication, 25 February 2021).

69 The strategy of the obsessional consists in taking such a position of waiting or prevarication in relation to the Other such that they, the obsessional, can hide/deny the lack of the Other, despite that they nonetheless remain the subject of this Other.

70 The two texts which best represent the respective contributions of these two intellectuals are probably Xavier Bichat's (1978) *Physiological Researches on Life and Death* (originally published in French in 1800), and Cannon's (1967) *The Wisdom of the Body* (originally published in 1932).

71 Lacan refers to "Laksanalaksana", a principle of Hindu esthetics that reads words always in their second or third meaning. For an account of Laksanalaksana, see Deshpande (2009).

72 It helps here, as Lee (1990) reminds us, to keep in mind Alexandre Kojève's commentary on Hegel's famous idea, as this would have served as the immediate background for Lacan's own use of the concept: Hegel said that all conceptual understanding (*Begreifen*) is equivalent to a *murder* ... For example, as long as the Meaning (or Essence) "dog" is embodied in a sensible entity, this Meaning (Essence) *lives*: it is the real dog, the living dog which runs, drinks, and eats. But when the Meaning (Essence) "dog" passes into the *word* "dog" – that is, becomes [an] *abstract* Concept which is different from the sensible reality that it reveals by its Meaning – the Meaning (Essence) *dies*: the *word* "dog" does not run, drink, and eat; in it the Meaning (Essence) ceases to live – that is it

does. And that is why the *conceptual* understanding of empirical reality is equivalent to a *murder* (Kojève, 1969, p. 140). Lacan of course makes his own psychoanalytic use of existing philosophical concepts, and was not as such beholden to Kojève's interpretation of Hegel (influenced by it as he no doubt was). Nonetheless it is worth noting – as we already have regards Lacan's use of (Kojève's) Hegel – that the above description importantly differs from – adds nuance to? – the idea that it is exclusively the symbol (or signifier) that represents the death of the thing.

73 This "pure desire" resulting from the coincidence of desire and death drive is invoked both in *Seminar VII* as "mè phunai" (1986, p. 361) and in the "sign of no" of Sygne de Coûfontaine as discussed in *Seminar VIII* (2001, p. 329).

74 In a way, Lacan's theory of the real is already fully operative in *Function & Field*. Lacan had in fact defined the concept at a conference address he gave two months earlier (July 8th 1953). He noted there that despite the title of his talk ("The Imaginary, the Symbolic, and the Real"), he had said nothing about the latter. He then went on to say: "I did say a little about it. The real is … the totality or the vanishing instant. In the analytic experience, it is when one bumps into something, for instance into the silence of the analyst" (Lacan, 2005, p. 53 [MDK's translation]).

References

Allouch, J. (2009) *L'Amour Lacan*. Paris: EPEL.

American Psychiatric Association. (2013) *Diagnostic and Statistical Manual of Mental Disorders* (5th Edition). Arlington, VA: Author.

Bénassy, M. (1953) Théorie des Instincts. *Revue Française de Psychanalyse*. 17, 1/2, 1–110.

Bergson, H. (1978) Time and Free Will: An Essay on the immediate data of consciousness. In K.A. Pearson and J. Mullarkey (eds.) *Henry Bergson, Key Writings*. New York / London: Continuum.

Bichat, X. (1978) *Physiological Researches on Life and Death*. Washington: University Publications of America.

Boileau, N. (2007) *Selected Poems*. London: Yale University Press.

Bonaparte, M. (1934) *Introduction à la Théorie des Instincts*. Paris: Denoël.

Borch-Jacobsen, M. (1991) *Lacan, The Absolute Master*. Stanford: Stanford University Press.

Bouvet, M. (1972) *Oeuvres Psychanalytiques I: La Relation d'Objet*. Paris: Payot.

Bowie, M. (1991) *Lacan*. London: Fontana.

Browning, R. (1887) *Parleying with Certain People of Importance in Their Day*. Boston/New York: Houghton, Mifflin, & Company.

Cannon, W.B. (1967) *The Wisdom of the Body*. New York: Norton.

Carroll, L. (1923) *Through the Looking Glass*. New York: Winston.

Clark, R. (2004) The Symbolic Order. *The Literary Encyclopedia*. Available at: https://www.litencyc.com/php/stopics.php?rec=true&UID=1082.

Deshpande, G.T. (2009) *Indian Poetics*. Mumbai: Popular Prakashan Pvt.

Dolar, M. (1999) Where does Power Come From? *New Formations*. 35, 79–92.

Dor, J. (1992) *Introduction à Lacan, 2. La Structure du Sujet*. Paris: Denoël.

Dunand, A. (1996) Lacan and Lévi-Strauss. In R. Feldstein, B. Fink and M. Jaanus (eds.) *Reading Seminars I and II: Lacan's Return to Freud*. SUNY Press: New York.

English Standard Version Bible. (2001) ESV Online. Available at: https://esv.literalword.com/

Evans, D. (1996) *An Introductory Dictionary of Lacanian Psychoanalysis*. London and New York: Routledge.

Fenichel, O. (1946) *The Psychoanalytic Theory of Neurosis*. New York: Kegan Paul.

Ferenczi, A. (1949) Confusion of the Tongues Between the Adults and the Child—*(The Language of Tenderness and of Passion)*. *International Journal of Psycho-Analysis*. 30, 225–230.

Fink, B. (2004) *Lacan to the Letter: Reading Écrits Closely*. Minneapolis: University of Minnesota Press.

Fink, B. (2006) Translator's endnotes. In J. Lacan (ed.) *Écrits*. London & New York: Norton.

Fink, B. (2011) *Fundamentals of Psychoanalytic Technique: A Lacanian Approach for Practitioners*. London: W.W. Norton.

Fleiss, R. (1949) Silence and Verbalization. A Supplement to the Theory of the 'Analytic Rule'. *International Journal of Psychoanalysis*. 30, 21–30.

Forrester, J. (1990) *The Seductions of Psychoanalysis: Freud, Lacan & Derrida*. Cambridge: Cambridge University Press.

Freud, S. (1896/2001) Further Remarks on the Neuro-Psychoses of Defense. In J. Strachey (ed.), *The Standard Edition of the Complete Psychological Works of Sigmund Freud*, Vol. 3. London: Vintage, pp. 157–185.

Freud, S. (1900/2001) The Interpretation of Dreams. In J. Strachey (ed.) *The Standard Edition of the Complete Psychological Works of Sigmund Freud*, Vols. 4 & 5. London: Hogarth Press.

Freud, S. (1901/2001) The Psychopathology of Everyday Life. In J. Strachey (ed.) *The Standard Edition of the Complete Psychological Works of Sigmund Freud*, Vol. 6. London: Vintage.

Freud, S. (1905a/2001) Three Essays on the Theory of Sexuality. In J. Strachey (ed.) *The Standard Edition of the Complete Psychological Works of Sigmund Freud*, Vol. 7. London: Vintage, pp. 209–226.

Freud, S. (1905b/2001) Jokes and their Relation to the Unconscious. In J. Strachey (ed.) *The Standard Edition of the Complete Psychological Works of Sigmund Freud*, Vol. 8. London: Vintage.

Freud, S. (1909a/2001) Analysis of a Phobia in a Five-Year Old Boy ('Little Hans'). In J. Strachey (ed.), *The Standard Edition of the Complete Psychological Works of Sigmund Freud*, Vol. 10. London: Vintage, pp. 1–147.

Freud, S. (1909b/2001) Notes Upon a Case of Obsessional Neurosis (The 'Rat Man'). In J. Strachey (ed.) *The Standard Edition of the Complete Psychological Works of Sigmund Freud*, Vol. 10. London: Vintage, pp. 151–249.

Freud, S. (1910/2001) Five Lecture on Psycho-analysis. In J. Strachey (ed.) *The Standard Edition of the Complete Psychological Works of Sigmund Freud*, Vol. 11. London: Vintage, pp. 1–56.

Freud, S. (1911/2001) Psycho-Analytic Notes on an Autobiographical Account of Paranoia (Dementia Paranoides)'. In J. Strachey (ed.) *The Standard Edition of the Complete Psychological Works of Sigmund Freud*, Vol. 11. London: Vintage, pp. 1–79.

Freud, S. (1914/2001) On Narcissism: An Introduction. In J. Strachey (ed.) *The Standard Edition of the Complete Psychological Works of Sigmund Freud*, Vol. 14. London: Vintage, pp. 67–102.

Freud, S. (1918/2001) From the History of an Infantile Neurosis (The "Wolf Man'). In J. Strachey (ed.) *The Standard Edition of the Complete Psychological Works of Sigmund Freud*, Vol. 17. London: Vintage, pp. 1–122.

Freud, S. (1920/2001) Beyond the Pleasure Principle. In J. Strachey (ed.) *The Standard Edition of the Complete Psychological Works of Sigmund Freud*, Vol. 18. London: Vintage, pp. 1–64.

Freud, S. (1926a/2001) Inhibitions, Symptoms and Anxiety. In J. Strachey (ed.) *The Standard Edition of the Complete Psychological Works of Sigmund Freud*, Vol. 20. London: Vintage, pp. 75–174.

Freud, S. (1926b/2001) The Question of Lay Analysis: Conversations with an Impartial Person. In J. Strachey (ed.) *The Standard Edition of the Complete Psychological Works of Sigmund Freud*, Vol. 20. London: Vintage, pp. 177–250.

Glover, E. (1931) The Therapeutic Effect of Inexact Interpretation: A Contribution to the Theory of Suggestion. *International Journal of Psychoanalysis*. 12, 397–411.

Gunkel D. J. (2014) Master Signifier. In R. Butler (ed.) *The Žižek Dictionary*. Durham: Acumen.

Hegel, G.W.F. (1991) *Elements of the Philosophy of Right*. Cambridge: Cambridge University Press.

Heidegger, M. (1996) *Being and Time*. New York: Harper & Row.

Hook, D. (2018) *Six Moments in Lacan*. London & New York: Routledge.

Jakobson, R. (1960) Linguistics and poetics. In T. Sebeok (ed.) *Style in Language*. Cambridge, MA: M.I.T. Press.

Jones, E. (1918) The Theory of Symbolism. *British Journal of Psychology*. 9, 2, 181–229.

Kojève, A. (1969) *Introduction to the Reading of Hegel: Lectures on the "Phenomenology of Spirit"*. Ithaca: Cornell University Press.

Koyré, A. (1953) An Experiment in Measurement. *Proceedings of the American Philosophical Society*. 7, 222–237.

Lacan, J. (1952) Intervention au Premier Congrès mondial de psychiatrie en 1950 qui fait suite aux exposés de Franz Alexander, Anna Freud, Mélanie Klein et Raymond de Saussure, dans le cadre de la Vᵉ section du Congrès mondial, "Psychothérapie, psychanalyse". In *Ce Discours a été Publié dans les Actes du Congrès*, Vol. 5. Paris: Hermann et Cie. pp. 103–108.

Lacan, J. (1956) Discours de Jacques Lacan (26 septembre, 1953). *Actes du Congrès de Rome, La Psychanalyse*. 1, 202–255.

Lacan, J. (1977) *The Four Fundamental Concepts of Psychoanalysis*. London: Hogarth Press & the Institute of Psycho-Analysis.

Lacan, J. (1986) *Le Séminaire, Livre VII, L'Éthique De La Psychanalyse*. Paris: Seuil.

Lacan, J. (1988a) *The Seminar of Jacques Lacan, Book I: Freud's Papers on Technique, 1953-1954* (edited by Jacques-Alain Miller, translated by John Forrester). New York and London: W.W. Norton.

Lacan, J. (1988b) *The Seminar of Jacques Lacan, Book II: The Ego in Freud's Theory and in the Technique of Psychoanalysis, 1954-1955* (edited by Jacques-Alain Miller, translated by Sylvana Tomaselli). New York and London: W.W. Norton.

Lacan, J. (2001) *Le Séminaire, Livre VIII, Le Transfert*. Paris: Seuil.

Lacan, J. (2005) *Des Noms-Du-Père*. Paris: Seuil.

Lacan, J. (2011) Overture to the 1st International Encounter of the Freudian Field. *Hurly-Burly*, 6, 17–20.

Lacan, J. (2021) *The Seminar of Jacques Lacan, Book IV: The Object Relation* (edited by Jacques-Alain Miller, translated by Adam Price). Cambridge: Polity.

Lee, J. S. (1990) *Jacques Lacan*. Amherst: University of Massachusetts Press.

Leenhardt, M. (1979) *Do Kamo. Person and Myth in the Polynesian World.* Chicago: Chicago University Press.

Lévi-Strauss, C. (1963) *Structural Anthropology.* New York: Base Books.

Lévi-Strauss, C. (1969) *Elementary Structure of Kinship.* New York: Beacon Press.

Lévi-Strauss, C. (1983) *The Raw and the Cooked, Mythologiques, Vol. 1.* Chicago: University of Chicago Press.

Lévi-Strauss, C. (1987) *Introduction to the Work of Marcel Mauss.* London: Routledge & Kegan Paul.

Liu, L. H. (2011) *The Freudian Robot: Digital Media and the Future of the Unconscious.* Chicago: University of Chicago Press.

Malinowski, B. (2002) *The Argonauts of the Western Pacific: An Account on the Native Enterprise and Adventure in the Archipelagoes of Milanesian New Quinea.* London: Routledge.

Masserman, J. (1944) Language, Behavior and Dynamic Psychiatry. *International Journal of Psychoanalysis.* 25, 1&2, 1–8.

Mauss, M. (2002) *The Gift: The Form and Reason for Exchange in Archaic Society.* London & New York: Routledge.

Miller, J. A. (1996a) An Introduction to Seminars I and II: Lacan's Orientation Prior to 1953 (I). In R. Feldstein, B. Fink and M. Jaanus (eds.) *Reading Seminars I and II: Lacan's Return to Freud.* SUNY Press: New York.

Miller, J. A. (1996b) An introduction to Seminars I and II: Lacan's orientation prior to 1953 (III). In R. Feldstein, B. Fink and M. Jaanus (eds.) *Reading Seminars I and II: Lacan's Return to Freud.* SUNY Press: New York.

Moland, L. and D'Haricault, C. (1856) (Ed.) *Le Livre de l'Enternelle Consolacion, Première Version Françoise de l'Imitation du Jésus-Christ.* Paris: Janet.

Muller, J. P. and Richardson, W. K. (1982) *Lacan and Language: A Reader's Guide to Écrits.* New York: International Universities Press.

Nishat-Botero, Y. (2018) *The Advent of the Subject: The Theory of Freedom in Lacan's Rome Discourse.* MA Dissertation. London: Kingston University.

Nobus, D. (2021) Personal communication (email, 25 February).

Quinodoz, (2004) *Reading Freud: A Chronological Exploration of Freud's Writings.* London: Routledge.

Rabelais, F. (1990) *Gargantua et Pantagruel, Le Tiers Livre*, III-IV. *Gargantua and Pantagruel.* New York / London: W.W. Norton & Company.

Regnault, F. (1967) La pensée du Prince. *Cahiers pour L'analyse.* 6, 22–52. Available in English translation as 'The Thought of the Prince' at: http://cahiers.kingston.ac.uk/pdf/cpa6.2.regnault.translation.pdf

Roudinesco, E. (1990) *Jacques Lacan & Co: A History of Psychoanalysis in France, 1925-1985.* Chicago: University of Chicago Press.

Roudinesco, E. (1993) *Jacques Lacan: Esquisse d'Une vie, Histoire d'un Système de Pensée.* Paris: Fayard.

Shepherdson, C. (2008) *Lacan and the Limits of Language.* New York, NY: Fordham University Press.

Verhaeghe, P. (2020) The Function and Field of Speech and Language in Psychoanalysis: A Commentary on Lacan's 'Discourse de Rome'. *Contours Journal*, 5: LaConference. Available at: https://www.sfu.ca/humanities-institute/contours/LaConference/paper1.html.

von Frisch, K. (1956) *Bees: Their Vision, Chemical Senses, and Language.* Ithaca, NY: Cornell University Press.

von Frisch, K. (1993) *The Dance Language and Orientation of Bees*. Cambridge, MA: Harvard University Press.

Wang, C. (2019) *Subjectivity In-Between Times: Exploring the Notion of Time in Lacan's Work*. London & New York: Palgrave.

Weber, S. (1991) *Return to Freud: Jacques Lacan's Dislocation of Psychoanalysis*. Cambridge: Cambridge University Press.

Wilden, A. Trans. & Ed. (1968). *The Language of the Self: The Function of Language in Psychoanalysis*. Baltimore: Johns Hopkins University Press.

Zafiropoulos, M. (2010) *Lacan and Lévi-Strauss* or *The Return to Freud (1951-1957)*. London: Karnac Books

Zenker, E. V. (1932) *Histoire de la Philosophie Chinoise*. Paris: Payot.

5

VARIATIONS ON THE STANDARD TREATMENT

Jamieson Webster

Context

This paper has escaped the kind of elaborate commentary that most articles in the *Écrits* enjoy. Its context, more or less cited by Lacan, seems to have side-stepped probing. There aren't any juicy details around the invitation to write the article by Lacan's friend and ally, the psychiatrist Henry Ey, the acceptance of the article by the *Encyclopedia* and its eventual removal in 1960, nor its reception, which seems minimal or confined to the converted. The last fact seems a shame as it is a paper addressed to the wider analytic community at the time: a great deal of the articles that Lacan cites are from the early 1950s, along with working with classics like Ferenczi, Fenichel, Reich, and Sterba. He is writing in the summer of 1954 after the first year of his infamous Seminar. The paper acts as a survey of the literature at the time on the question and criteria of so-called 'standard treatment' – or in French 'cure type' – interrogated dialectically through condensed presentations of Lacan's thought and his work in Seminar I (1988) on Freud's papers on technique. Thus we get a picture of Lacan's knowledge of the developments in psychoanalysis over 50 years and a forceful insertion of his place in this movement, in this paper in particular, as the one who stays true to the standard treatment as outlined by Freud. This takes place on the threshold of having thrown his hat in the ring by beginning a yearly seminar that would continue for 28 years and which forms a parallel body of work to his major publication, Écrits.

A word on the title deserves mention, for throughout the article there is a slippage between standard treatment and typical cure. In French, the title is *Variantes de la cure-type* and yet both *treatment standard* and *cure type* are used to convey the norm for psychoanalytic work. While the English translation tends to stick with the word 'standard' and 'treatment' the article itself tries to effect a displacement from the many accepted notions of treatment toward the specificity of a psychoanalytic cure. 'Standard' feels more formal and normative than 'typical' which still has the colloquial connotation of type as if it were

DOI: 10.4324/9781003264231-5

a choice of one among others. In French, it can also be used as an insult – close to how we say 'typical' sardonically. Many have commented that this is Lacan's first use of the word 'cure'. The article is often paired with the 1958 treatise on psychoanalytic technique 'The Direction of the Treatment and the Principles of its Power' (Lacan, 2006) which has been the more focal article. But both concern themselves with the means and ends of treatment, the direction of treatment in the sense of its telos, end or termination, and what the end tells you about the way or pathway *to* that end. Both of these articles outline a specifically Lacanian vision of a psychoanalytic cure (even if he would call it Freudian). So while the *standard treatment* and the *direction of the treatment* are the central signifiers in these technical papers in English, in both articles 'cure' slips through as the word of great import for Lacan.

Etymologically, the cure goes back to the Latin *cura* that means care, and Lacan moves away from a medical model, which sees illness as a momentary perturbation in a system that should be kept homeostatic, to a conception of care or concern that entails something ongoing and whose final aim is not transitory or a return-to-the-norm or standard but a new state all together. The mention of care/cure brings to mind Heidegger who has a stealthy presence in this article, as he does in much of early Lacan. Care has two meanings: worries or troubles and concern or attention, care as a burden and care as solicitude. Heidegger points to care as stretched between earth and the divine; the burden that pulls you down, and the concern that lifts you up. Care becomes synonymous with Being or Dasein which for Heidegger is an existential category that goes beyond our individual being and which Lacan plays with, especially in his use of Other and other. Care, in this Heideggerian context, is elevated to a mode of Being which solicits us back to ourselves from escape, anxiety, insignificance, and alienation. It opens us back toward a sense of time and the future. The play between care and cure, means and ends, feels critical to understanding what is at stake in the very title of this article. What do we mean by psychoanalytic care and psychoanalytic cure? As you will see, this is a part and parcel of a question of the ethics of psychoanalysis.

There are other hidden virtues to 'Variations on the Standard Treatment,' not least of which is the context of the article which forced Lacan into a more systematic review of the literature which makes its appearance in surprising allegiances and detailed readings (often quite critical) of work by some major figures like Anna Freud, Edward Glover, Michael Balint, Sandor Ferenczi, Wilhelm Reich, and Theodor Reik, and some minor figures like Richard Sterba, Alice Balint, Max Gitelson, and Richard P. Knight. The latter was the president of the American Psychoanalytic Association (APA) during the time Lacan was writing and gave a fascinating survey of the state of psychoanalysis (Knight, 1953). Lacan's rhetorical style is not as vitriolic as it is in the 1958 paper ('Direction of the Treatment') (Lacan, 2006), as he hadn't suffered the betrayal of his colleagues yet at the SFP (Société Psychanalytique de Paris). We must keep in mind that the crisis surrounding Lacan's practice of the short session began roughly in 1951. Furthermore, his move away from the Société Psychanalytique de Paris to Société Francaise de Psychanalyse took place during the time that he was working on this article. However, he was still part of the larger community of analysts at the time (he wasn't excommunicated from the International Psychoanalytic Association (IPA) until 1963), part of the Freudian body, and not yet forced to be a Lacanian to the extent that he was excluded from the 'authorized' Freudian association. His position was certainly in jeopardy, and he was perceived as a threat, but the lengths to which the institution would go could not have in any way been clear in the summer of 1954. Again, the translation of the title from French cure to English treatment speaks to something important that mirrors this situation: in French, at the time he is writing, he can be seen as attempting to effect a displacement from treatment to cure in the direction of his own reading of Freud; in English, reading from the future, he is put in the position of commenting on the standard treatment from the position of being a deviant.

I think it is important to read the article with both temporal moments in mind, especially since the article was emended in 1966 for the publication of the *Écrits*. Finally, it is important to note that the debates that Lacan engages with in terms of psychoanalytic technique rage on today. The field is still riven by certain impasses on the definition of treatment that Lacan tries to unearth in this article 60 years prior. His personal exasperation, the gravity of his tone, and the tragicomedy he depicts of mid-century psychoanalysis, are, on the one hand, absolutely applicable to today's milieu, but on the other hand, given that we are in a new moment defined by the decline of psychoanalysis with its re-marginalization in the world of both medicine and the humanities, the article can strike one as prophetic *and* pitiful. The psychoanalysts, even as the public and the major institutions abandon them, continue to wage their narcissistic wars of minor differences, without making much of the theoretical headway that Lacan calls for in this paper. As Lacan says in 'Variations on the Standard Treatment,' 'what is at stake is...less a standard, than standing' (227, 5). Even as that standing has been lost, in part because of the fevered attempt to maintain their position of power and not the pathway of a psychoanalytic cure, psychoanalysis rages on.

I *'A Bat Question': examining it in the light of day*

'Variations on the Standard Treatment' – The title, Lacan announces, is a pleonasm that is lame, twisted, abject, a distortion. It's an amazing set of words to describe the title of an article that Lacan was assigned and which was eventually, and perhaps not surprisingly, rejected. 'Standard' implies without variation and yet, in creating a standard one also delimits a margin of variation. To encircle a center, one must define the outside periphery. The two – standard and variation – are interdependent on one another. More often than not value becomes a part of this kind of system of measurement, where the standard is good and the deviations are bad or lesser than. Lacan worries that this way of speaking about standards is simply a normative enterprise, a critique very much in the air of the French milieu, especially when tied to questions of science, technology, modern medicine and psychiatry. Lacan appeals to Foucault's Naissance de la Clinique (The Birth of the Clinic) in making the point that what he refers to a 'our 'clinical approach'' (300, footnote 2) still maintains 'an originally repressed moment in the physician who extends it', this physician being 'the lost child of this moment' (300, footnote 2).

So, what are these variations? And what does it mean to be charged with the task of speaking of variation? Mustn't we first know what is standard, and perhaps even why it is considered the standard before we can speak about this outside edge? This is the distortion that is intrinsic to the question, what Lacan calls the stopping point that is also a point of entry into the problem. Lacan is asking us not to stop at whatever is vague or seemingly impossible about the question of standards and variations, but rather to see what the distortion il-luminates. To do so, we must first stop at the question of what 'standard' psychoanalytic treatment means and enter there before we can move on to consider a question of variations on the standard. Certainly, standards were *the* pressing question at the time Lacan was writing because there were already questions about his variations on the standard psychoanalytic technique, and he was forced to hide his practice of variable length sessions. So while Lacan begins this essay playfully, one can also hear the sense of urgency – what standards!? And if we don't know, and yet use this as the basis for a kind of normative or moralistic judgment, are we not truly lame in all the senses of the word running from halting to injured to feeble to dull? This twisting in the use of standards is tantamount to what Lacan is calling a bat question, alluding to Aesop's fable of the bat, meaning we do not know where we belong, to the kingdom of birds or the kingdom of beasts, and so have no friends. We psychoanalysts, he insinuates in his footnote (300, n.1), are abject.

If Lacan begins by declaring psychoanalysts abject, then what is fascinating is that what comes to the rescue – only two paragraphs in – is the public. A strange place to put the fate of psychoanalysis, but interestingly, Lacan throughout this article, lauds the public for what they inherently know or sense, against the abject knowledge of psychoanalysts at the time he is writing this article. What the public knows is that variation implies neither the adaptation of treatment to a 'variety' of cases, nor to 'variables' that influence the field of psychoanalysis, but rather to a strange, almost hypersensitive, concern for what he calls 'purity of means and ends' (269, 7). The public gets this and therefore grants us a more meritorious status, understanding that what is at stake 'is clearly a rigor that is in some sense ethical' without which a treatment, 'even if it is filled with psychoanalytic knowledge, can only amount to psychotherapy' (269, 8).

How, we might ask, can Lacan claim that the public knows such a thing? Especially, when the references embedded in these questions concern the critique of an accepted worldview structured by the power of psychiatric knowledge? Reflecting on this paper over 50 years later, at a time that is certainly not the 'hey-day' of psychoanalysis – which usually refers to the 1950s psychoanalysis in America – I can still say that there is something true about what I believe Lacan is referencing in this nod to doxa or public opinion. Namely, that the public – meaning not only the psychoanalytic initiates – has the sense that something special (pure, rigorous, different) is meant by psychoanalysis as a treatment. You often see it when a patient asks about the couch in the room: What happens *there*? Even the perennial jokes about psychoanalysis lasting a lifetime implicitly acknowledge the depths that are to be traversed and the difficulty of the end or termination of such a treatment. In the common criticisms of psychoanalysis pitted against say cognitive-behavioral treatment, we can see an acknowledgment that 'getting to the bottom of it' is simply too costly (usually meaning either time, money, and/or the suffering – and not necessarily symptom relief – involved in searching for the truth).

Lacan goes on, and one might consider this sentence the thesis of this section, to say:

> This rigor [concerning the means and ends of psychoanalytic treatment] would require a formalization, by which I mean a theoretical formaliza-tion, which has hardly been provided to date because it has been confused with a practical formalism – that is, a [set of rules] regarding what is done and what is not done. (270, 1)

The theoretical formalization of psychoanalysis is what Lacan spent his life working on. He wanted to go back to the most basic terms without assuming we knew what was meant, from unconscious to drive to transference; to go back and re-read Freud with fresh eyes, return to Freud, and use theory in order to create a more formal and structural understanding of what is at stake in a psychoanalytic cure. It was this original rigor that he felt was palpably lost in mid-century psychoanalysis and its emendations by ego-psychology and object-relational theory. The technique was standardized formally simply as a set of rules – five days a week, lying on the couch, do not accept gifts, pay for missed sessions, interpret only in late mid-phase analysis, etc. – by the institution of psychoanalysis. And what was done was decided without defining the basic tenets of psychoanalysis. This can be seen today when candidates in analytic training conduct what are called 'control analyses' in order to become graduate analysts. The outcome of a proper control case is often entirely dependant on whether the patient comes to the office five times a week and lies down on the couch, or, in a more bureaucratic iteration, has completed a defined number of hours or weeks of therapy in a given year. If this is not the case (for example if a patient comes less, takes a break, decides they want to sit up) and an argument erupts in the overseeing committee as to why it is still a proper 'control' psy-choanalysis, the varying positions are often so irreconcilable that the case is liable not to count towards a candidate's graduation. The same problem exists with respect to the candidate's 'training analysis' that is judged not on the basis of its effects, meaning that the candidate seems to know how to occupy the position of analyst with his or her patients, but rather on whether the analyst is properly accredited by the institution and the candidate has complied with hourly requirements of analysis for graduation. This is exactly the problem that Lacan is addressing in this article: how can it be that only a set of formal procedures defines psychoanalysis…and yet, he agrees that there should be something like the outlines of what a standard psychoanalytic treatment entails. But not even the psychoanalysts seem to know! Speaking to this disjunction between formalized rules and theoretical formalization, as the task of speaking about 'Variations on Standard Treatment,' is how Lacan defines his assignment; a project that he seems almost destined to have received.

Lacan now moves to how the analyst treats questions of cure, what many call the 'efficacy' of treatment. Lacan posits that modern medicine and psychoanalysis are twins in their lack of concern for basic statistical knowledge: they diagnose and cure based on set scientific knowledge (say anatomy for the medical doctor and Freudian metapsychology for the psychoanalyst) that guides the doctor who must confront the singularity of each case (270, 3). If you tell a doctor that 75% of patients improve from a certain surgery, while it is encouraging, it doesn't determine what he knows, how he knows, what he does, and how he views the outcome of his procedure with a given patient whose physiology, history, and current state – both normal and pathological – are absolutely unique. In the case of psychoanalysis, it is even more 'innocent,' Lacan says, for the analyst is taught from the get-go to be wary of any 'haste in concluding' or hastened attempt to cure, meaning, improving is not even on the agenda for the analyst (270, 3). Nor is there any certain knowledge concerning diagnosis or etiology. Psychoanalysts cannot be concerned with improvements or fact-finding, for these could function as a powerful ruse in a treatment. A 'transference cure,' which Freud defined as a moment when a patient's symptoms suddenly disappear early in treatment as a way of avoiding the work of analysis, is clearly a false cure. It is a cure in the transference, as a moment of transference (in order not to have to face analysis, to prove the analyst right or wrong, to hide one's symptoms from the analyst's watchful eye, etc.) and so not a real cure, which involves a more fundamental structural change.

Lacan often makes this point, I think because it is so fundamentally counterintuitive and peculiar to psychoanalysis: we are taught not to care if our patient's symptoms improve. In fact, we are taught to distrust improvements more often than not. As well, patients tend to get much worse in treatment before they get better. So the psychoanalyst is someone who makes you sicker, distrusts if you get well, and, to take this one step further, is taught to be deeply suspicious of any desire to cure in him or herself, what Lacan names *furor sanandi*, fury for health or the rage to cure (270, 4). He goes on to say that Freud himself was so deeply worried by a potential desire to cure, that if there was an innovation in the technique that seemed based on this desire, he immediately raised the question, 'Is that still psychoanalysis?' (270, 5). So here the question of standards and deviations points not to a formalism in technique, but rather a formalization in the analyst whereby the analyst purifies himself of the desire to cure which defines the line dividing psychotherapy from psychoanalysis.

It is my contention that already Lacan is showing us that what is important is the position the analyst occupies as a psychoanalyst, something he will come back to again and again, especially in the fourth and final section. The analyst acts as the inner support of an inter-subjective dynamic that keeps the question from the patient about him or herself alive and leaves the listening ear of the analyst open or purified. So, while it delimits a center – what we have been looking for all this time with the question of standards – the center is in fact an empty center. This delimited, but vacant site is what Lacan refers to when he speaks of the analyst as the dummy in the game of bridge. This is different from the silence of an undisputed truth or the refuge of a refusal to justify one's actions that are apriori *tried and true* – what might characterize how contemporary analysis situates the analyst (270, 7). The analytic position is one the analyst does not identify with or take as equal to him or herself; it is merely a space occupied by the one who welcomes discourse, who supports a question but does not answer the question, leaving that answer to come from the patient. It involves a kind of radical openness from the inside, but at the point where one experiences a fundamental limit; in the case of the analyst the limits of love and knowledge. This opening is at once intimate and foreign, a wound and a cure. Lacan calls this 'extraterritoriality' (270, 8) and later names it 'extimacy' which is a neologism that combines exterior and intimacy. The unconscious is a kind of intimate exteriority or exterior intimacy for each of us. Lacan contrasts this aspect of the refuge that he calls ethical with the omnipotent refuge of ill-defined standards and formalistic control that characterize contemporary psychoanalysis. Further, the corrupt version of 'extra-territoriality' is the one where psychoanalysis can appeal to other forms of knowledge, like science, for validation (especially today with the vogue of neuro-scientific proof that acts, as Lacan sometimes called it, as an insurance policy), and then reject scientific standards when an appeal to the uniqueness of psychoanalysis suits them (270, 8). This is a refuge that is neither ethical nor rigorously scientific, but rather the means of further dissimulation.

Lacan turns to Edward Glover's 1954 article 'Therapeutic Criteria of Psychoanalysis' in the *International Journal of Psychoanalysis* in order to demonstrate this very crisis at work in the current theorization of psychoanalytic criteria (271, 3). Bruce Fink points out that, quite uncharacteristically, Lacan almost always has positive things to say about Glover whose rhetorical flair approximates Lacan's own unlike most other dull and standard analytic writing (see Fink, 2014a). This article is particularly bleak and vitriolic about the current state of psychoanalysis, no doubt part of the reason Lacan quotes it so extensively. Glover surveys the small elite group of analysts working in Great Britain trying to 'ascertain what were the actual technical practices and working standards of analysts' (Glover, 1954, p. 95). Out of 63 points, only six reached a complete agreement, and only one of the six could be considered fundamental – the necessity for analyzing the transference. Lacan will come back to this factor, what he calls the robustness of transference, in order to say more about his own ideas of treatment. What is crucial is that Lacan uses Glover – who was a prominent analyst addressing his cohort at the IPA congress in 1953 – to show how little analysts agree on treatment criteria. In fact, the most damning statement by Glover is that while analysts clearly do not practice or maintain the same standards, and the institutes are 'riven by differences' which lead to practices that must be as different as 'chalk from cheese,' they put on a unified front, not only for the public, but in relation to one another where there is a

> sedulously cultivated assumption that the participants in such discussions hold roughly the same views, speak the same technical language, follow identical systems...practice the same technical procedures, and obtain much the same results...which are held to be satisfactory. Not one of these assumptions will bear close investigation (Glover, 1954, p. 96).

Meanwhile, he continues,

> we have next to no information about the conduct of private analytic practice...we have no after-histories worth talking about. Certainly no record of failures. This lack of verifiable information, when added to the loose assumptions I have already set out, fosters the development of a psychoanalytic mystique which not only baffles investigation but blankets all healthy discussion. (Glover, 1954, p. 96)

The problem, seemingly, will only grow worse and worse, or as, Glover says, criteria of psychoanalysis will become increasingly 'perfectionist, undefined, and uncontrolled' (p. 96).

Lacan takes up the charge here of a growing *mystique* as the effects of group-psychology on psychoanalysis, where maintenance of standards is no longer about 'healthy discussion' or 'scientific' understanding, but falls more and more 'within the ambit of the groups interests' and power. 'What is at stake is thus less a standard, than standing' (272, 5). Lacan puts the nail in the coffin: what is meant by standard technique is simply what you have to do (or say you do) to be considered one of the group. In fact, Glover makes an important point in his paper that Lacan does not reference regarding allegiance to groups and its effects on psychoanalytic technique. Glover (1954) points out that we must include the psychoanalysis of the analyst as one of the technical modifications of psychoanalytic practice, for an analyst who comes from years and years of analysis practiced with allegiance to a tradition of interpretation, will not have the courage to confess the failure of his training and set about a sound analytical re-orientation. 'On the contrary he is much more likely to preserve his self-respect by maintaining a fanatical conviction on the special virtues of the tradition on which he has been nourished' (1954, p. 99). What Glover is pointing out is that since interpretation seems governed by allegiance to one's group, and not necessarily based on some truth coming from the analysis, this will only strengthen group dynamics and fanaticism. Glover's conclusion to this important article is that the extension or delimitation of therapeutic criteria depends on the 'degree to which we can succeed in eliminating...the influence of a defensive, esoteric, but so far unconfessed mystique' (1954, p. 99). And, 'although elimination of the esoteric is supposed to be one of the tasks of training analysis there are in my view few signs that this important aim has so far been achieved' (p. 100). The negative institutional effects extend to the very core of psychoanalytic practice and the formation of the next generation of analysts. If what is transmitted is only some kind of group allegiance, some vampiric system of mimesis, then, as Freud must ask, 'is that still psychoanalysis?' (270, 5).

Thus, Lacan says, 'only a global apprehension of the divergences, which is able to grasp them synchronically, can determine the cause of their discord' (272, 9). Psychoanalysis must be approached through its historical unfolding (like a good Hegelian), something Lacan does not just in this article, but also throughout his work. He contextualizes the changes in theory from the focus on the unconscious to the ego, the shift from interpreting language and re-presentation to object relations and intersubjective phenomena, the de-emphasis of the Oedipal triangle in favor of the dyadic mother–child relation, and the dilution of transference interpretation with the hype surrounding countertransference analysis. One must see the discord of diverging theories as a coherent trajectory around a central axis, like the 'rigor with which the shrapnel of a projectile, in dispersing, maintains its ideal trajectory' (273, 8). Indeed, like an unfolding psychoanalysis, symptoms can mutate, get better or worse, go underground, and reappear. What is important is the direction of the treatment, what Lacan feels invariably underlies these changes. It is the analyst's job to have a sense of this direction as the one who directs the treatment. This is true for Lacan even when the analyst is not *directive* in his stance of general neutrality and adherence to the rules of free association. Can we do this work of finding the direction, the trajectory, with psychoanalysis as our subject? Psychoanalysis our patient? And might we then understand better both standard treatment and the place of variation?

It is for this reason, Lacan says, 'that the question of variations...can find an unforeseen advantage' (273, 10). To go back just a bit, this is what Lacan is up to when he mentions looking at the current state of psychoanalysis and the dispersion of concepts, and getting a sense of a 'massive phenomenon of pas-sivity, and even of subjective inertia, whose effects seem to grow with the spreading of the movement' (273, 1). How would the psychoanalyst understand these symptoms? Why is there an increasing inertia in psychoanalysis? And furthermore, why is transference the only concept that weathers this storm (from the beginning assessment by Glover)? I think Lacan's answer is threefold and this is how he ends the first section:

1   That the psychoanalytic inertia on the one hand, and fragmentation on the other, is related to 'seeking...recognition' (273, 11) – a factor behind the spreading movement or perhaps an effect of it – which cannot but evoke certain intersubjective effects which are outlined in the mirror stage. This includes the interplay between the inertia of the unified image and an increased sense of fragmentation. Psychoanalysis misrecognizes itself in its projected image, wrongly seeks recognition from the image, further eclipsing a relation to the Other, which is the only source of recognition. Ego–ego relations predominate in this struggle. In the mania of the mirror, one must combat any sense of inferiority or weakness in the form of a master-slave dialectic. The action moves from aggressivity to absurd self-rejoicing. While the structures that govern 'misrecognition' should be internal to the theory of psychoanalysis, instead it is played out in its movement. He will come back to this more strongly in the next section with the question of the ego.

2   Beyond the mirror, the thing still insists. The thing, *das Ding*, insists behind every imaginary or even symbolic screen (273, 5). Lacan links this to the robustness of the concept of transference, which survives the distortions or misrecognitions of the growing movement of psycho-analysis. It is in the transference that the thing makes its appearance, insisting, repeating and so defining the very trajectory of the analysis. If in Glover's analysis of the situation of psychoanalysis the 'interpretation of the transference' was the only important criteria to survive, Lacan feels this is the case because it is there, in the transference that will always insist in a treatment, where whatever there is to be found will be found! Analysts cannot escape from the manifestations of transference, whatever their theoretical orientation. Lacan writes:

People even go so far as to rejoice in the fact that the weakness of invention has not allowed for more damage to the fundamental concepts, those still being the concepts that we owe to Freud. The latter's resistance to so many attempts to adulterate them becomes the *a contrario* proof of their consistency. This is true of transference which manages to weather the storm of popularizing theory and even popular ideas. It owes this to the Hegelian robustness of its constitution: Indeed, what other concept is there that better brings out its identity with the thing, the analytic thing in this case, cleaving to it all the ambiguities that constitute its logical time? (273, 4–273, 5) Lacan then goes on to link transference to logical time, temporality, to history and its unfolding, which he says Freud inaugurated when he theorized transference and repetition together. Lacan adds to these fundamental questions about the transference asking if it is a return or a memorial, real or fantastical, a need to repeat 'or the repetition of a need' (273, 6). These are important questions concerning what it is that repeats in an analysis. What returns through the transference? These are also questions analysts have stopped asking or seeking to define, while they quibble about formalities. Lacan here is putting these questions front and center, questions he would go on to try to answer throughout his work.

3   Finally, at the very end of this section, Lacan himself retains only one criterion, since he says, 'it is the only one at the disposal of the physician who orients his patient in the treatment' (274, 3). 'This criterion,' rarely said because it is considered tautological, 'can be stated as follows: a psychoanalysis, whether standard or not, is the treatment one expects from a psychoanalyst' (274, 3). What is compacted into this final statement is a fascinating reversal, typical of Lacan. It is not the physician that we are orienting here with criteria, but rather the analyst who orients his patient to psychoanalysis. So, let us take our criteria from that fact: how does the analyst orient his patient? The patient must demand from the analyst psychoanalysis for it to properly begin! The patient must begin with a question, addressed to the analyst, with an implicit demand for psycho-analysis. This is one of the basic tenets of beginning a treatment and Lacan's concept of preliminary sessions, which must bring a patient to this point for the psychoanalysis to properly begin. Often patients begin without really asking for an analysis, and may in fact come because their partner sent them, or they want the analyst to make a symptom go away but they have not asked a fundamental question, which inherently demands psychoanalysis. So, we are back again to the center of analysis being the analyst put in the position to support the patient's coming to ask a question; the irony being that Glover stated that no questions are any longer really being asked...So, according to Lacan, no one is assuming the position of psychoanalyst any longer. Reading this final criteria, I think we can also hear Lacan telling the analyst that they receive all the recognition that they need when able to place themselves in the position of the analyst and bring a patient to demand psychoanalysis from them. Again we return to a question of the position an analyst occupies, but does not identify

with, nor control. This is what gives the analyst their standing and could begin to orient any question of standards. Nothing more, nothing less.

II From the psychoanalyst's pathway to its maintenance, considered from the viewpoint of its deviations

Lacan begins with a joke that becomes part of his rhetorical style throughout this section. The threat that variation exacts on standard psychoanalysis (in the same measure that Lacan was perceived as such a threat) indicates that the existence of psychoanalysis is rather precarious and requires a 'real man' to maintain its pathway (274, 6). From now on, the analyst who is called upon to shore up the profession will be referred to as 'the real man.' This is funny on a number of levels. The machismo of the real man analyst will be a useful *a contrario* image for what Lacan would like to put forth. Also, that machismo is posited as a response to the feeling that one's identity is under threat, or simply, a response to ambiguity. Further, the idea of analysis depending on who the analyst is, as a 'real' person, against understanding what it means to occupy the psychoanalytic position, obviously goes against any traditional ideas of the psychoanalyst's neutrality. There is also an inherent truth in the phrase 'real man' beyond its parodic image to the extent that 'the real' is an important concept for Lacan. The analyst is oriented towards the real as what is beyond both the imaginary and symbolic system of representation (as we said in the last section, in respect of *das Ding*). One may say the analyst is oriented to this beyond – be that trauma, the bedrock of castration as Freud termed it, the body and affects, or even the figure of death and the work of mourning – which speaks to a question about the end of the analysis.

Finally, there is a kind of historical prophetic truth that touches on this question of the movement of psychoanalysis. The only other analyst excluded from the international body besides Lacan was Wilhelm Reich who will come to figure prominently in this chapter (remember, at the time the article was written, Lacan had not yet been 'excommunicated' as he liked to call it from the International Psychoanalytic Association). In his rage against the 'psychoanalytical careerists' (Reich, 1974, p. ix) and the defamation that surrounded his career, Reich wrote a scathing parodic book titled *Listen, Little Man!* in 1946. He betrayed him and who he feels tends towards the misuse of power, as 'Little Man'. While Lacan is certainly not taking up Reich's rhetorical style, there is a strange echo of Reich who was, rightly or wrongly, also expelled for his variations on the standard treatment.

Lacan begins his parable: 'the real man' is solicited to see what effect the ambiguities of psychoanalysis have on him in his role of maintaining its pathway (274, 6). But if the question of the limit remains common, meaning the limited pathway he must travel in conducting a standard psychoanalytic treatment, it is because no one sees where the ambiguity ends, especially when the end of psychoanalysis remains ambiguous, no less what one does or why.

Should 'the real man' spare himself the effort of having to define this end-point? Well, Lacan says, the real man can take his word from the authorities who make it a rather confusing affair, as we are about to see in Lacan's survey of the literature on termination (and which we already got a taste of in Glover (1954) (see particularly his thought on p. 97 on 'stalemate' analyses (1954, p. 97)). Or, paradoxically, he can rigorously misrecognize the endpoint by avoiding any experience of a limit, which nonetheless implies that he has registered its place (274, 7). This isn't *just* a rhetorical flourish. Lacan's comments about the forced choice presented to candidates in psychoanalytic training continue to have relevance to this day, namely, in respect of identifying with an established doctrine, and/or rigorously avoiding what is difficult in psychoanalysis. If what is difficult is being avoided – namely the questions that inevitably arise as one confronts something new in each patient – the analyst senses its existence in the very act of avoidance. This likely results, Lacan speculates, because clinicians aren't provided with the tools to handle this difficulty of the unprecedented, because it falls outside the purview of established standards. The literature on termination, no less technique, is still remarkably impoverished.

This situation is what Lacan is calling, 'the bad faith of instituted practice' where one is duped by one's action more than performing any actions of real consequence (274, 7). I have often come across candidates in supervision who cling to their identifications with their previous supervisors – 'routines whose secrets are dispensed by clever analysts' like gifts that they 'reserve themselves the right to detect' (274, 7) – to avoid the real confrontation in the treatment, in the transference. It is this rigorous avoidance, buttressed by the logic of identification, which I believe Lacan is speaking to. Further, this logic undermines any possible scientific claims of psychoanalysis. As Bruce Fink characterizes the conundrum: 'It shifts the focus from a standard approach to treatment, to a standardization of talent among analysts, who – as Lacan (2006) quips in 'Direction of the Treatment' – heal not by what they say or do but who they are. A training institute's goal is thus to standardize who they are, to standardize their so-called personalities' (Fink, 2014a, p. 71), to make them 'real men'.

So even if this master with all his gifts declares, like Freud, that one 'should not form too lofty an idea of this mission', this is only 'false humility' (275, 2). What he calls the 'path of true humility' (275, 3) would require nothing less than a confrontation with the rather unbearable ambiguity of the psychoanalytic situation in and of itself, which isn't some special secret for initiates, but is within everyone's grasp: 'it is revealed in the question of what it means to speak, and one encounters it simply by welcoming discourse' (275, 3). What Lacan is pointing out is that the very premise of psychoanalysis – inviting someone to speak to you about him or herself – immediately erupts in unbearable ambiguity. Every analyst, no less any human being, understands the anxiety that makes its presence felt when solicited to speak about what is most intimate, to speak freely to another person. Furthermore, this is an ambiguity that resides in the very act of speaking and listening, not just speaking to a psychoanalyst. What Lacan is introducing for the first time here is the emphasis that he puts on speech and language in psychoanalysis. This is incredibly important because while he posits it as a basic tenet of the situation of analysis and a truth of Freud – especially the early Freud of who analyzed dreams, jokes, and slips – the structural aspects of language are something that remained unrecognized or theoretically formalized by contemporary psycho-analysis: from the division between the subject of the enunciation and the subject of the enunciated (or statement), to the signifier and the signifying chain, and the unconscious as structured like a language. So, the analyst not only supports the patient's question about themselves, but also their speech.

This will now be brought to bear on our tale of 'the real man' analyst! To begin, if we 'mean to say' something, like in the colloquial phrase 'what I meant to say was,' there is already a recognition of an ambiguity at the heart of speaking that Lacan calls a 'double entendre' that is up to the listener to hear and decide upon; whether the listener follows what this 'means to say' means to say or what it does not say or does say in spite of what is meant (275, 3). Or, as he puts it, 'whether it is what the speaker means to say to him by the discourse he addresses to him or what this discourse tells him about the condition of the speaker' (275, 3). Lacan is speaking to a fundamental division in the subject, which was often thought of since Freud as that between conscious and unconscious, but here is specifically linked to the condition of being a speaking being or '*parletre*.' We are not in control of our message. The act of speaking illuminates two different subjects: (1) the subject that says I, the subject that means to say, the subject of the statement, and, (2) the subject that is spoken of, what Lacan calls the subject of the enunciation, the subject that appears in a discourse. We might term one the ego and the other the subject of the unconscious. The more elusive 'subject of the unconscious' can be recognized by *both* the speaker and the listener, but requires attention to the beyond of what is intentionally trying to be conveyed. This is, in one sense, the task of the analyst, and Lacan highlights the inter-subjective dimension of recognition in the act of listening. 'Thus not only does the meaning of discourse reside in he who listens to it, but the reception he gives it determines who says it – namely, whether it is the subject to whom he gives permission and lends credence,' the subject of the statement, 'or the other that his discourse delivers to the listener as constituted,' the subject of the enunciation (275, 3).

A point often made is that this is not a theory of speech as *communication* which assumes a direct circuit from speaker to listener, from point A to point B and back. There is, for Lacan, a radical gap, not just in oneself, but between self and others, which necessitates a decision or choice about what to attend to. This a–symmetrical structure is made all the more extreme by the rules of psycho-analysis, in particular, the one rule given to patients, modeled on Freud's idea of free association: to speak without stopping, without holding anything back, without regard for rationality, coherence, politeness, or shamefulness (275, 4). Lacan says that the hope seems to be that we can see this gap between word and thing, speech and meaning, what Lacan calls constituting speech and constituted discourse in all its glory! As the analysis proceeds, by speaking and speaking and speaking, meaning flies out from underneath intention. At some point, Lacan imagines, the analyst might pin his hopes on the patients finally finding themselves equal to what they were saying. What is said and the act of saying, could join together in a great unity, with the force of revelation! We finally mean what we are saying! But – and Lacan doesn't let us down gently – it will never be so. Such are the structural laws of language and the 'rarely noticed' limits in which free association takes place (275, 4).

The analyst must retain 'complete responsibility' in his position as the listener, and, what's more, he solicited this responsibility when he invited the patient to speak, something that acts as 'a secret summons' that will not be dismissed even if the analyst remains silent (276, 1). Speaking and listening is the engine of the transference, and nothing more. It is not some mysterious meta-psychological substance that oozes from the unconscious. It is a factor of language. Lacan returns us here to a question of ethics pointing to the weight of welcoming words and the responsibility of the analyst facing this deep division in the subject and the ambiguity of speech that will never be resolved, either by the analyst or by the patient, whatever fantasy we might have about it. Again, Lacan is defining something absolutely critical to how he views the analytic position and places it in the formal situation of psychoanalysis, not as a set of procedures or some mystical property of psychoanalysis, but as the pathway initiated by a 'talking' therapy.

It is at this point that he will now turn to how 'contemporary psycho-analysis' deals with interpretation, and he will spare no one. Lacan begins by pointing out how uneasy analysts seem in the face of defining interpretation, that their theories are awkward and formless, using words like 'analyzing' instead of 'interpreting', and even at points shying away from interpretation altogether (276, 2). It is often recommended that analysts not 'interpret' for many, many years into an analysis. While this is true for Lacanians who tend to avoid 'meaningful' interpretations, playing with the speech that is more ambiguous or oracular, waiting for the analysand to find their way with meaning, many of the other schools veer away from interpretation in favor of other techniques like confrontation, explanation, insight, mirroring, holding, all of which move further and further from speech and language while keeping to the idea of conveying 'meaning' both in what needs to be said to the patient (explanation, confrontation), or not said but done for the patient's benefit (mirroring or holding). The vogue for analyzing countertransference, rather than interpreting transference – meaning the analyst thinks about his own feeling and ideas about a patient rather than responding interpretively to what a patient has said – is just one more move away from the one action an analyst is to take, namely, for Lacan, to respond to what a patient has said in a way that opens a new truth. Lacan quips that it's a good thing the students of 'the real man' are too ashamed to make him explain what they are supposed to be doing (276, 4).

For the next few pages, Lacan is going to go into the question of the analysis of the resistances, which had come to replace the classical idea of interpretation 'of the material,' as ego-psychology gained dominance with Anna Freud in London and then with émigré analysts in the United States. The proof for the value of interpreting resistance is said to be that it produces new material (276, 5). For example, a classical resistance interpretation will either point to a break in free association, a lack or point of stoppage – 'You are reluctant to speak today,' 'You did not associate to the dream you mentioned in passing' – or, it will specifically address a refusal to speak about some material – 'You do not want to address my upcoming vacation,' 'You never say anything about your father when you speak of your parents divorce,' and so on. The patient will then speak to what they were previously resistant to – the dream, the vacation, the father – and then that material can be interpreted. Lacan points out that there is still a question here because if the analyst then goes on to interpret the material, which is what he was supposed to do in the first place and is the focus of Freudian technique, 'will we be justified in wondering whether the term 'interpretation' has the same meaning at these two different points in time' (276, 5), meaning interpreting from the get-go or interpreting after an interpretation of the resistances. This is the crux of Lacan's question to the justification for this shift in technique: if you have set up the analysis as interpreting the resistances or, its later incarnation as defense interpretation, and only after, interpreting the material (be it an interpretation of fantasy, sexuality, Oedipus, etc.), does the interpretation of resistance fundamentally alter the material to be interpreted? And further, does this shift in technique create other effects in the field of psychoanalysis as a whole? What happens when the psychoanalyst is in the position to constantly know what the analysand isn't, and should be, speaking about?

The shift towards the analysis of the resistances is pointed to with the changes in Freud's thinking marked by the 1920s and a failure to achieve the same results (276, 2–277, 1). There was a feeling that the unconscious was closing back down after its initial opening. Prior to this 'turning point' it was in deciphering the 'material' that we learned the symptom's secrets. The removal of symptoms and the restoration of memory are the bi-directional pathway of treatment: when one is reached, so is the other (277, 1–277, 5). In this pathway, the unconscious is defined for Lacan as a clearly constituting subject 'since it sustained symptoms in their meaning before it was revealed, and we experienced the unconscious directly, recognizing it in the ruse of disturbances in which the repressed compromises with the censorship' (277, 3). If the patient was given an interpretation of the symptom and the symptom persisted – and it should be added, that the material kept pointing to this same solution or interpretation – then the analyst concluded that this resistance must be analyzed. This is where this deviation in the technique that has now become standard, began. However – and here is where Lacan's addition of his insight into speech, language and the divided subject becomes important to analyzing this emendation of classical technique – if the original focus on 'interpreting the resistance' is a momentary deviation in the standard treatment, this means that it still puts its faith in interpretation and takes the unconscious as a constituting subject (277, 3). As the focus shifts towards the analysis of resistance as a standard technique, there will be major ramifications: 'should the deviation go on to seek his resistance outside of this discourse, it will be irremediable. No one will come back to question the constituting function of interpretation regarding its failure' (277, 4). Lacan has just turned standard technique, meaning standard at the time he was writing, on its head, as the premier deviation! The very first deviation in psychoanalytic technique whose central focus was always the interpretation of the material, was interpretation of the resistance. With these two reversed, Lacan wonders if we will ever come back to the important Freudian task of listening to what is said?

Lacan points out that Freud spoke of resistance as early as 1895 locating resistance in the verbalization of chains of speech or interconnected units composed of pieces of memories, things heard and seen, all (see Freud's (1895) *Project for a Scientific Psychology*) wrapped around a core trauma. This is how Freud conceptualized both the difficulty patients had spoken about the origin of their symptoms, as well as why they often veered away from it onto seemingly unconnected associations. Seeing how the patient moved from one set of thoughts to another – a set of thoughts that seemed unrelated but eventually could be brought into line with the original repressed or resisted thoughts – was the beginning of the creation of the technique of free association. In this early model, there is both resistance at work in a chain and between chains, all of which bend around a pathogenic nucleus or what Lacan would later call the traumatic 'Real.' The analyst can gauge how close or distant he is to this nucleus by virtue of the intensity of this resistance. Resistance in a chain is different from that between chains to the extent that the first involves moving through a series of related associations that form one articulated chain or thought, whereas moving between chains implies moving closer to the traumatic core, getting closer to the kernel of truth. The emphasis for Lacan in this model of resistance is in a technique that looks at the very text of what a patient comes to say, hearing elisions, distortions, gaps, and holes, in the process of association. Freud would then come back to resistance again with the development of the structural model (277, 1–277, 5). Here, resistance is not just taking place within discourse, but more generally in the psyche as a whole, where there is resistance implied by the very conflict between the structures of the mind: id, ego, super-ego. The second model of resistance, asks the question 'who is resisting?' Even, Lacan says, if 'the ego' is the answer, this is taken solely from what he calls the 'undiscriminating angle of its

157

dynamics,' its relation to the other agencies of id and super-ego, or its resistance in the context of the material of a session or series of them (278, 3). Lacan is pointing to the fact that if the direction of the treatment is paramount – meaning here the approach towards the pathogenic nucleus – then the question of resistance is simply part of the dynamic unconscious, whether it's the ego resisting, or the personal subject, or the super-ego, or part of the dynamics of speech and transference. The problem is,

> that by reversing the correct choice that determines which subject is welcomed in speech, the symptom's constituting subject is treated as if he is constituted – like material, as they say – while the ego, as constituted as it may be in resistance, becomes the subject upon whom the analyst henceforth calls the constituting agency. (278, 6)

This change is thus a complete reversal; it is no longer the unconscious which is given voice in speech as the primary constituting agency, with the constituted structures of the ego, super-ego, and id acting as points of resistance, but now the unconscious that is constituted, a bunch of set material, with the ego called upon to be the force of agency and change, to be the constituting subject in the analysis.

Many ego psychologists say that when they speak of the ego in this way that they are talking about the person in his totality, and in particular because Freud links the ego with the 'perception-consciousness system' from the original topographic model (278, 6–279, 3). This is for Lacan a mistake, a grave mistake, and a misreading of Freud. First, Lacan points out that Freud said that the super-ego, not the ego, is the first guarantor of an experience of reality; it is the heir of the Oedipus complex (278, 7). Reality is not so much reality, as something about the dissolution of the Oedipus complex and what Freud (and Lacan) called the castration complex. Also, Freud (1900), in Chapter VII of *The Interpretation of Dreams*, split the perception and conscious system, which had always been soldered in a pre-Freudian view of the conscious rational subject. He placed perception on the side of the unconscious, and consciousness as a secondary effect. Thus ego-psychology seems to return to a pre-Freudian worldview, uniting the perception of reality and consciousness in the figure of the autonomous thinking ego. The ego, on the other hand, was always depicted by Freud as rather empty, without any energy or content of its own, close to the censor in the first topography, and like a besieged bureaucrat, forced to negotiate between the demands of reality (which are not synonymous with it), the super-ego, and the id. How is this the constituting force of psychoanalysis and what does it mean to make this the central subject? Lacan goes on to say that this move is essentially bankrupt (278, 6–279, 4). Harsh and definitive words! It is the return of a reactionary ideology that had, since Freud (and especially in the philosophy that surrounded Lacan), been given up. And Anna Freud, like a Sphinx, prophesizes the ego's return in the opening remarks of her (1936) book

The Ego and the Mechanisms of Defense naming the ego *unpopular* in order to be the force of the ego's supposed resurrection (279, 2). But, Lacan points out, the ego was never unpopular; it was simply one among several structures. But with psychoanalysis turned into Ego-psychology, the ego will make a violent return, and desire, Antigone-like, will be buried alive. The father of the discovery of unconscious desire is killed by his daughter's ego.

As attention to language and the constituting subject of the unconscious are sacrificed by these 'turning-point' authors, the more nuanced Freudian concept of resistance, as the logical network of chains of signifiers that appear in the approach to the traumatic pathogenic nucleus, is as such obscured, confused, and finally replaced by the idea of ego defense (279, 5–280, 2), a move which loses the way the unconscious structured like a language is spoken in session. The constant trope of ego-psychology was that analysis needed to attack the defenses of the ego (which paradoxically strengthens weak egos) and adapt the patient to reality through bringing about more rational compromise formations (symptomatic compromises between the drive, reality, and super-ego). From the work of Hartmann and Lowenstein, who wanted to integrate psychoanalysis with the experimental findings of psychology, to recent advances in neuroscience (see Solms and Turnbull, 2002; Gabbard and Weston, 2003) concerning 'executive functioning,' the ego in ego-psychology is maintained as the 'control center' which is to be precisely that, controlled and in control, smooth functioning, practical, and efficient. For Lacan this goal or endpoint of treatment is not psychoanalytic, it is ideological and based on a world-view, that of 1950s American expansionist capitalism or a 'theology of free enterprise' (see Lacan's footnote 11, p. 302).

The 'real man' analyst is getting a new twist in his caricature. His maintenance of the pathway of psychoanalysis begins to look more and more like the pathway of an attack on the patient in the name of a certain vision or image that becomes the therapeutic ideal (279, 5–280, 2). Lacan again relies on Glover (1954) who points out that while dynamic criteria would seem the most suitable for orienting psychoanalytic criteria, it doesn't take long to realize the difference in emphasis on the roles of libido and aggression in symptom formation, 'differences which are expressed in the modern tendency to separate the analytical sheep from the goats in accordance with the degree to which they 'analyze the aggression', to use the cant phrase' (Glover, 1954, p. 97). The emphasis in ego-psychology is on aggression: the analyst is depicted as aggressively taking on defenses, the language used is aggressive, the patient's transference is always thought of as negative and suffused with aggression. The more aggressive you are able to be in psychoanalytic institutes dominated by ego-psychology, the more proof that your aggression was sufficiently analyzed. It is for this reason that Lacan thought the new psychoanalytic ideal of health was one modeled on the aggressiveness of the American lawyer. Just enough to get what he wants.

So even if the theory of the ego admits that drive and defense are locked in a tight dialectic, when one looks at the literature on defense analysis (Lacan here specifically points to Fenichel) one can see that the defenses are perceived to be a kind of Kafka-esque labyrinthine fortress; you take on one defense only to find out that it hides another which is considered *more* essential. If the drive finally appears in all its supposed brute nakedness – let's say some expression of aggression by the patient in the face of this attack – it is often concluded that the aggression is only there in order to further hide or hold on to one's defenses (279, 5–280, 2). The process seems infinite, especially when the covering is no truer than what is hidden by it. The whole process reads like an unending military siege and 'psychoanalysis degenerates into an immense psychological mess' (280, 2). What used to be considered a 'negative therapeutic reaction,' namely a treatment where negative feelings stagnate it and which becomes a battleground, is now the model, no less the sign of progress. Libido, or desire, falls by the wayside. As an aside, it is interesting to fast-forward to 2004 when Peter Fonagy and Mary Target, chief executives of the Anna Freud Center, declare that sex needs to be put back in psychoanalysis (Fonagy and Target, 2004).

As attention to speech falls away, signs of defense and resistance are sought in the non-verbal inter-subjective realm – how a patient enters the session, his tone, his posture, how he leaves, how he handles the frame from rescheduling to payment to breaks. This is very different from attending to the flow, the tone, the interruptions, the melody of the session (280, 4). Lacan says that 'an attitudinal reaction in the session will hold our attention more than a syntactical error and will be examined more in terms of its energy level than its import' (280, 4). He goes on: 'the more we separate the authenticity of the analytic relationship from the discourse in which it is inscribed, what we continue to call its 'interpretation' derives ever more exclusively from the analyst's knowledge' (280, 5). What he is pointing to here is that there is a sliding from attention to language ('syntactical error') to resistance to defense to the non-verbal or outside-language, which then shifts the focus from the patient's discourse to the analyst's knowledge. More and more, it is not what the patient says, but what the analyst knows, who must then communicate that knowledge to the patient (280, 5).

Because the analyst's ego and knowledge become the central player, someone like Wilhelm Reich, whose early work *Character Analysis* is seen as a precursor to defense analysis, would have to admit that the analyst must insist on his or her interpretations (280, 2–281, 1). In Sterba's article from 1934 'The Fate of the Ego in Analytic Therapy,' referenced by Lacan, Sterba states:

> Since there are in the transference and the transference resistance two groups of forces within the ego, it follows that ego-dissociation induced by the analyst must take place in relation to each group... First of all, the analyst gives an interpretation of the defense, making allusion to the instinctual tendencies *which he has already divined* and

against which the defense has been set up. With the patient's recognition that his attitude in the transference is of the nature of a defence, there comes a weakening in that defense. The result is a more powerful onslaught of the instinctual strivings upon the ego. The analyst then has to interpret the infantile meaning and aim of these impulses...*In order that all these interpretations may have a more profound effect, it is necessary to repeat them.* (emphasis mine, p. 123)

The emphasis is on the deployment of what the analyst knows and divines. What insists is not the unconscious but the analyst. In fact, for Sterba (1934), what this introduces into the patient is a dissociation or split, in which the analyst finds an ally with one part of the ego in order to attack the other. Look at the language Sterba uses:

> the therapeutic dissociation of the ego is necessary if the analyst is to have the chance of *winning* over part of it to his side, *conquering* it, *strengthening* it by means of identification with himself and *opposing* it in the transference to those parts which have a cathexis of instinctual and defensive energy. (1934, p. 120, emphasis mine)

Furthermore, this is achieved, according to Sterba through 'the explanations' given to the patient by the analyst, which bring about 'a new point of view of intellectual contemplation' (1934, p. 121). It is amazing to see that Lacan isn't simply exaggerating! Sterba admits that he turns the patient against him or herself by effecting an identification with himself through intellectual explanations of what he divines are the 'infantile' impulses to be won over by reality. Of course, what Lacan adds to this is that the reality is of course only Sterba's view of reality, and psychoanalysis is now only a relation between two egos, one for the other.

A fascinating twist to this tale, unmentioned by Lacan, is Sterba's (1934) conclusion to this essay in a turn to the question of speech. He quotes Herder in order to support his idea that the objectifying process of ego-dissociation, originates in the first act of speech where we single out a clear observation from the mass of sensations, and name it. We are divided from ourselves by the first production of speech! Therapy, as talking therapy, is justified by Sterba (1934), as a like contribution to the humanizing of mankind. While this is a strange echo of Lacan, the differences between these two thinkers couldn't be more extreme. This original division is alienating for Lacan, while it is simply humanizing for Sterba. Lacan emphasizes speech. Sterba's version of interpretation is thus, for Lacan, suggestion and intellectualism, an exacerbation of self-consciousness, and ultimately foreign to truth, because Sterba has forgone the constitutive power of speech, in the name of knowledge, in particular the constituted body of *apriori* psychoanalytic knowledge. In the end, Sterba says nothing about what a patient comes to say, only what the analyst must say to him. Ironically, the attack on Lacan by ego-psychology and others will be that it was Lacan who intellectualized psychoanalysis!

This grounding of psychoanalysis in the analyst's ego remains unchanged and is instead confirmed, Lacan says, even if we turn to the other side of the theoretical divide, namely to object relations theory (281, 1–281, 6). There, all you find is the idea of the introjection of analyst's ego in the form of a good object as some kind of mystical meal that is supposed to combat the primitive parts of the patient (funnily enough). This is exactly the same thing as identification with the analyst, but from a wildly different theoretical system. Again, object-relational technique, not mentioned here by Lacan but investigated elsewhere (see *The Direction of the Treatment and the Principles of its Power* (Lacan, 2006) or Seminar VI *Desire and its Interpretation* (Lacan, 2002)), amounts to the insistence on certain interpretations, especially the divination of the patient's transference through attention to the non-verbal. Finally, when one looks at what is said on termination, and here Lacan turns to Hoffer's 1950 article 'Three Psychological Criteria for the Termination of Treatment,' all criteria eventually amount to

> the substitution of the patient's infantile super-ego by the analyst's super-ego. I think it is not advantageous to call it a substitution. It is a change in the patient's ego due to identification; it affects of course the ego-ideal and therefore the super-ego, but the mechanism involved is identification within the ego with the functions of the analyst. (Hoffer, 1950, p. 195)

Hoffer admits that psychoanalysis aims to substitute the patient's ego for the analysts. I might argue that many ego-psychologists, Kleinians, and contemporary theorists offer a more subtle interpretations of termination. Sometimes the identification with the analyst is an identification with what is called the 'function as analyst' separate from the analyst as transference fantasy. For others, termination is seen as the modification of the ego-ideal which unravels the vicious reign of the super-ego, happening through a confrontation with what is possible and impossible given who we come to know ourselves to be in a psychoanalysis. There might be some room for comparison here with Lacan's own views of the end of treatment where the analyst falls away as an idealized transferential figure, or identification with one's symptom and one's unique ways of being that are created by an analysis. However, the problem still remains that a technique that maintains a focus on the analyst's perception of reality and the patient's ego is problematic. It is, by a confusion of logic that Lacan is at pains to point out, almost destined to be an act of substitution ego to ego (281, 1–281, 6).

So, once these many formulations are demystified of their depiction of psychoanalysis as a learning process or a strengthening dissociation, a substitution that acts as a humanization, or even a totemic meal that modifies the super-ego, what they signify for Lacan is that in ruling out any foundation of his relationship with the subject in speech, the analyst can communicate nothing to him that the analyst does not already know from his preconceived views or immediate intuition – that is nothing that is not subject to the organization of the analyst's own ego. (281, 6)

If we accept this deadlock at the place where the patient is utterly subjected to the analyst's ego, we have to ask 'what must the analyst's ego be if it assumes the role of being the measure of truth for all of us and for each subject who puts himself in the analyst's hands' (281, 7). If we play by your rules, by your measure of truth, how, Lacan seems to be pleading, can another's truth enter into this? Or, to render the question Heideggerian, what happens to 'Being' in an analysis that it is increasingly annexed by the analyst's ego? What aspect of the analyst's being might hold in the discovery of truth that is supposed to be the pathway of psychoanalysis? While Lacan is going to go deeper into the question of the ego in the next section, it isn't until the final section, section IV, that he really comes back to this.

III On the ego in analysis and its end in the analyst

So we've moved from an impasse in section I to an aporia in section II. Lacan begins section III, more or less asking how anyone can see the ego as the point of strength for the analyst (281, 6–282, 5). The good or strong ego is at stake everywhere in the additions to the classical technique from the healing power of empathy to the importance of assessment, and the use value of counter-transference analysis. In each of these cases, the ego is put forward as the subject's collateral or safety, and for Lacan, this is no foundation upon which to build oneself or psychoanalysis (282, 4). Freud, in 'Analysis: Terminable and Interminable' (1937), is, as Lacan stresses, abundantly clear on this topic: 'analysts in their own personalities have not invariably come up to the standard of psychical normality to which they wish to educate their patients' (282, 5). The analyst's ego is not a model of health or normality, it is not the standard in 'standard treatment' or the type in a 'typical psychoanalysis.'

To demand such an image from the analyst only adds to the weight that Ferenczi (1955) acknowledges as the extreme and ongoing difficulties that the analyst faces in his task as an analyst: during long hours of listening to patients, analysts must split themselves between a focus on the patient, self-control, and intellectual activity; they cannot give free play to narcissism or egoism, and even in fantasy, only very minimally (282, 5–283, 3). There isn't much in everyday life that makes these kinds of demands and Ferenczi (1955) wonders if the analyst might need some kind of ongoing mental hygiene. Though Ferenczi is labeling it ultimately inadequate, aren't these extreme constraints the reason that the analyst's analysis is so crucial? What the analyst must bring about in himself in order to endure the task of being a psychoanalyst seems to Lacan to not be a strengthening of the ego, but rather it's effacing (283, 3–284, 1). We efface our egos in order to give way to the patient and their 'subject-point' (283, 3) of interpretation. This can only take place on the basis of the analyst's personal analysis, *especially its end*. We might recall that Glover stated that personal analysis seems to have failed to bring anything about except fanaticism and mystification, and that in Lacan's perusal of the literature, psychoanalysis is unable to conceptualize its end. If you don't know where you are going, how are you going to get there? This confusion continues unabated until the answer 'identification with the analyst's ego' becomes the *raison d'etre* for all schools, chalk and cheese, in mid-century psychoanalysis. 'Where' then 'is the end of analysis as far as the ego is concerned?' Lacan asks (283, 4).

At this point, Lacan wants to put this question to the test with a kind of case study using Reich's *Character Analysis* as our subject (283, 3–285, 4). Reich seems an apt figure because his book laid the groundwork for ego-psychology and provides a kind of extreme example of where this thought may take one. Reich moved on to an analysis of the body without the use of language or speech, focusing on orgasmic energy and the control of what he called Orgone energy. Lacan says that Reich's theories force us to look closely at how the tensions that analysis creates and seeks to resolve are characterized, symptomatically, in personality.

> The whole theory that Reich provides of it is based on the idea that these structures are a defense by the individual against the orgasmic effusion whose primacy in lived experience can alone ensure its harmony. The extremes this idea led him to are well known – they went so far as to get him ousted by the analytic community. But, in ousting him not unjustifiably, no one ever really knew how to formulate why Reich was wrong. (284, 2)

As Bruce Fink (2014a) points out in Volume I of *Against Understanding* (and he is one of the few commentaries I found which specifically focused on this analysis of Reich), Lacan is using a deconstructive method *avant la lettre:*

> [Lacan] says that the notion of armor suggests a defense against something that is repressed (hence armor is structured like a symptom), whereas what we deal with in psychoanalysis is, rather, an armorial, coat of arms, or set of heraldic signs (*armoirie*). Heraldic signs are designed to visually impress people and display one's prestige.
>
> (Fink, 2014a, p. 77)

Although Reich conceptualizes what he is doing in analytic treatment as breaking through the subject's defenses, Lacan seems to suggest here that at the end of such 'treatment' the subject is still carrying around the weight of his defenses; it is simply that 'the mark bordering on the symbolic that they formerly bore…[has] been effaced' (Fink, 2014a, p. 77). Lacan is beginning his elucidation of why Reich was wrong by pointing out that if the personality is a symptom, defensively structured like armor that the subject carries around, this armor has significance (284, 1, 284, 5). It is not simply there to be attacked to get to the thing (which is in any case impossible). The armor is actually an armorial, a coat of arms, with traces of a subject's history and pre-history, namely, what the subject inherits.

The armor as a signifier, not the signification of armor, is what the work of analysis is focused on for Lacan: unraveling one's history through signifiers, the weight of past-identifications, one's desire as desire of the Other, inter-generational transmission of trauma, and finally, the mark as the mark of death and finitude:

> It would seem to Lacan that the mark should, instead, be considered indelible, as it is the mortal mark of death. A family coat of arms brings you into being within a certain tradition or family line, but it also seals your fate: you are destined to die in the service of x, y, or z. According to Lacan, Reich tries to exclude the mortal mark we bear when he refuses to accept Freud's notion of the death drive.
>
> (Fink, 2014b, p. 103)

Reich's refusal of the death drive as the most radical psychoanalytic discovery is what – so Lacan insinuates – forces Reich to go too far (284, 5–285, 4), to pursue the Thing, *jouissance* itself! Consider his orgone theory: achieving absolute or-gastic potential was destined to become more and more literal, an imaginary object that one must have full access to and control over (with orgone boxes and machines that tried to capture its energy in the atmosphere), eventually seen as access to God or God-likeness. So while Reich refuses the death drive, his work, for Lacan, is the death drive incarnate; or, to put it another way, this is the ideal precisely as death driven. While Lacan does eventually speak about mystical *jouissance,* it is not something we ever have controlled access to. It will always be Other, and always only appear through a representational system. Surface is depth. Reich's stance, in the end, is fundamentally paranoid – consolidating and personifying the position of the other – which Lacan linked early on in the mirror stage to both the mania of the ego and the image of mastery as absolute knowledge. Reich's life ended in actual persecution by the law in 1956 – a fate brought down by many paranoiacs – and his death in prison in 1957.

> Reich's error can be explained by his deliberate refusal of the signification that is tied to the death instinct, which was introduced by Freud at the height of his conceptual powers, and which is, as we know, the touchstone of the mediocrity of analysts, whether they reject it or disfigure it. (284, 5, 285, 1)

Having deconstructed Reich, Lacan now goes on to elaborate upon his view of the ego, reviewing his work on The Mirror Stage. First of all, he says, if we follow neurosis and the structure of desire, we do not find some Valhalla of orgasmic energy and total satisfaction, we do not find some original naturalistic relation to the other, sex, and pleasure that had merely been distorted by neurosis, but something else (284, 5–285, 4). What we glean from the analysis is something about the structure of desire and the twisted development of the human personality: the alienation of desire, the desire for desire, the desire for recognition, all of which are modulated and structured through the vicissitudes of sexuality in the forms of sexual perversion that Freud (1905b) chronicled in the *Three Essays on the Theory of Sexuality*. When one looks closely at sexual perversions we find both the dominance of narcissism and the precariousness of desire, the splitting of the subject into 'existence and facticity' (subject, object, and Other, contained in the positions laid out in a perverse fantasy, for example the aggressor, the victim, and the witness). We find also the ambivalence that rests on passionate love linked to the ego-ideal and the hate that follows from such inevitable dependence on the other (285, 4). For Lacan, in these early works of Freud, we have some of the most important tools at our disposal for clinical understanding, especially regarding the structure of symptoms and fantasy. We can see the multiple positions unconsciously assumed by the patient, the place where desire and symptom run up against one another, and, in following the vicissitudes of sexuality, we will find what has historically marked a subject.

Lacan links these findings not only to Freud's (1921) *Group Psychology and the Analysis of the Ego*, but eventually to *Civilization and its Discontents* (1930) (285, 4–286, 3). The ego, far from being the object of aversion as Anna Freud (1936) states in her prophetic sinister music, is everywhere in Freud during this period. If we turn from sexuality to the question of aggression, what we see in Freud's work from this period is that it has nothing to do with some natural aggression linked to Darwinian survival and evolution but what Lacan calls our 'dehiscence from natural harmony':

> The rending of the subject from himself, a rending whose primordial moment comes when the sight of the other's image, apprehended by him as a unified whole, anticipates his sense that he lacks motor coordination, this image retroactively structuring this lack of motor coordination in images of fragmentation…It is thus at the heart of experiences of bearing and intimidation during the first years of life that the individual is introduced to the mirage of mastery of his functions, in which his subjectivity will remain split, and whose imaginary formation, naively objectified by psychologists as the ego's synthetic function, manifests instead the condition that introduces him to the alienating master/slave dialectic (286, 3–286, 4).

This is man's 'fruitful illness', his Hegelian 'happy fault' (286, 5), namely his being divided from himself: in the case of Freud the split between conscious and unconscious, or for Hegel, the divide between essence and appearance which he links to the fall of man and original sin. Lacan shows how man's relation to the image, its mark, introduces him both to the vicissitudes of life and death specific to the human being who apprehends himself, outside himself, in an image: 'only to man does this image reveal its mortal signification and, at the same time, that he exists' (287, 1). The ego, for Lacan, is always only half the subject, and represents a point of loss, a gap, a rending, in human development, what Freud always indicated with the idea of the lost-object. It is no wonder that the subject clings to the image as a place where he attempts to recognize himself – There I am! But this maneuver only divides the subject rather than uniting him with himself. As in the earlier discussion of speech, this division cannot be overcome. The psychoanalytic theory seems to have come to ignore this basic Freudian truth.

What does this mean for technique? Lacan agrees that analysis brings the narcissistic mirage into full being in the regression of treatment, in particular as a demand for recognition by the analyst (287, 4). How does the analyst respond to this? On the one hand, the response can elicit a powerful transference love whose presence and passion for presence dominates the analysis. Love for the analyst and the analyst's self-love are in a *danse macabre* as the patient's idealization meets with the analyst's narcissism. Analysis becomes interminable. On the other hand, a lack of response often provokes the aggression and hatred of a negative transference. The analyst's aggressive interpretations are met with aggression by the patient *ad infinitum*. The analysis is often prematurely terminated. This is well documented in the literature although the iatrogenic nature of the phenomena is less well scrutinized. What the analyst knows less well, Lacan says, is that 'what he says in his response is less important here than the place from which he responds' (287, 6)

Lacan will come back to this at the end of this section, but it is probably one of his most important remarks – in this section certainly, but perhaps in the entire article. It goes back to the question of the position of the analyst. Here, he is linking the place from which the analyst responds to this question of death, the position of the analyst being to maintain the presence of death in a refusal of closure, the only master in the game being death (death precisely as 'the absolute master' (289, 2)). The analyst will not play the master. Any figure of mastery other than death will lead to a closure of the unconscious. Therefore 'the subjectification of death' (289, 3) is linked, for the first time, to the psychoanalytic cure. It is a very Heideggerian rendering of the project of analysis, something that would wane over time in Lacan's work. Nevertheless, the import of the structure of death as the mediating term retains its centrality through to the end of Lacan's teaching. The reason for bringing these remarks forward at this point is that Lacan is here synthesizing the co-ordinates of the dilemmas of the ego in psychoanalysis. If the analyst increasingly 'falls under the sway of the illusions of his own ego' (282, 2) where the 'shaping of the subject by the analyst's ego serves merely as an excuse for the analyst's narcissism' (288, 3) the question is, how does death intervene in order to avoid this distortion of psychoanalytic treatment?

Of course, Lacan will offer another critique before concluding this section; this time turning to an analyst from Ferenczi's Hungarian school, Michael Balint (288, 5–289, 5). Balint is best known for his concept of the 'basic fault' (Balint, 1979) which echoes Hegel's happy fault alluded to earlier by Lacan when discussing the mark of death or the dehiscence at the heart of man. Balint (1979) locates the basic fault in the inter-subjective dyadic relationship between mother and child. Again, Lacan is playing with a figure that acts like his double in the text with a question of how far the synchrony between them goes. This is the very play of his critique. Indeed both figures talk about the necessity of knowing how to count to three in analysis – to know the difference between the subject alone, the subject as part of dyad, and the subject in triangular relations – as well as following this 'something missing' as it plays out in analytic treatment. It seems important to add that Balint was critical of the psychoanalytic institution in much the same line as Glover and Lacan. Annie Tardits, in her book *The Trainings of the Psychoanalyst*, says of Balint's criticisms of analytic training in his 1948 article 'On the Psychoanalytic Training System':

> Analytic training had taken the form of primitive initiation ceremonies: esoteric knowledge, dogmatic exposes, authoritarian techniques, submission to, and identification with, the initiator on the part of candidates. Contrary to the official aim of analysis to produce a strong and critical ego, training has become the 'formation of a superego'.
>
> (Tardits, 2000, p. 53)

While Lacan does not cite this earlier article of Balint, he does cite Balint's later (1954) article on the analytic training system at the very end of 'Variations on the Standard Treatment', lauding Balint for clarity with regard to the problems of the institution (298, 4)! Like Lacan's analysis of Ernst Kris in 'The Direction of the Treatment and the Principles of its Power' (again on a section questioning the function of the ego), one always finds Lacan engaged with a double in a battle to the death! Perhaps Lacan is not only explaining his theoretical position, he is also acting it out before our very eyes. Lacan concludes this *pas de deux* as the one who situates death in its place, while these others seem unable to, and *their* ego increasingly takes center stage.

Looking at Balint's article 'On the Termination of Analysis' Lacan is going to bring the question of the end of analysis into focus with how Balint works with his notions of the ego, the primary ambivalence of love and hate, and the basic fault linked to the pre-oedipal or the mother-baby dyad (288, 5–289, 5). Looking at Balint's (1950) article on the termination we find that once again, the author must bemoan the failure of any attempt to establish theoretical standards, that the standards one does have are rather 'perfectionist', and that 'we are not able to define what would constitute an admissible deviation from our criteria' (Balint, 1950, p. 198). This is right in line with much of what Lacan has been saying. However, when Balint turns to his own experience of termination with patients, Lacan cannot but go for the jugular. Balint feels he leads his patient's to what he calls 'mature genital love', developing their 'capacity for testing the reality with regard to his objects', the patient feeling like he is going through a 'kind of re-birth', 'taking leave of something very dear' in a 'deeply felt grief' which is 'mitigated by the feeling of security' (1950, p. 197). Balint continues: 'Usually the patient leaves after the last session happy but with tears in his eyes and – I think I may admit – the analyst is in a similar mood' (p. 197). While this is his idea of termination, Balint is forced to admit that this only happens rarely. 'Still,' he says, 'I remain convinced that in the main my description is correct' (p. 197).

As Balint goes on to talk about the cases that achieve lesser results, he completely undermines himself. He states that, if the beginning of a treatment was 'spoilt' it was 'hardly possible to remedy the situation' and these cases 'usually ended in a state of partial success, seldom of dissatisfaction or resentment, in spite of sincere goodwill and honest efforts from both sides' (Balint, 1950, p. 198). A 'feeling of having missed something' persists long after the analysis (p. 198). How, we might ask, can standards not be a perfectionist if 'spoiling' leads to such a catastrophic mutation of termination? It is not clear if it's the analyst's ideal – the mutual oozing of emotions and fluids – or the patient's (which in any case would seem to be an inevitable confrontation in analysis in the form of disappointment), that is the cause of such 'partial success'. Lacan's description of Balint here is brutal! But the contradictions of Balint's position are perhaps best summed up by Balint himself who, without irony, concludes his 1952 article 'On Love and Hate' depicting termination thus:

> In some cases the result of treatment will be health behind barriers of hatred, a costly but not-too-bad protection against the wish to regress. In other cases the result will be a perpetual dependent identification, defending by idealization the object against our hatred. And lastly, in favorable cases, the lasting marks of this fateful primary object relation, of the primary transference, may amount only to unforgettable memories, sweet and painful at the same time. When describing such fortunate people, may I quote again the traditional ending of fairy-tales: 'And they lived happily ever after!'
>
> (Balint, 1952, p. 362)

It is not a far cry to say that the fortune – both fortune finding and fortune telling – of the ending here belongs only to the analyst. It is not the patient's neurotic idealization – be it in the form of masking regressive hatred or de-pendence – that is the problem here; it is rather the analyst's ideal that is everywhere in these papers on technique and termination. Trapped in their own imaginary, the analyst can do very little with the inevitable imaginary phenomena that surface in a patient's discourse, except perhaps to be sunk by it, or, once in a while, manage to join it in some sort of identification-fueled emotional soup.

The vague warm mist of Balint's fairy-tale ending can hardly make up for the more common ends that serve as a depiction of the herd mentality of the ego in Freud's (1921) *Group Psychology and the Analysis of the Ego* and the vicissitudes of narcissism and aggression in *Civilization and its Discontents* (1930). The cure here is no cure, and Lacan is poking fun at Balint's idea that primary love and genital sexuality magically come to fruition. This primary love emerges for Balint from the dyadic analytic relation, which Balint (1952) himself depicts at other moments as voracious, beset by the feeling of a basic fault (or lack!), and destined to erupt in hate and disappointment as a repetition of the vicissitudes of the mother-baby relationship. To twist the knife, Lacan says that this point is most clearly articulated in an article by Balint's first wife, Alice Balint (1949): 'Love for the Mother and Mother-Love'. She says,

> to sum up, the child who has outgrown his infancy is no longer so agreeable to the mother (thinking still in terms of instinctual maternity), nevertheless he clings to her and does not know any other form of love but that of his naïve egoism. This naïve egoism, however, becomes untenable, because there is no mutuality at base. Thus the child is faced with the task of adapting himself to the wishes of those whose love he needs. It is at this point that the rule of the reality sense starts in the emotional life of man. (p. 257)

There is no mutuality. What then is Balint attesting to as possible for a dyad at the end of analysis? What 'happily ever after' is there?

There is no reality except for the reality of death for Lacan. This is crucial. It is death – not reality – that must be brought to bear on the dyad or the ego–ego relation behind the dyad. It must be 'reduced to the only face that sustains it behind their masks: the face of the absolute master, death' (289, 2). And what better description of this death mask is there than Alice and Michael Balint's depictions of the fate of the dyad? The mother's love is destined to abandon the child; the child is destined to feel a huge fault or lack in his mother's love and subsequently in himself. All attempts to fend against this, to twist his desire to that of his Mother, will ultimately fail. The effacing of the ego takes place in respect to both of the limitations of the imaginary and the ego's literal 'being destined to die'. The ego, Lacan says, finds its ideal terminus (from origin to end) in 'the subjectification of his death' (289, 3). A confrontation occurs with lack, with loss, with failure, with the gap or the 'want-to-be' that structures subjectivity and inter-subjective relations.

> And this is supposed to be the end required of the analyst's ego, about whom we can say that he must acknowledge the prestige of but one master – death – in order for life, which he must guide through so many vicissitudes, to be his friend. (289, 4)

Lacan often linked death to Freud's (1937) conception of the 'bedrock of castration' in his late article 'Psychoanalysis Terminable and Interminable'. The end of analysis was this bedrock, meaning the place where the phallic mirage dissipates, like morning mist, at the first ray of light; an event no patient willingly wants to endure. Sickness, Freud says, is often preferable. The termination of treatment here is more like a shattering than any fairy-tale happily ever after.

This extreme 'subjectification' of death is the only way that an analyst can then bring another to this ecstatic limit of the self. Thus, Lacan says, 'assuming he has eliminated all the illusions of his ego in order to accede to 'being-toward-death,' no other knowledge, whether immediate or constructed, can be preferred by him to be made a power of, assuming it is not simply abolished thereby' (289, 5). What is fascinating in this final statement is that Lacan delicately answers the criticism made by Balint and Glover regarding the problems of psychoanalytic training, because if the analyst can assume his position as 'being-toward-death' then knowledge will no longer have the force of mystique, perfectionism, or esoteric authoritarianism (289, 5). No one is a master when death takes its proper place, and if this doesn't wipe out knowledge all together (perhaps in an elevation of non-knowledge), knowledge at least loses its imaginary power of fascination. Knowledge as a form of mastery is not the economy that psychoanalysis will deal in. The analyst is only the subject *supposed* to know. 'Thus he [the analyst] can now respond to the subject from the place he wants to respond from' (289, 6). It is this shift from knowing to supposed knowing that provides the place from which the analyst can respond to his patient's desire for recognition. It is from this place that technique will take its bearings.

'This brings us to the following question: What must the analyst know in analysis?' (289, 9). Lacan wonders what kind of knowledge is knowledge of death and also what death does to knowledge. Who wants to have anything to do with this necrophiliac version of psychoanalysis? Even if one might characterize the analyst as a kind of death-like creature – silently expectant, passive, indifferent, blank, maybe even dumb – and this allows the analyst to subordinate himself to the subject's truth, Lacan's vision is more radical than what can look like a kind of psychoanalytic posturing. How does this confrontation with death transform the analyst to take on the difficulties of day in and day out analytic work (for example as characterized by Ferenczi (1955) earlier on)?

In fact, given Lacan's characterization of what takes place, couldn't we imagine that it makes the psychoanalyst a worse analyst? Or, might we imagine that after the analyst's analysis, he or she might want nothing to do with analysis any longer? That the analyst may want to get on with life rather than turn right back around and help others in this death-work? This raises fascinating questions concerning the masochism of the analyst; how a cure effects the desire of the analyst to be an analyst; why the possibility of not wanting to be an analyst must be part of any training analysis and its end; and finally what termination means about the position the analyst is able to occupy. Lacan sometimes characterized this as the confrontation with the impossible, which took on many guises throughout his lifetime: from the figure of death, to castration, the shattering of the Real, to his iteration on there being no Other of the Other, no final judgment, no Woman, no sexual relationship, to his late work on the limits of love and knowledge, and the subjective destitution of the psychoanalytic cure. Finally, he says that the analyst falls as an object of desire, that when the analyst falls sometimes they are also flushed like a piece of shit! One must hear the iteration of this series of negative propositions about the cure in contrast to how Balint (1952), for example, characterized his vision of fairy-tale termination! Having taken us to the limits of love and knowledge, let us go back to a question of what the analyst must know.

IV What the psychoanalyst must know: how to ignore what he knows

The problem of the ideal in the form of the analyst's ego is taken up again in this last section in order to talk about its potential subversion. The problem of the ego, in the end, proves critical to the cure in the same manner in which the repetition compulsion becomes repetition in the transference in order to open out in both rememberings and working through. So far from the ego being simply an obstacle, Lacan now makes the claim that just because it belongs to the imaginary 'does not mean that it is illusory' (290, 1). If one looks at imaginary numbers in mathematics, or an ideal point in geometry, we see how they act as 'the pivotal point of transformation,' a nodal point in a 'convergence' of forms and figures, determined *by* reality, not against it (290, 1). Much later, in Seminar XX, Lacan (1998) spoke of finding the center of an ellipse – which has no center but is structured by two foci – dropping down to an imaginary point. Something about the ideal as a structure of the ego (remember here Freud's early division of the ego into ego–ideal and ideal–ego in his (1921) paper on *Group Psychology*, the ego–ideal being there a predecessor for the super-ego) must be highlighted by analysis. Applying this question to the analyst's ego, what transformation takes place there in relation to the ideal?

It seems clear, Lacan conjectures, that while the analyst does not know what he is doing, and changes 'nothing in 'reality'', still, psychoanalysis 'changes everything for the subject' (290, 3)? Notions like 'distortion of reality,' 'wishful thinking,' or 'magical thinking', as something to be corrected by analysis, are not at the core of transformation for Lacan; they are simply an 'excuse for ignorance' (290, 3). Terms like distortion or wish have proven themselves in the history of the psychoanalytic literature to be indices of the analyst's imaginary power – his knowledge considered as a privileged point – exploiting the naïve faith of the patient who sees him as a man 'not like the others' (290, 5). What reality? Or rather, whose? Once we are asking a question of who determined the outlines of a supposed reality, namely the construction of a fantasy around a certain ideal, we are closer to the nodal ideal point of any imaginary form. Lacan's infamous example of this can be found in his reading of Freud's (1919) 'A Child is Being Beaten' in his seminar *The Logic of Fantasy* (Lacan, 2011). In the imaginary masturbatory scene of a father figure beating many children there is, says Lacan (1966–1967), often a hidden instrument – be it a horse whip, or a paddle with engravings, or an ivory cane – that is full of significance. The subject is indicated by this ideal point, this instrument, which is often saturated by symbolic content if one looks closely at the fantasy, a factor that itself is hidden by the *jouissance* engendered by the scene. This eclipsing of the subject by his or her fantasy is seen in the very structure of Freud's work, summing up fantasy in the form of a disembodied sentence; the subject doesn't even assume a role in the sentence or scene that defines his enjoyment (as in Freud's (1919) '*A Child is Being Beaten*').

Lacan breaks off this discussion suddenly and returns to his claim that what the analyst does is support speech, asking the question: 'What is speech?' (291, 2). Lacan is immediately in the contradictory and somewhat tautological position of explaining what speech is with speech, and with having to articulate the meaning of meaning. Speech is not reducible to meaning, and meaning is not reducible to speech (290, 1–291, 8). However, speech does 'give meaning its medium in the symbol that speech incarnates through its act…it is thus an act and, as such, presupposes a subject' (291, 3–291, 4). When speech functions as an act, when it deploys meaning by summoning the symbolic, it brings a subject into being. Lacan brings up the declarations, 'You are my wife' and 'You are my master' which signify 'I am your husband' and 'I am your disciple' (291, 5). Nevertheless, this can be heard by the listener in two ways: as a statement about the relationship between speaker and listener, or as a description. The speech act on the side of the subject is what Lacan will call 'true speech,' (291, 6) while 'true discourse' is based in knowledge as 'correspondence to the thing' (291, 6); in other words, speech that says 'I' and speech that says 'that'. Speech that says I constitutes a truth the less it is based on true discourse and the more it is based on a subject's investment in and recognition of their own being. True discourse is constituted as knowledge of reality, outside of the inter-subjective dimension. The ego position of the analyst or analysand is often an investment in true discourse at the expense of true speech. 'That's the way it is', split off from its other half, 'because that's the way I say it is.'

Lacan calls this bifurcation of speech the 'inter-accusation' of speech that acts like the Charybdis and the Scylla that the analyst must navigate (291, 9). One always accuses the other of lying. Freud, in *Jokes and Their Relation to the Unconscious* (1905a) in a section on skeptical jokes, acknowledges this division in speech:

> 'Two Jews met in a railway carriage at a station in Galicia. 'Where are you going?' asked one. 'To Cracow', was the answer. 'What a liar you are!' broke out the other. 'If you say you're going to Cracow, you want me to believe you're going to Lemberg. But I know that in fact you're going to Cracow. So why are you lying to me?''...The joke...is making use of the uncertainty of one of our commonest concepts. Is it the truth if we describe things as they are without troubling to consider how our hearer will understand what we say? Or is this only Jesuitical truth, and does not genuine truth consist in taking the hearer into account and giving him a faithful picture of our own knowledge?...What they are attacking is not a person or an institution but the certainty of our knowledge itself, one of our speculative possessions.
>
> (Freud, 1905a, p. 115)

The joke about lying plays with an ineradicable uncertainty due to the division between what Freud calls Jesuitical truth and genuine truth. Freud says that what is attacked in playing on the uncertainty of truth in speech, is the certainty of knowledge in general. That is why these jokes are called skeptical jokes. Lacan will make a similar point when he says that true discourse accuses true speech of lying since it points to the promisorial nature of any declaration; no-one (290, 7–291, 8). Ambiguity is always present since the future outruns the speaking person in question, who is always 'outstripped' (291, 7): 'You want me to believe you are going to Lemberg.' One can always accuse the person of lying. When someone says, 'I love you,' the retort is often, as the famous song goes, 'and what about tomorrow?' One has to say 'I love you' again and again and again. Nevertheless, on the side of true speech, it questions true discourse as to what it signifies, since one signification leads to another to another (291, 8). 'What do you mean when you say you love me?' 'What do you love about me?' 'When did you decide you loved me?' and so on. As a lover's discourse shows us, it cannot catch up to the thing. 'True discourse seems to be doomed to error' (291, 8). This is perhaps most obvious in the unending questions of children ('Why is the sky blue?', 'What is air?', 'Who made air?' 'What is time?', 'How do you know?' and so on...) which often leads back to an ur-question as to why the parent is answering the child's questions to begin with, in other words, the position they occupy as the one who supposedly knows. The child demands an answer on the level of true speech, not true discourse, its forgotten or obscured other half.

This struggle in speech – speech always working by way of ruses, trickery, error, and ambiguity – nonetheless seeks to stabilize itself inter-subjectively through conviction, agreement, or simply the committed stasis of continued battle (291, 8–292, 6). For Lacan however, there is a difference between re-cognizing these structural laws and working with them, and the way in which we can get lost in speech as a result of the power struggle, especially in 'the discourse of conviction, due to the narcissistic mirages that dominate' there (292, 4). The subject misrecognizes him or herself; something Freud focused on in his 1925 article 'On Negation.' It is often the case that when a patient insists on how great the analyst is, and how they aren't angry with them in the slightest for canceling their session, that they mean precisely the opposite in their unconscious. 'You are great' = 'I hate you'. The mirages of narcissism must be transparent to the analyst if they are not going to take this utterance at face value and bask in a sense of greatness. However, an insistence on one's knowledge of the 'I hate you' still participates in a mirage of narcissism. One has to support the patient's coming to say, 'I hate you' for such and such particular reason.

How does this support of authentic speech happen? Lacan begins with a rather bleak pronouncement: authentic speech is forbidden to the patient except in rare moments of one's existence – hence the need for psychoanalysis. Nevertheless, truth speaks and can be read in one's very being at 'all the levels at which it [speech] has shaped him' (293, 1). Lacan once again grounds being through an inter-subjective foundation at the level of speech, a foundation that can be read by the psychoanalyst. Lacan becomes very theoretical at this point. He says, that what the analyst must do is 'silence the intermediate discourse in himself in order to open himself up to the chain of true speech, that he can interpolate his revelatory interpretation' (293, 3). The best way to understand this cryptic statement is to turn to his reading of Freud's (1909) case of the Rat Man (292, 7–294, 4).

Lacan's claim is that Freud solves the riddle of the Rat Man's obsessional neurosis in opening up to a 'word chain' that unpacks the Rat Man's history, providing 'the meaning by which we can understand the simulacrum of re-demption that the subject foments to the point of delusion in the course of the great obsessive trance that leads him to ask for Freud's help' (293, 5). The Rat Man came to Freud because he couldn't stop thinking of a rat torture (told to him by his cruel captain in the army) being performed on his father and his lady love if he proves unable to return a payment for his eyeglasses made by another soldier in the military. However, through a series of tricks using obsessional logic, he landed himself with impossible duty to pay back lieute-nant A by paying back lieutenant B. His father also happened to be dead, which somehow didn't prevent the possibility of rat torture in the afterlife. Following the logic of this delusional 'simulacra' of redemption, Freud traced the word 'raten'/rats to 'ratten'/installments through a series of associations circling around an infamous unpaid gambling debt of his father's from his days in the army leading to his discharge. The unconscious accusation concerned a monetary/characterological problem of his father, which, in the long run, led to the father's marrying the Rat Man's mother for money and not the woman he loved. This cast a shadow over the whole of his parent's marriage (292, 7–294, 4), and, at the point that the Rat Man fell ill, his mother was hypocritically asking the Rat Man to make a similar 'calculation' in his choice of a wife. In other words, she was asking him to marry a woman for her wealth and not the one he loved, forcing the Rat Man into a fate similar to his parents in the model of a reverse Oedipus complex. Lacan points out that in his symptom, the Rat Man unites the real Oedipal couple, his father and his lady love, showing his desire to marry the woman he loves and not follow his mother's ultimatum and repeat his family history.

This chain, unpacked by Freud, is in fact not made up of

> pure events (all of which had, in any case, occurred prior to the subject's birth), but rather of a failure (which was perhaps the most serious because it was the most subtle) to live up to the truth of speech and of an infamy more sullying to his honor. (293, 5)

Questions of trauma and truth still haunt psychoanalysis. Truth in this case is something different from veridical truth as 'real' events; it is what Lacan would call subjective truth. Furthermore, the father and the lady love are precisely the nodal point of transformation in the case, a point where two 'narcissistic images' are subverted by a hidden symbolic content, the two as besieged by rats/installments', 'undoing this chain in all its latent import', 'summoning the subject', 'less as a legatee than as its living witness' (294, 2). The Rat Man is witness to a truth about his family, a truth that precedes his very birth, leaving its stamp on his life. We are back to the analysis of Reich's armor as an armorial. The Rat Man's coat of arms would have a rat and money inscribed on it in the section that depicts the history of marriage in this family. This is the ideal point of the imaginary that is subverted in a reading of its signification. In pointing out that the Rat Man is more a witness than a legatee, Lacan indicates that analysis gives him back a choice regarding this legacy, in other words, the Rat Man is brought to a point where he can live-up to his truth. This nodal point acts as a symbolic debt. It is something owned and assumed, something that cannot be fulfilled, and which must as such be lived with. It cannot, like a real debt, be paid off, as is the case in the Rat Man's presenting predicament with the money for his glasses (293, 4–294, 4). In fact, the Rat Man goes on to marry the woman he loves, sadly just before dying in the war.

Perhaps most important with regard to technique, Lacan says that Freud was able to touch on this crucial point because a 'similar suggestion' had been made to Freud himself by his family and proved critical in his self-analysis (294, 4). Lacan conjectures that if Freud had not rejected this decree by his own family, and analyzed his relationship to money as it circulated in his family mythology, he may have missed it in the Rat Man. One assumes this is because he would have to blind himself to his failed choice and its continued consequences, upholding the mirage dictated by his family. While the effects of Freud's narcissism in his clinical work are a subject of much investigation, especially in the Dora case (Freud, 1905c), still, Lacan says, 'the dazzling comprehension Freud demonstrates…allows us to see that, in the lofty heights of his final doctrinal constructions, the paths of being were cleared for him' (294, 5). In other words, Freud's self analysis – as a clearing of being, or bringing being into a clearing (to put it in Heideggerian terms) –worked, and it is precisely this which allows Freud to open himself to the linguistic chain and read the Rat Man's story. While this of course points to the importance of reading Freud's cases closely, it also brings us to our last stop in the discussion of the analyst's knowledge – 'namely, the contrast between the objects proposed to the analyst by his experience and the discipline necessary to his training' (294, 6).

The first object proposed to the analyst by his experience seems to be 'the rebelliousness of facts' (294, 7) of which there is no better voice than Theodor Reik's (1948) work *Listening with the Third Ear*. Reik was contesting both the training protocols and technique of the ego-psychologists, especially their exclusion of lay-analysts and THEIR emphasis on interpretation of the resistance. He eventually set up a counter-institute to the New York Psychoanalytic Institute in downtown Manhattan, called National Psychological Association for Psychoanalysis (NPAP). Lacan says that Reik reminds us, even if he fails to theorize it, that interpretation is close to divination in its original juridical meaning as the one who supports 'speech's accusation in a trial' (295, 1). On the question of training, Lacan says that we know that malaise reigns. He points the reader to Dr. Knight's 1953 address to the American Psychoanalytic Association 'The Present Status of Organized Psychoanalysis in the United States' (295, 2). While Knight characterizes the problems as one of a quickly growing institution (whose numbers he obsessively details in his talk), we know today that the same institution, facing bankruptcy because of a lack of new members, continues to have problems of malaise and infighting. In a section on professional standards and training, Knight characterizes the situation: 'the spectacle of a national association of physicians and scientists feuding with each other over training standards and practices, calling each other orthodox and conservative or deviant and dissident, is not an attractive one, to say the least' (Knight, 1953, p. 210). It is interesting to note that the 'Board of Professional Standards' of the American Psychoanalytic Association sued the American Psychoanalytic Association over disagreements on training standards, in particular the rules determining who could function as a training analyst for candidates, in 2013. 'Standard' continues to be the signifier of battle in psychoanalysis! Lacan goes on to quote Knight at length concerning changes not only in training – from one structured around a master figure, to one resembling the structured bureaucracy of a medical school – but also in respect of trainees, namely from self-motivated, introspective, theoretically well-read individuals, to anti-intellectual, professionally hasty, clinicians (295, 1–295, 4). Lacan goes on to remark:

> It is quite clear, in this highly public discourse, how serious the problem is and also how poorly it is understood, if it is understood at all. What is desirable is not that the analysands be more 'introspective' but rather that they understand what they are doing; and the remedy is not that institutes be less structured, but rather that analysts stop dispensing predigested knowledge in them, even if it summarizes the data of analytic experience. (295, 4)

This is one of the most direct criticisms and subsequent recommendations regarding training in Lacan. The question of a non-imaginary knowledge is central, even the most fundamental, when considering the experience of the analyst and his training.

Psychoanalytic training is not about the transmission of a set body of knowledge (295, 4–296, 5). To jump to his conclusion:

> the positive fruit of the revelation of ignorance is non-knowledge, which is not a negation of knowledge, but rather its most elaborate form. The candidate's training cannot be completed without some action on the part of the master or masters who train him in this nonknowledge— failing which he will never be anything more than a robotic analyst. (297, 5)

An experience of non-knowledge, as the most elaborate form of knowledge, is critical to the formation of a psychoanalyst. Whether this is something about the candidate's experience in analysis or supervision, or an experience with teachers who know not to fetishize knowledge, who proceed Socratic-like, a revelatory encounter with ignorance is essential. Most of the knowledge accumulated in the course of an analyst's experience concerns the imaginary. Lacan characterizes this experience as a 'natural history of the forms of desire's capture and even of the subject's identifications' that had never before been this rigorously cataloged (296, 2). It is not of use to him in his action as an analyst. While depicting the capture of desire in true discourse is notoriously difficult – since it is about the truth of illusion and the limits of illusion, which are never stable – it is of little help to the analyst since it concerns the deposit and not the mainspring (295, 4–296, 5). In other words, it does not concern what generates the world of the imaginary, what constructs the veil.

One of the main bifurcations in Post-Freudian theory concerns the division between biologizing drive theorists on the one hand, and cultural humanists on the other. Both suffer from problematic ideals seen in their respective ideas of 'drive harmony based on individualist ethics' and Darwinian science or humanist ideals of group conformity that Lacan calls the 'covetousness of 'engineers of the soul'' (296, 4). Both have a tendency towards domination. The 'ideal of 'drive' harmony' (296, 4), Lacan conjectures, holds little water when one takes into account the basic scar or unhappy fault of the Freudian subject, while an orthopedic vision of cultural sublimations of one's wound seems to offer very little advantage. Of course, what both of these visions leave out is language. Psychoanalysis, for Lacan, is best when subordinated to its unique purpose, which is a consideration of what is most particular about a subject. The universal 'wisdom' of science or cultural morality has little place in this ethic of the particular that is unique to Lacan's reading of Freud. What is required is not-knowing.

What Freud says about psychoanalysis as a science is that it is a science that puts itself in question with every new case (296, 5–297, 5). Every case should bring what psychoanalysis thinks it knows into question. And imagine here the modesty and flexibility of the analyst! This dictum clearly indicates for Lacan the path that training should follow: in other words, pre-digested knowledge will be of no help when analyzing a case. In fact, the analyst cannot analyze unless he 'recognizes in his knowledge the symptom of his own ignorance' (297, 2). The desire to know is a symptom, maybe even *the* symptom, and must be treated like the neurotic's desire to love, which is what the 'best analytic writers' point to when they say that the reasons one wants to be an analyst must, above all, be analyzed. Lacan refers the reader in a footnote to Maxwell Gitelson's 1954 article 'Therapeutic Problems in the Analysis of the 'Normal' Candidate' – a now legendary paper – where he specifically takes up the challenge of Dr. Knight's address, and the new ecology of candidates. Gitelson says that their professionalism is the first line of an intellectual defense, that the imago of authority is now psychoanalysis itself, which makes it hard to analyze even in cases where candidates 'sincerely affirm their intellectual acceptance of analysis' (1954, p. 178), and their normalcy works as a denial of the unconscious, especially in their phallic ambition which is an oral substitute and defense against regression. They thus have great difficulty in 'surrendering' to the uncertain gratification and postponed solutions demanded by analysis, while the current analytic training system fosters these defensive solutions, rather than working against them, especially in its system of codified knowledge. This is especially true when the analysis of candidates, the so-called 'training analysis,' is seen as a learning process distinct from therapy or regular analysis, in other words, as dealing in knowledge as though between a teacher and a student. To play the student (in line with eventually being the teacher-analyst) is a fantastic, or perhaps better, phantasmatic, obstacle seen at the very core of the decision to become an analyst. If the institution supports this phantasm, isn't the pathway of psychoanalysis lost?

And so we come back to the 'closing' up of the unconscious predicted by Freud in the 1920s as the turning point of analytic technique, linked by Freud to the potential effects of analysis becoming more wide-spread. 'Indeed the unconscious shuts down insofar as the analyst no longer 'supports speech,' because he already knows or thinks he knows what speech has to say' (297, 6). The patient cannot recognize his truth in what the analyst says, since it does not have the structure of truth as revelation, namely as the encounter with something new and absolutely specific to the patient. This is often the surprising effect not only of what Freud says to a patient, but also its status as a truth for Freud, a truth he encountered in his own analysis. Lacan here is elaborating on his earlier point regarding Freud's interpretation of the Rat Man's injunction to marry for money and not love. True speech must be true for both parties. They are united in the interpretation. This is a quite radical point and one not often seen in the literature on technique. It puts at the center the necessity of the analyst's analysis being a certain kind of experience of unconscious truth. It similarly centralizes the re-discovery of the co-ordinates of this truth in the coming-to-say of interpretation. 'Speech reveals an unconscious subject' (298, 2). This is true not only for the patient, for the analyst must speak at some point as well.

For Lacan, we can only listen to and speak through the unique signifiers at play in a case if we silence conscious knowledge and foreground the patient's – and the analyst's – unconscious voice. This returns us to Lacan's question about the Being of the analyst and how Being and desire structure one's role as analyst; 'the analyst must know, better than anyone else, that he can only be himself in his speech' (298, 2). Interpretation must be as surprising to the analyst as it is to the patient, as if what the analyst said literally fell out of the analyst's mouth. All of Lacan's emphasis on oracular speech finds resonance here, but with the added element of a lack of knowledge or intention. He can't just speak oracularly. His speech takes on the co-ordinates of an oracle, since it comes from elsewhere. The analyst will re-discover his own truth, in a new form, in every case. This real avowal in relation to the truth, by the analyst, the use of his being which acts even in silence, allows the patient to find his 'own desire' *in* the analyst, as other, in accordance with the laws of speech. While this might seem in danger of being nothing more than a narcissistic identification on the part of the analyst it is the maintenance of Being on the level of the truth of speech that prevents it from being thus (298, 3–299, 2). Lacan points out that narcissism is always the rejection of the commandments of speech; one would see in an analysis of this nature the ferocious reign of the super-ego opened up by this solidification of the imaginary. I have often been a patient's second (or third or fourth) 'therapist'; and while some symptoms might have resolved, their super-ego is as harsh as ever, especially in their discourse about themselves as symptomatic – I have such and such problem, and its for this and this reason. They are thoroughly objectified. In Lacan's late paper 'l'étourdit' (Lacan, 2009) he addresses the fantasy of final judgment, in other words, the dictates of the super-ego, encountered as a kind of vanishing point in an analysis. The subject is the one that always vanishes, and no judgment – usually partaking of the good/bad variety – can stabilize this subject. This instability, this vanishing act, is preferable to the avid stability of an objectified self. The subversion of the super-ego in the direction of this vanishing is necessary on an institutional level, Lacan claims, if psychoanalysis is going to function as such. In 'Variations on the Standard Treatment' that vanishing must take place on the plane of knowledge. So here we have the bi-directional co-ordinates of treatment: speech and Being on the one hand, and the imaginary and the super-ego on the other.

Lacan then enters into one last parody of the modern-day analyst (298, 3–299, 2). Here the analysand in training analysis confirms his knowledge of his Oedipal problems by confessing that he is in love with the woman who opens the door to his sessions, who he believes is his analyst's wife. Lacan's quip here is that this titillating fantasy is just conformism (in the model of Gitelson's (1954) normal candidate) and is hardly a lived knowledge of Oedipus, which in any case, would strip him entirely of this fancy when all is said and done, since Oedipus leads one through the narrow straights of castration. What will happen, Lacan asks, when we ask this little chap who proves to be nothing other than 'a follower whose head is full of idle gossip' to add his 'two cents' worth to the question of variations in treatment?' (298, 5). Brutal! The analyst has no standard with which to judge a variation having discovered nothing but his own conformity in his analysis! And the hushed conditions surrounding training analysis (and which continue to this day) must not drive ideas concerning the means and ends of psychoanalytic treatment further into the shadows.

It is fascinating to note that the recent lawsuits by and against the American Psychoanalytic Association centered on the question of training concerns arguments over formalities – who is allowed to be a training analyst, who judges, by what criteria – rather than any substantive question about treatment and termination and what role it plays in the formation of analysts. To this day, many, many analysts have admitted that they needed the second analysis after their training analysis, since the first was a sham. These are the peculiarities and real dangers of the training of a psychoanalyst. 'A hundred mediocre psychoanalysts do not advance analytic knowledge one iota' (299, 2). Jumping slightly ahead, Lacan states, in no uncertain terms that

> in order to situate analysis in the eminent place that those responsible for public education should grant it, its foundation must be laid open to criticism, without which it will degenerate into effects of collective subornation. It is up to the discipline of analysis itself to avoid these effects in the training of analysts and to thus bring clarity to the question of its variations. (300, 2)

It is fascinating to realize that at this late moment in this paper that Lacan outlines a program of study for the psychoanalyst. Nothing could be further from what actually takes place in a psychoanalytic training (299, 2–300, 6). He advocates studying:

a   The history of science prior to Aristotle, namely the study of dialectic in Plato and even the pre-Socratics
b   Mathematics
c   Human Sciences
d   Linguistics in its most modern and concrete developments;
e   Rhetoric
f   The modern notion of history so as to understand the function of history in the subject's individual life
g   The theory of symbols so it might be restored to its universal function meaning the study of whole numbers, game theory, and set theory (299, 3–300, 1).

A very Lacanian agenda, but nonetheless, what we find here is a study of knowledge that cannot be directly applied in analysis – can we imagine an interpretation using the theory of whole numbers? – although it can be used in order to orient the analyst to what is being said, to the structures of re-presentation. Only at that point, Lacan boldly points out, can the analyst open himself to the unconscious chain, to the production of truth that is both beyond his and his patient's mastery. For Lacan, this is why an analysis must rectify one's relationship to desire, which cannot be short-circuited in the imaginary if it needs to hold to this pathway of truth. There is nothing but the desire for analysis, for the psychoanalysis to carry on, for the psychoanalysis to be psychoanalysis and not something else; purified, as he said in the very beginning, in its means and ends. Only then, he says, will we understand the extreme discretion of Freud when he says of 'standard treatment' (and here Lacan cites Freud directly):

> I must however make it clear that what I am asserting is that this technique is the only one suited to my individuality; I do not venture to deny that a physician quite differently constituted might find himself driven to adopt a different attitude to his patients and to the task before him. (Freud, cited in Lacan, 300, 5)

Of course, Lacan points out that this is not a sign of Freud's profound modesty – some sort of idealization of Freud that masks profound aggression – but rather a truth about the analyst's relation to knowledge. The analyst must know that he cannot proceed by way of mimicry of Freud, which in any case would only be formalistic, but must rather find his scale of measurement along the path of non-knowledge. To take this one step further, Lacan here implies that every analyst must reinvent psychoanalysis, must invent his own being and attitude and way as an analyst, and that Freud leaves this open; demands it even. So in a way, the 'standard treatment' decrees variation, this individual variation as invention of oneself as an analyst. Lacan ends saying you can only be your own being, which is no doubt best done in speech, personal variation, style. And if you haven't encountered this necessity by the time you make your way into the analyst's chair, he grimly states, you will be lost and you will always be lost. How else can one make their way with the unconscious?

References

Balint, A. (1949) Love for the Mother and Mother-love. *The International Journal of Psychoanalysis*. 30, 251–259.

Balint, M. (1950) On the Termination of Analysis. *The International Journal of Psychoanalysis*. 31, 197–198.

Balint, M. (1952) On Love and Hate. *The International Journal of Psychoanalysis*. 33, 355–362.

Balint, M. (1954) Analytic Training and Training Analysis. *The International Journal of Psychoanalysis*. 35, 355–362.

Balint, M. (1979) *The Basic Fault: Therapeutic Aspects of Regression*. London/New York: Tavistock Publications.

Breuer, J., and Freud, S. (1957) *Studies on Hysteria*. Oxford, England: Basic Books.

Ferenczi, S. (1955) The Elasticity of Psychoanalytic Technique. In *The Selected Papers of Sandor Ferenczi, M.D., Vol. III, Final Contributions to the Problems and Methods of Psycho-Analysis*. New York: Basic Books.

Fink, B. (2014a) *Against Understanding Volume 1: Commentary and Critique in a Lacanian Key*. London: Routledge.

Fink, B. (2014b) *Against Understanding Volume 2: Cases and Commentary in a Lacanian Key*. London: Routledge.

Fonagy, P., and Target, M. (2004) Playing with the Reality of Analytic Love: Commentary on Paper by Jody Messler Davies "Falling in Love with Love". *Psychoanalytic Dialogues*. 14, 4, 503–515.

Foucault, M. (1963) *Naissance de la Clinique*. Paris: PUF [*The Birth of the Clinic* (New York: Pantheon, 1973)].

Freud, A. (1936) *The Ego and the Mechanisms of Defense*. London: Hogarth Press.

Freud, S. (1895) Project for a Scientific Psychology. In J. Strachey (ed. and trans.). *The Standard Edition of the Complete Psychological Works of Sigmund Freud, Volume 1*. London: Hogarth Press.

Freud, S. (1900) The Interpretation of Dreams. In J. Strachey (ed. and trans.). *The Standard Edition of the Complete Psychological Works of Sigmund Freud, Volumes 4 & 5*. London: Hogarth Press.

Freud, S. (1905a) Jokes and Their Relation to the Unconscious. In J. Strachey (ed. and trans.). *The Standard Edition of the Complete Psychological Works of Sigmund Freud, Volume 8*. London: Hogarth Press.

Freud, S. (1905b) Three Essays on Sexuality. In J. Strachey (ed. and trans.). *The Standard Edition of the Complete Psychological Works of Sigmund Freud, Volume 7*. London: Hogarth Press.

Freud, S. (1905c) Fragment of an Analysis of a Case of Hysteria. In J. Strachey (ed. and trans.). *The Standard Edition of the Complete Psychological Works of Sigmund Freud, Volume 7*. London: Hogarth Press.

Freud, S. (1909) A Case of Obsessional Neurosis. In J. Strachey (ed. and trans.). *The Standard Edition of the Complete Psychological Works of Sigmund Freud, Volume 10*. London: Hogarth Press.

Freud, S. (1919) A Child Is Being Beaten. In J. Strachey (ed. and trans.). *The Standard Edition of the Complete Psychological Works of Sigmund Freud, Volume 17*. London: Hogarth Press.

Freud, S. (1921) Group Psychology and the Analysis of the Ego. In J. Strachey (ed. and trans.) *The Standard Edition of the Complete Psychological Works of Sigmund Freud, Volume 18*. London: Hogarth Press.

Freud, S. (1925) Negation. In J. Strachey (ed. and trans.). *The Standard Edition of the Complete Psychological Works of Sigmund Freud, Volume 19*. London: Hogarth Press.

Freud, S. (1930) Civilization and Its Discontents. In J. Strachey (ed. and trans.). *The Standard Edition of the Complete Psychological Works of Sigmund Freud, Volume 21*. London: Hogarth Press.

Freud, S. (1937) Analysis Terminable and Interminable. In J. Strachey (ed. and trans.). *The Standard Edition of the Complete Psychological Works of Sigmund Freud, Volume 23*. London: Hogarth Press.

Gabbard, G. O. and Weston. D. (2003) Rethinking Therapeutic Action. *International. Journal of Psychoanalysis*. 84, 824–841.

Gitelson, M. (1954) Therapeutic Problems in the Analysis of the 'Normal' Candidate. *The International Journal of Psychoanalysis*. 35, 174–183.

Glover, E. (1954) Therapeutic Criteria of Psycho-analysis. *The International Journal of Psychoanalysis*. 2, 95–100.

Hoffer, W. (1950) Three Psychological Criteria for the Termination of Treatment. *The International Journal of Psychoanalysis*. 31, 194–195.

Knight, R.P. (1953) The Present Status of Organized Psychoanalysis in the United States. *Journal of the American Psychoanalytic Association*. 1, 2, 197–221.

Lacan, J. (1988) *The Seminar of Jacques Lacan, Book I: Freud's Papers on Technique, 1953-1954* (edited by Jacques-Alain Miller, translated with notes by John Forrester). New York and London: W.W. Norton.

Lacan, J. (1998) *The Seminar of Jacques Lacan, Book XX, Encore: On Feminine Sexuality, the Limits of Love and Knowledge, 1972-1973* (edited by Jacques-Alain Miller, translated by Bruce Fink). New York and London: W.W. Norton.

Lacan, J. (2002) *The Seminar of Jacques Lacan, Book VI: Desire and its Interpretation, 1958-1959* (edited and translated by Cormac Gallagher). London: Karnac.

Lacan, J. (2006) *Écrits: The First Complete Edition in English*. Trans. B. Fink. New York: W. W. Norton & Company, Inc.

Lacan, J. (2009) L'étourdit. *The Letter*, 41, 31–80.

Lacan, J. (2011) *The Seminar of Jacques Lacan, Book XIV: The Logic of Phantasy, 1966-1967* (edited and translated by Cormac Gallagher). London: Karnac.

Reich, W. (1974) *Listen, Little Man!* New York: Farrar, Straus and Giroux.

Reik, T. (1948) *Listening with the Third Ear: The Inner Experience of a Psychoanalyst*. New York: Farrar, Straus, and Giroux.

Solms M., and Turnbull O. (2002) *The Brain and the Inner World: An Introduction to the Neuroscience of Subjective Experience*. New York: Other Press.

Sterba, R. (1934) The Fate of the Ego in Analytic Therapy. *The International Journal of Psychoanalysis*. 15, 117–126.

Tardits, A. (2000) *The Trainings of the Psychoanalyst*. London: Karnac.

6

ON A PURPOSE

Owen Hewitson

Context

Unlike most of the other papers in the *Écrits*, 'On a Purpose' was written especially for the publication of the collection in 1966. It acts as a preface to what Lacan offers as two samples of his Seminar – an introduction, and a response, to Jean Hyppolite's commentary on Freud's paper 'Verneinung' ('Negation').

Commentary on the text

There are two main themes condensed into this short text. First, a restatement of what had throughout the 1950s been the main tenor of Lacan's work: the advocacy of a close reading of Freud's texts, with special attention paid to the signifiers Freud had chosen to employ. The importance given to Freud's German terms – *verwerfung* [foreclosure] referenced in the first page of this paper (301, 4); and *verneinung*, the central term of the two papers which follow – testifies to what Lacan calls a 'literal commentary' (304, 9) which he admires in Hyppolite's contributions, and which Lacan himself pursues.

Second, the uses of topology in conceptualizing the central ideas that Freud and psychoanalysts since had grappled with: the internal and external worlds, repetition compulsion, and signifying insistence. Although he does not elaborate on these in depth here, Lacan's reference at the end of the text to where he does – in the Seminar he was giving that year (Seminar XIII, 1965–1966) and one he had given previously (Seminar X, 1961–1962) – allow us to trace a path between the condensed references to topology in this paper and the extended discussions he offers the audience of his Seminar.

Lacan begins the paper by looking back a decade, with a lament to the demise of the journal *La Psychanalyse*[1] that he saw as a Francophone bulwark against 'the slippery slope' (304, 4) down which he believed international psychoanalysis to be heading. *La Psychanalyse* featured – but was not limited to – contributions from members of the Société Française de Psychanalyse (SFP)[2] and Lacan was its editor. Its first issue, which he references at the start, was published in 1956 on

DOI: 10.4324/9781003264231-6

the subject of speech and language. Lacan made three contributions in the form of his 'Rome Discourse' (reprinted for the *Écrits*), his translation of Heidegger's article 'Logos', and his dialogues with Hyppolite which follow 'On a Purpose' in the *Écrits*.

It is interesting to note the addition of non-psychoanalytic voices (Martin Heidegger, Jean Hyppolite, Émile Benveniste) as contributors. Lacan maintains that this was not for its own sake or in the service of 'some vain semblance of dialogue, even and especially philosophical' (305, 6). His decision to turn to philosophers and linguists rather than other psychoanalysts of his time indicates that he thought there was a dearth of thinking within the psychoanalytic community on the subjects of speech and language.

Just as Lacan turned his back on many of his psychoanalytic peers, so – he believed – they turned their backs on him, causing the message of *La Psychanalyse* to fall on deaf ears. He derides the fact that, in his view, 'the journal was disavowed in psychoanalytical circles right from its very introduction' (304, 5). Perhaps this lack of reception can explain why Lacan himself so steadfastly eschewed publication until 1966, jokingly referring to it here with the pun *poubellication* (304, 6). Equally though, perhaps Lacan would have preferred – at least at the time of *La Psychanalyse* – for his work to be read as a reading rather than as a presentation of a theory itself, given that he reminds his reader of how 'for the preceding three years already I had been legitimating my work as a *literal commentary* on Freud's work' (304, 9).

To understand what he means by this, we should bear in mind that in the ten years prior to the publication of the *Écrits* Lacan was heavily influenced by structuralist theory, and it is the 'structural reason' for paying attention to what he labels the 'literality of any text' (305, 2), that he privileges in this paper. The support for this 'literality' is to be found in the signifier, a term which he borrows from structural linguistics originating in the work of Ferdinand de Saussure at the turn of the century. This, he argues, is key to why psychoanalysts should concern themselves with language. Broadly speaking, this agenda can be read as the 'Purpose' referred to in this paper's title.

There is perhaps a no better representation of the application of structuralist theory to the Freudian discovery than the first few pages of Freud's (1901/ 1953) *The Psychopathology of Everyday Life*. The somewhat self-congratulatory reference Lacan makes in the opening paragraphs of this paper – highlighting the term *signor* in Hyppolite's commentary on that work – is a reference to the example Freud's book begins with, and indicates the closeness to the letter of Freud's text that Lacan is espousing.

In those pages, Freud repeats an account, first given in 1898 in his paper 'The Psychical Mechanism of Forgetfulness', of his failure to remember the name of Signorelli – the painter of the fresco featuring the Antichrist at Orvieto cathedral – during a conversation with a traveling companion. Freud's analysis centers on the connections between the signifier *Signorelli* and what he sees as repressed thoughts concerning sex and death. The unconscious takes advantage of the materiality of other signifiers in the conversation to instead make conscious two substitute terms: the names of the painters *Boticelli* and *Boltraffio*. If *Signorelli* is what Lacan calls later in the *Écrits* 'The broken tip of the memory's sword' (373, 4), the logic behind its forgetting depends on the link to the associations Freud produces in its place, drawn from the rest of the conversation. The crucial point for Lacan is that these associations matter not in their meaning but in their pure materiality as signifiers.

In referencing this example in the opening paragraphs, Lacan provides a succinct – we might say 'laconic' – message: that an attention to the text of Freud's work mirrors the attention needed in psychoanalytic work to the 'textual' nature of the formations of the unconscious. This is what Lacan means by the *'requirement to read'* (304, 10) that he saw lacking in the psychoanalytic community of his time, which demands what his student Jacques-Alain Miller (1988) later called a 'discipline of the signifier'. 'In short', Lacan says cuttingly, 'people read Freud in the same way that they write in psychoanalysis – enough said' (306, 7).

To return to the paper's title, the 'purpose' of this however is not the elucidation of structuralist theory, but to serve the 'practical stakes' (303, 4) of the training of psychoanalysts, a project at the heart of Lacan's teaching. Although we can say that this 'purpose' traverses Lacan's work from the 1950s onwards his re-reading of Freud is not simply a re-treading; the project of the 'Return to Freud' is not – he is eager to point out – a regression (306, 8). Moreover, from the late 1950s up to and including the publication of the *Écrits*, Lacan's agenda is far from being wholeheartedly structuralist. For several years already, through his Seminar, Lacan had been fascinated with the use of topological models to express the nature of human subjectivity. And it is to these models that he turns, not to qualify but to enrich the reading of Freud's work that had interested him hitherto.

The applicability of topology to psychoanalysis becomes clearer if we think of how both fields attempt to describe a series of relations not impacted by temporal, geographic, or affective proximity. Freud himself attempted, over the course of his life, to construct several models to represent the human psyche, but these were topographical rather than topological. To illustrate the difference, Lacan refers to the classical psychoanalytic idea that resistances increase in strength the closer in proximity they come to repressed content. Noting this relation at a theoretical level is one thing; adopting, at a more practical level, 'an inflexible discipline in following its contours' to reveal the 'veiled irreducibility in which the primacy of the signifier is stamped' (305, 10) is another. But it is through characterizing the sexual dimension of the phenomena of resistance as an 'awkward detour [*biais*]' (306, 1) that Lacan expects the reader to recognize a reference to the topology on which his conception of subjectivity from this point forward is based. Indeed, 'My return to Freud', he writes '...is based on the subject's topology, which can only be elucidated by a second twist back [*tour*] on itself' (306, 10).

There were several topological models which interested Lacan at this point in his work, which he is describing here with reference to the 'twist'. In the only footnote to this paper, he notes how he employed these models in his Seminar on identification in the academic year 1961–1962[3] and has returned to them through 1965–1966. The two models to which he gives the most attention are known as the cross-cap and the Moebius strip respectively. Both have the same topological properties which show peculiar characteristics. Formed by taking a strip of paper, twisting it, and then conjoining the two ends, the Moebius strip is a model whereby the 'outside' becomes continuous with the 'inside' insofar as a line traced on its surface can never be said to be either on the surface or below it. The cross-cap shares this same property in the way that its surfaces intersect one another. What interested Lacan about these topological forms is how they help us rethink crucial problems in psychoanalysis, like what we mean by 'the unconscious'. Such models problematize the relation of inside to outside, the surface to depth, and illustrate the way that satisfaction is always missed by the demand that grasps for it (a process which Lacan believes gives rise to desire).[4] For example, just as the Mobius strip has no underside, so Lacan argues – as in Seminar I (1988: 191) there is no difference between the repressed and the return of the repressed.[5] The practical lesson therein is that a psychoanalyst should not mistake what is on the surface for what is superficial (Figures 6.1–6.3).

The topological models Lacan employs around this time also oblige us to conceive of a hole as constitutive of subjectivity. He tells us immediately, however, that this is not a hole in knowledge, but at 'a place which is closer that pressures us to forget it' (306, 2). Where might this be? Although he does not say explicitly, Lacan had spent the academic year 1959–1960 theorizing what he referred to as 'the Thing' [das Ding], a point beyond symbolization or imaginary representation where the Freudian pleasure principle reaches its limit. A proximity to this point produces exactly the effects Lacan describes here – it 'causes the subject to flee its jouissance…due only to the anxiety provoked by the experience that deflates it' (306, 3). Between the late 1950s and the publication of the Écrits this idea of 'the Thing' underwent various other incarnations, and we can find shades of it in the notion of the agalma in Seminar VIII on transference from 1960 to 1961, after which time it develops into the theory of object a from Seminar X on anxiety in 1962. Although Lacan believes we can see Freud himself encounter this same impasse as early as Beyond the Pleasure Principle in 1920, we should not be surprised, he suggests, that post-Freudian analysts recoiled from the 'indecent intimacy' which a practice based on its confrontation demands, choosing instead to petrify it with 'the confused images into which the worst translations run headlong' (306, 6).

The point of his topological return to Freud, Lacan says towards the end of his paper, is not an attempt to achieve absolute knowledge but instead to highlight 'the position from which knowledge can reverse truth effects' (307, 1). His idea here is that science sutures the joint between knowledge and truth,

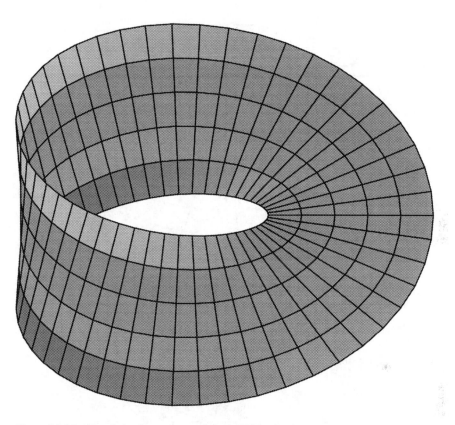

Figure 6.1 Moebius Strip. Image sourced from Wikipedia Commons.

something which is echoed later in the *Écrits* in the paper entitled 'Science and Truth'. There he states that the division between knowledge and truth is the essential division of the subject and that the subject of science has hitherto been the only thing that has joined these two together (727, 3). In discussing this idea he uses the Moebius strip to give it representation: just as how any point traced along the Moebius strip shares the same origin – it is neither top nor bottom – 'the division in which these two terms come together is not to be derived from a difference in origin' (727, 3). Given this, in the present paper he asks why we should not 'undertake a new operation' – that of psychoanalysis rather than science – 'where this joint remains gaping in our lives?' (307, 1).

In concluding his short paper Lacan opposes the topological models he had been using in his Seminar to present human subjectivity – the Moebius strip, the cross-cap, and the torus – to the model of the sphere in Antiquity. Just four months before the manuscript of the *Écrits* was sent to the printers in October 1966, Lacan was speaking to the audience of his Seminar on precisely this theme. There he told them that the difference between Antiquity's sphere and

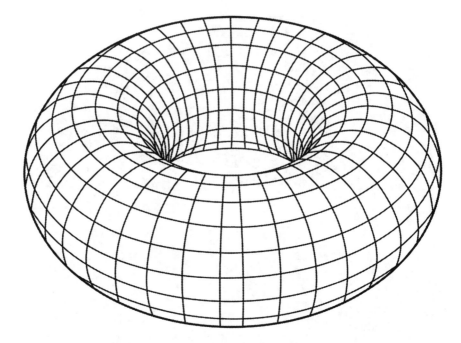

Figure 6.2 Torus. Image sourced from Wikipedia Commons.

the torus lies in the 'unrepresentable' hole in the latter and that this best represents object *a*, the object-cause of desire, because it shares the characteristic of having no specular or symbolic representation.[6] We can therefore understand why in the current paper Lacan claims that his purpose in using topology is to 'try to close in on that cause', a cause which is 'connected with a subject's formation' (306, 1).

At the very end of the article, we find the idea that *Ananke* is exercised *in* the *Logos*; or, destiny in discourse. Although Lacan would have been aware of Freud's use of the term *Ananke* to mean Necessity – and Bruce Fink's (2006) translator's footnote (793) tells us the same – the fact that Lacan refers here to 'great Necessity' suggests that it is more the subject's destiny which is at stake rather than simply that which is necessary. This is borne out by the connection Lacan makes to Freud's discovery that a repetition compulsion [*wiederholungszwang*] marks the subject's division. For Lacan, repetition points to what he calls an 'insistence' of the signifier (corresponding to *Logos* or discourse here), and one of the uses of topological models in his Seminar prior to this paper was to show that the continuous, non–orientable surfaces of the Moebius strip, the cross–cap, and the torus demonstrate how we should conceive of this repetition. In Seminar IX in 1962 for instance he described these models as being 'well designed to represent for us signifying insistence

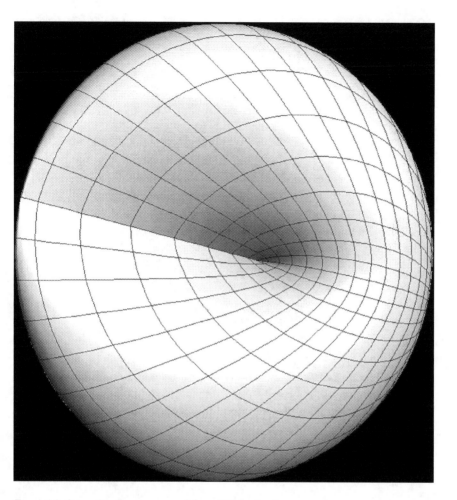

Figure 6.3 Cross-Cap. Image sourced from Wikipedia Commons.

and especially the insistence of repetitive demand' (session of 28th March 1962). This helps us to understand the paper's somewhat cryptic last line – the 'index' that commands repetition to continue corresponds to the *Logos* or this same insistence of the signifier.

Notes

1 *La Psychanalyse* was the journal of the Société Française de Psychanalyse and under Lacan's directorship served both as the mouthpiece for that group and the principle source of Lacan's published teaching prior to the *Écrits*. Its first issue featured Jean Hyppolite's commentary on Freud's 'Negation' paper, which Lacan references here, as well as Lacan's introduction and response to Hyppolite, which are reproduced in the

Écrits immediately after 'On a Purpose'. Other significant papers from the *Écrits* published first in *La Psychanalyse* include 'On a Question Prior to Any Possible Treatment of Psychosis' (volume 4), 'The Instance of the Letter in the Unconscious or Reason Since Freud' (volume 3), and 'The Function and Field of Speech and Language in Psychoanalysis' (volume 1). Its final edition was in 1964, though Lacan's final direct contribution was in 1962.

2 The Société Française de Psychanalyse (SFP) was the French psychoanalytic association created by Lacan and Daniel Lagache in 1953 as a reaction against what they perceived as the failures in the major French group of the time – the Société Psychanalytique de Paris (SPP) – to perform its role as a scientific organization furthering psychoanalytic research. However, following internal disputes around Lacan's own status as a training analyst of the SFP – the relinquishing of which would be the price of the group's approval by the organization Freud established, the International Psychoanalytic Association – the SFP was dissolved in 1963 and many of its former members followed Lacan to form the Ecole Freudienne de Paris (EFP) in 1964.

3 Session of 28th March 1962.

4 See Lacan's unpublished Seminar IX, session of the 30th May 1962.

5 See also the interview with Lacan in *L'Express*, May 1957, available at http://braungardt.trialectics.com/sciences/psychoanalysis/jacques-lacan/interview-jacques-lacan/

6 Session of 1st June 1966 in Lacan's unpublished Seminar XIII.

References

Fink, B. (2006) Translator's Endnotes. In J. Lacan (ed.) *Écrits: The First Complete Edition in English*, London: Norton.

Freud, S. (1898/1953) The Psychical Mechanism of Forgetfulness. In J. Strachey (ed.) *The Standard Edition of the Complete Psychological Works of Sigmund Freud, Vol 3*. London: The Hogarth Press and the Institute of Psycho-Analysis, pp. 287–298.

Freud, S. (1901/1953) The Psychopathology of Everyday Life. In S. Freud (1966–1974) (ed.) *The Standard Edition of the Complete Psychological Works of Sigmund Freud*. Trans. J. Strachey. London: Hogarth, vol. VI.

Freud, S. (1920/1953) Beyond the Pleasure Principle. In S. Freud (1966–1974) (ed.) *The Standard Edition of the Complete Psychological Works of Sigmund Freud*. Trans. J. Strachey. London: Hogarth, vol. XVIII.

Lacan, J. (1961–1962) *Le Séminaire IX, L'Identification*, unpublished.

Lacan, J. (1988) *The Seminar. Book I: Freud's Papers on Technique*. Trans. J. Forrester, ed. J.-A. Miller. Cambridge: Cambridge University Press.

Miller, J.A. (1988) A and a in Clinical Structures, Acts of the Paris-New York Psychoanalytic Workshop, 1988, reproduced at http://www.lacan.com/symptom6_articles/miller.html.

7

INTRODUCTION AND RESPONSE TO JEAN HYPPOLITE'S COMMENTARY ON FREUD'S "VERNEINUNG"

Russell Grigg

Context

These two chapters, 'Introduction to Jean Hyppolite's Commentary on Freud's "Verneinung"' and 'Response to Jean Hyppolite's Commentary on Freud's "Verneinung"', are the written-up versions of Lacan's introductory and concluding comments on a talk Hyppolite gave at Lacan's seminar on Freud's writings on technique on 10 February 1954 (Lacan, 1975/1988: chap. 5). Hyppolite's talk, given the year he was appointed director of the École normale supérieure, is published as an appendix in John Forrester's translation of this seminar (Lacan, 1975/1988: 289–297) and, in a revised translation, as 'A Spoken Commentary on Freud's "Verneinung" by Jean Hyppolite' (1966/2006) in *Écrits* (746–754). 'Introduction' and 'Response', as I shall refer to them, were initially published in the first issue of *La Psychanalyse*, the journal of the newly founded *Société Française de Psychanalyse*, on 1 January 1956. There are only minor editorial differences between the two versions of each text. The comments Lacan made at the seminar itself are, however, quite different from the published versions. For while Lacan gives the impression (317, fn. 1) that 'Introduction' and 'Response' are only slightly modified transcripts of the comments he made at the seminar, they were both in fact largely rewritten, particularly the latter, for publication in *La Psychanalyse*.

The context is a presentation by the philosopher Jean Hyppolite of one of Freud's most abstract and theoretical papers, 'Negation' (Freud, 1925/1961). As one would expect from such an eminent philosopher as Hyppolite, whose translation of and commentary on Hegel's *Phänomenologie* remain defining works, his paper is abstract and theoretical, philosophical rather than clinical. Yet despite this theoretical approach, Lacan has his eye very much on the clinical issues. This is in keeping with the theme of the seminar of that year,

DOI: 10.4324/9781003264231-7

Freud's papers on technique, and with another of Lacan's preoccupations at the time, namely his exploration of how psychoanalysis might best account for the differences between neurosis and psychosis – a question that would become the major theme of his 1955–1956 seminar which he entitled *The Psychoses* (Lacan, S3, 1955–1956) and the related text, 'On a Question Prior to Any Possible Treatment of Psychosis' (445–488).

These two chapters address three major topics, all clinical.

The first, which covers most of 'Introduction', is a discussion of resistance and its implications for technique, which was the topic for the first six weeks of Lacan's seminar that year, with Hyppolite's commentary and Lacan's introduction and response taking place in week five.

The second concerns the structural difference between neurosis and psychosis. Lacan refers to both 'Introduction' and 'Response' at his seminar on the psychoses on 16 November 1955 and 15 February 1956 (S3, 1955–1956: 12–13 and 149–151), which would have been around the time or shortly after he was working on these two chapters for publication as articles in *La Psychanalyse*. As this timing would suggest, there is overlap between the seminar on psychosis and the chapters, especially 'Response'. The timing might also explain why his response to Hyppolite's commentary at the seminar itself and the version subsequently published as 'Response' are so substantially different.

Indeed, it is in relation to the account of foreclosure developed in his seminar on the psychoses and in 'A Question Prior to the Possible Treatment of Psychosis' that 'Response' holds the most interest. Lacan traces Freud's use of the German term 'Verwerfung' to argue that even in Freud, for whom repression remains the basic mechanism at work in paranoid psychosis, there is evidence of a nascent alternative explanation for the phenomena of psychosis, so radically different from what we find in neurosis. And so, in 'Response' we see the beginnings of a crucial distinction between two separate structures: *Verdrängung*, repression, in neurosis and *Verwerfung*, foreclosure, in psychosis. However, what makes 'Response' of particular interest is that it is not merely a prelude to later developments on paranoid psychosis that form the central issue of inquiry in *Seminar III*, but is also specifically focused on the phenomenon of hallucination as such and thus complements the detailed treatment of *Verwerfung* in his seminar on the psychoses and 'On a Question Prior to Any Possible Treatment of Psychosis'. Hallucinations are certainly discussed in *Seminar III,* but only insofar as, or at least predominantly as, the hallucinations of a paranoid psychotic, Daniel Paul Schreber. In 'Response', on the other hand, the emphasis is on hallucinations in statu nascendi, which locates them more on the side of schizophrenia.

Along with the topic of foreclosure and psychosis in 'Response', Lacan discusses acting out in reference to a case previously presented by American ego psychologist Ernst Kris (Kris, 1951) – a case that, since Lacan, has come to be known as that of the 'fresh brains' man. In both texts, Lacan mounts a strong criticism of ego psychology, and while the critique that Lacan makes of ego psychology may seem outdated, even obsolete, more than half a century after Lacan first announced his return to Freud, the discussion remains significant for what it can still teach us about the important clinical matter of acting out and its relationship to interpretation. Kris's case, which Lacan discusses for the first time in *Seminar I*, has acquired something of an iconic status in Lacan's oeuvre, being mentioned in at least six of his seminars – most notably, his seminar on desire and its interpretation on 1 July 1959 (S6, 1958–1959: 471–486) and in his seminar on the logic of fantasy on 8 March 1967. The most important discussion of Kris's case in a text takes place in the *Écrits* chapter entitled 'The Direction of the Treatment and the Principles of Its Power' (500–503). The present chapter will briefly refer to some of the details in Lacan's discussion of Kris's case but I leave the broader discussion for the chapter on 'Direction of the Treatment'. I will, however, discuss the comparison made by Lacan between acting out, as in Kris's case, and hallucinations, as illustrated by Freud's case of the Wolf Man.

Overview

The significance of these papers is, then, threefold: the analysis of resistance and the critique of ego psychology's emphasis on interpreting the resistance; the knotting of Freud's paper on negation with the key concept of foreclosure, which Lacan introduces to account for the structural differences between neurosis and psychosis; and the phenomenon of acting out and its similarities with that of hallucination.

Discussion

I Introduction to Jean Hyppolite's commentary on Freud's *"Verneinung"*

The chapter opens (308, 1) with a reference to a major theme of Lacan's seminar of that year on Freud's writings on technique (Lacan, S1, 1953–1954: 19), namely the concept of resistance in the context of contemporary understanding of psychoanalytic technique.

The critique that ensues is directed at American ego psychology, one of the two major currents of psychoanalysis in Lacan's day, and whose three most significant theoreticians were Ernst Kris, Rudolph Loewenstein and Heinz Hartmann. This is not the place to go into a description of ego psychology, since it has been the subject of extensive discussion in the literature. Suffice it to say that Lacan, a regular reader of contemporary psychoanalytic journals, comments in *Seminar I* that these three authors 'propose theoretical principles which have very important technical applications', and tells his students that 'it is very interesting' for them to read the work of the ego psychologists since

195

they will be instructive for them as a 'very significant failure' (S1, 1953–1954: 25). Here he discusses an article by Ernst Kris (1951) that along with articles by Heinz Hartmann and Rudolph Loewenstein deals with interpretation from the perspective of ego psychology, which considered that the technique of analysis should proceed first and foremost by the interpretation of resistances. Lacan traces its 'failure' to an inadequate understanding of what resistance is.

This is the background against which Lacan (308, 2) claims that since Freud the psychoanalytic concept of resistance has become theoretically diluted, and that this is particularly concerning in light of the primacy Freud gave to the analysis of resistances. Understand that this is not a critique of analyzing resistance per se but rather a critique of how resistance is to be understood, and also note that the translation of the last sentence of this paragraph (308, 2) is misleading. The sense is that analysts (and he has Ernst Kris in his sights, as we see below) justify, on the basis of a particular order of priority, '*ordre d'urgence*', a technique that misunderstands what it is applied to, namely resistance. The allusion is to Kris's recommendation, which he takes to be Freud's, that 'analysis should start from the surface, and that resistance be analyzed before interpreting content' (1951, 16), which is to establish a particular order of priority in interpretation: resistance first, and only then unconscious content. But, Lacan maintains, this is a technical principle that follows from an impoverished theory that fails to recognize the 'dialectic' (309, 1) immanent in psychoanalytic practice. What this means for Lacan is that the resistance encountered by an analyst does not exist prior to the encounter but is the effect of the analyst's very interpretation. Ego psychology's mistake is to think that resistance implies that there is something – an unacceptable thought, an undesirable desire – that the subject withholds in the analysis. Of course, free association is inherently an impossible task and there are always things that are held back. But analytic interpretation has to be viewed as dialectical because it is capable of creating something that was not there before.

There is a risk, Lacan writes (308, 3), that the guidelines for psychoanalysis become rigid formulas rather than indications for the technique that are based on an understanding of the 'truth' of the analytic experience; Freud had this understanding, and we too can achieve it through the work he left us. There are those, on the other hand, who hide behind the primacy of technique by appealing to supposed 'advances' in the technique that derive from nothing more than 'dumbed-down' versions of analytic concepts.[1] To put this remark in context, at this time American psychoanalysts were beginning to publish handbooks on psychoanalytic technique[2] in the belief that the findings of psychoanalysis could be gathered together in a manual for use by practitioners.

In what follows Lacan teases out the implications of neglecting the fact that psychoanalysis is a dialectical process in the above sense. He begins with a critique of how resistance is understood and then broadens the discussion out to criticize other technical issues. Having lost the special sense in which Freud uses the term 'resistance', and rather than reflect on the nature of resistance,

Lacan says (309, 2), psychoanalysts have resorted to using the term in its ev-eryday sense. Taking 'to resist' to be a transitive verb, analysts ask what it is that their patients are resisting, and conclude that they must be resisting their 'tendencies', which manifest themselves both in their neurosis and in their resistance to avowing them to their analyst. Moreover, Lacan continues, the analyst encounters this presumed resistance in the analysis and quite naturally concludes that the patient is being defensive. But 'defense' is yet another term that is currently misunderstood in analytic circles, the modern practitioner being unaware of the use Freud makes of the term for whom a defense is integral to the formation of a symptom.[3]

Lacan (309, 3) considers an objection to his criticism of the ego psychol-ogists: by focusing at the lowest level of the confusion over the very idea of resistance, don't you, Lacan, his imaginary critic asks, succumb to critiquing them for what they think rather than for what they do?[4] Lacan responds by pointing out that the 'precepts' they employ do nothing to remedy the consequences of the original confusion over their technique. Lacan (309, 3–310, 1) then illustrates this point with six examples of these precepts:

1   Understand that a subject can communicate only about his ego and via his ego (a thesis in which we see the return of 'common sense')
2   The aim of the analysis is to reinforce the ego, or at least its healthy part (and heads nod in agreement)
3   Use this blueprint for how to proceed with the analytic material (with the readymade, certified plans in our pocket)
4   Interpret from the surface to the depths[5]
5   Analyse aggressiveness
6   Leave the dynamics of anxiety to the end.

Lacan (310, 2) references Freud's *Studies on Hysteria* in which Freud speaks of three different 'stratifications' of resistance in the analysand's discourse. Around a pathogenic nucleus of ideas, there is a rich threefold stratification of ideas. There are the 'longitudinal' strata which follow the diachronic unfolding chain of the analysand's discourse in which memories occur in reverse chronological order; the 'concentric' strata, where ideas are organized con-centrically around the nucleus and the distance from the nucleus is in indirect proportion to the resistance the ideas encounter; and the third strata in which signifiers are linked thematically by their content, overlap one another and vary radially from the nucleus (Breuer and Freud, 1893–1895/1955: 288–290). The metaphor of the musical score, famously used by Lévi-Strauss (Lévi-Strauss, 1978) in his work on myth, is an addition of Lacan's. This passage from Freud was mentioned in Lacan's seminar three weeks before Hyppolite made his presentation (S1, 1953–1954: 22), but the commentary from 'some time ago' is no doubt a reference to the extended discussion in 'The Function and Field of Speech and Language in Psychoanalysis' (240ff).

Lacan (310, 3) now turns to his own understanding of resistance and, re-jecting out of hand any 'mechanistic' reading of Freud, characterizes (310, 4) resistance in terms of truth. This could almost be a definition: resistance is the phenomenon that structures every revelation of truth in dialogue. The translation has 'psychoanalytic dialogue', but in speaking in terms of truth Lacan intends to include *all* dialogue, psychoanalytic or not. In fact, we see that this paragraph emphasizes the continuity between the phenomena of repression analyzed by Freud and 'all censorship of social origin'. Hence Lacan's remark that repression is a 'discordance' (continuing the musical metaphor) between signifier and signified that allows the truth to be expressed 'between the lines' – a reference to a work by Leo Strauss (1952, the date in *Écrits* is incorrect) on persecution and the art of writing which Lacan cites again in 'The Instance of the Letter in the Unconscious, or Reason Since Freud' (423, 7). Strauss speaks of writing 'between the lines' as the writer's way of expressing his meaning covertly when faced with persecution should he speak openly. This is how Strauss puts it:

> Persecution, then, gives rise to a peculiar technique of writing, and therewith to a peculiar type of literature, in which the truth about all crucial things is presented *exclusively between the lines*. That literature is addressed, not to all readers, but to trustworthy and intelligent readers only. It has all the advantages of private communication without having its greatest disadvantage-that it reaches only the writer's acquaintances. It has all the advantages of public communication without having its greatest disadvantage-capital punishment for the author. But how can a man perform the miracle of speaking in a publication to a minority, while being silent to the majority of his readers?...An author who wishes to address only thoughtful men has but to write in such a way that only a very careful reader can detect the meaning of his book.
>
> (Strauss, 1952: 25, emphasis added)

The remark that 'truth is identical to the symbols that reveal it' (310, 4) entails that truth is expressed in and through signifiers, which anyone who wishes to make the truth known can take advantage of. Lacan then makes the important, even crucial claim that the 'true' subject (310, 5), the subject of the un-conscious, 'proceeds no differently' from Strauss's writer in expressing his truth through his symptoms; that is, not only are his symptoms expressed in sig-nifiers but also in the form of speech addressed to the Other, which is not a person but a place, a 'locus' required by the structure of discourse. As an analysis unfolds, the analyst comes to be situated increasingly in the place of the Other, the place to which the message is addressed, and thus becomes the receiver of the subject's discourse, including the 'language of his symptoms' (310, 5). The transference emerges as the moment at which the analyst comes to be situated in the place of the Other. As Lacan states in his 1957 text 'Psychoanalysis and its Teaching', 'It is only owing to the place of the Other that the analyst can receive the investiture of the transference that qualifies him to play his legitimate role in the subject's unconscious' (379, 6). And a direct consequence of the fact that the language of the subject's symptoms is 'not so much deciphered by the analyst' as 'more and more solidly addressed to him' is that in the transference the major lines of the symptoms become both sharper and increasingly intensified.

The effect of an analysis depends on the extent to which the 'empty discourse' (311, 2) at the beginning evolves, under and through the transference, to the point where the subject's words approximate the truth expressed by his symptoms. The emphasis here is on the verb 'approximate', for the trajectory is at best asymptotic in that his words will only ever approach a limit; there will always remain a gap between the truth of the symptom and what the subject is capable of putting into words. As we see below, Lacan understands that the existence of this gap is the source of resistance. I would therefore speculate that when Lacan says that the formulation that the truth can only ever be approximated is 'of more general import' than that concerning repression, it is because the role censorship plays in the latter is not of universal application.

In the analysis, then, the subject will approach the limit of what he can put into words – and this is the point at which resistance emerges, 'linked to the psychoanalytic dialogue' (311, 3) in the form of a word, phrase or 'trait' that is specifically addressed to you, the analyst, by the analysand in his utterances on the couch. The resistance 'punctuates' his speech; his words 'tilt' (bascule) towards the presence of the analyst.

As Lacan describes it (313, 4), this is no ordinary presence, however. It has the three following features:

1   it is the 'purest relationship a subject can have with a being', all the more deeply felt the less qualified he takes this being to be;
2   it is no longer veiled by the everyday discourse, conventions and beliefs of the 'they' (the term refers to Heidegger's concept of '*das Man*'); and
3   it is characterized by a pause, or 'suspensive scansion', in discourse frequently accompanied by a moment of anxiety.[6]

It is, Lacan considers (311, 6), usually a mistake to ask what these thoughts are, unless one knows what to expect in reply; and it is even a stupid mistake, though one commonly made, to ask for the express purpose of allowing the subject to give voice to his aggressiveness towards the analyst.

At this point (311, 7–312, 2), Lacan is stating in clear terms that resistance is imaginary: it is an 'ego phenomenon', and one of the purest forms of this phenomenon that we encounter in analysis. The thought to hold onto at this point is that the ego is constituted, in these imaginary captures, 'by another and for another' (312, 1), and that this ego-other imaginary relationship has the feature of alienation that Hegel discerned in the famous 'master-slave' dialectic. The lesson for the analyst is that in the transference he will be the support, or the 'prop', for the subject's alter ego; and this is why analyzing the resistance is imaginary and will have profound effects in the imaginary register.

The unnamed 'colleague' Lacan mocks (312, 3) for observing that a primary condition for analysis is that the subject 'have some sense of the existence of the other' is Sacha Nacht. See Nacht and Lebovici (1956). Incidentally, Lacan makes several, invariably scornful references to Sacha Nacht in *Écrits*, whom he sometimes refers to as 'Midas', and nowhere refers to him by name.[7]

Lacan (312, 4) ridicules Nacht's claim on two grounds. First, since there is no ego without other, the issue is what sort of otherness is at stake; and second, if there is anything that will satisfy the demand for prior knowledge concerning what will help orientate the analysis at the outset, it is knowing what, for each neurotic structure, are the ego's 'alibis', a word which Lacan uses with a meaning it carries in French, but not in English, of special pleading, excuse, pretext, or specious justification. In this sense, then, 'alibis' are defensive strategies of the ego.

And so, Lacan continues (312, 5–6), the moment when associations stop becomes a crucial moment at which the imaginary and reciprocal access of ego to other emerges – which is why the questions who is speaking and to whom are one and the same. But the moment also allows the possibility of opening up a question concerning the imaginary place the subject occupies, for the place is not the same for every neurotic. A suitable 'punctuation', or interpretation, would be one in which imaginary and symbolic overlap, where analysis of the resistance, which is an ego function, and analysis of unconscious material coincide. These remarks take us back to (312, 6) and answer the question of how to respond to the subject's silences. To give a concrete example of such a moment in an analysis, consider the moment in the case of the Rat Man when the latter is in agony in his attempt to recount to Freud the details of the repugnant rat torture that the cruel captain had delighted in relating to him. The Rat Man, unable to finish his account, gets up from the sofa and implores Freud to spare him the agony of continuing. Freud writes,

> I assured him that I myself had no taste whatever for cruelty, and certainly had no desire to torment him, but that naturally I could not grant him something which was beyond my power. He might as well ask me to give him the moon. The overcoming of resistances was a law of the treatment, and on no consideration could it be dispensed with.
>
> (Freud, 1909/1955: 166)

As simple as this response is, it sits perfectly at the juncture of the symbolic and the imaginary at a moment of great distress for the analysand. Freud seizes the significance of the imaginary dimension and reassures the Rat Man that he has no reason to attribute the sadism of the cruel captain to Freud, while at the same time he invokes the symbolic framework of the analytic set-up by reminding the Rat Man of the rule of free association by which both analyst and analysand are bound.

Lacan (312, 7–313, 2) contrasts his approach with that in which the immediate assumption is that the subject's silence is a sign of his aggressiveness towards the analyst, even a result of his need for love. His response is to say that this is ho-hum, since where words are expected the silence of the speaker, and even more so the silence of the analyst, produces the field of 'violence' even without – particularly without – one's intervention. This is to be taken as a guideline for analytic intervention. Silence of and by itself produces a 'sense of the other' in the imaginary mode and so provokes aggression as an imaginary reaction to the 'presence' of the other. And this is something, says Lacan, that you will, or should, learn to handle in supervision. It is entirely predictable that, by interpreting the analysand's aggression towards you and even the 'need for love' it conceals, you will expose the subject's defensive strategies. This is to be expected because in the realm of the imaginary, when 'speech gives up', the ego's relationship to the other is dominated by aggression. See Theses II and III of 'Aggressiveness in Psychoanalysis' (82–101) for a detailed analysis of the place of aggressiveness in the clinical setting.

In reading the two paragraphs on Clausewitz (313, 3–4), it seems that Lacan has possibly embraced a widespread confusion over Clausewitz's ideas about 'total' and 'absolute' war (Clausewitz, 1832/1976). The notion of total war describes an armed conflict that mobilizes the entire available resources of a state, including its population as well as its economic, political and legal systems, where everything is subordinated to the single aim of military victory over the enemy. 'Absolute war' on the other hand refers to war as an ideal type in which it is pursued to its logical, 'absolute' limit free of the moderating effects imposed on it by the demands of politics, society and the material realities of the situation. As it happens, because actual wars invariably rely upon political decisions and economic realities, absolute war is impossible in practice. And thus, contrary to Lacan here, war is never purely in command because it is an extension of political expedients.

If the above comments are correct, then these paragraphs (313, 3–4), which are difficult to understand, might be read in the following way. I stress that what follows are some speculative remarks on what these two paragraphs mean.

First, it is unclear what the 'social warfare' is, but if in the present context we take Lacan's comments to be a metaphor for the analytic experience (and there are many places where Freud employs military metaphors), then we might say that the fact of engaging in the analysis will lead to moments of imaginary 'battle' that the analyst must learn to recognize. They are moments in which the adversary becomes something different from, 'other than', what he was – that is, no longer a subject of speech but an imaginary object in a dual relationship – and at these moments it is crucial that the analyst keep in mind the overall 'stakes' that will ultimately enable a fair and 'equitable' outcome in the place of ongoing imaginary, and thus irresolvable, claims.

Two passages in Lacan support this reading. The first is the reference (313, 7) to Freud's battle metaphor where each move in an analysis is to be considered in relation to the subject's overall strategy. The second occurs in Lacan's seminar on 17 February 1954, which is one week after Hyppolite's presentation and Lacan's introduction and reply, in which Lacan is discussing Anna Freud's position on 'the analysis of the defences'. Lacan says (S1, 1953–1954: 65),

> Anna Freud started by interpreting the analytic relation in accordance with the prototype of the dual [imaginary] relation, which is the relation of the subject to her mother....This path would not take her very far. She should have distinguished between the dual interpretation, in which the analyst enters into an ego-to-ego rivalry with the analysand, and the interpretation which moves forward in the direction of the symbolic structuration of the subject, which is to be located beyond the present structure of his ego.

This naturally leads to the observation that 'the most effective response to a defense is not to bring to bear upon it the test of strength' (314, 2); that is, not just *a* response, but *the most effective* response. Why? First, because to do otherwise is not just less effective but squarely ineffective and, second, because a defense is a demand, and to respond to demand, even negatively, is to alter the dialectic of speech in such a way that the desire becomes adulterated.

This concludes the discussion from 313, 5 to 314, 1 and opens some considerations on defenses.

Lacan calls the analysis of the defenses a 'pedantic form of suggestion' (314, 3) because it invites its practitioners to want to 'have the last word', and consider the protest or skepticism of their analysands as various forms of defensive resistance to their interventions.

Incidentally, the phrase, 'why his daughter is mute' (314, 3) alludes to Molière's *Le médecin malgré lui*, *The doctor in spite of himself*, and the sentence, '*Voilà pourquoi votre fille est muette*', 'And that's why your daughter is mute' (Molière, 1914, p. 22), which in Molière's play is a vacuous expression that concludes a verbose and incomprehensible speech employed as a pseudo and obscure explanation intended to cut short any further discussion.

Lacan's point is that the analysis of defenses invites the analyst to unload responsibility for the purported lack of progress in the analysis back onto the analysand. This is captured very nicely by Z★ in *Seminar I* who says (Sem 1, 26), 'I believe that, from the clinical point of view, the notion of resistance clearly represents an experience that we all encounter at some time or another with almost all the patients in our practices – he is resisting and it makes me furious'. Z★'s declaration fits well the characterization of the 'dialectic of the ego and the other' (314, 4) that matches the analysand's situation in the analysis to the analyst's prejudicial view about his 'ill will'.

It is possible to see in this imaginary aggressiveness of the analyst the true lining of the famous *furor sanandi*, or rage to heal, described by Freud as a universal inclination of the curing class, and which explains Lacan's remark that 'there is no other resistance in analysis than that of the analyst'. This is such a significant factor, Lacan thinks, that this 'biased belief', or prejudice, is essentially what the conditions of training analysis boil down to. Training analysis involves a 'true dialectical conversion' *of the analyst* that can only be maintained through ongoing practice. Note that this is consistent with Lacan's later views, right down to his final text, 'Preface to the English Edition of *Seminar XI*' (Lacan, 1977/2018), in which Lacan asserts that there is no such thing as a born analyst; in the present context the observation is that, if we are born to anything, we are born into a relationship to the other that is antithetical to the place of an analyst. It is for this reason that Lacan maintains that there is something ascetic about the place of a psychoanalyst. As he says in 'Function and Field' (264, 4), this place requires a 'long subjective ascesis' that never ends because 'the end of training analysis is not separable from the subject's engagement in his practice'.

This moment at which the resistance manifests itself transparently in the transference is also apparent in other forms of 'syncope', as Lacan calls them (315, 4–6), referring to other contexts in which the absence or omission of words is comparable to the analysand's reticence on the couch. He gives two examples: a dream and the forgetting of names.

In his *Introductory Lectures on Psychoanalysis*, Freud (1915–1916/1961, 118), refers to a patient who retains just a single word of a dream, 'channel', to which she has no associations; but in her next session the following day, she recalls the witticism about the Frenchman who, when the Englishman quoted the saying, 'Du sublime au ridicule il n'y a qu'un pas', responds, 'Yes, the Pas de Calais', which is the region of France bordering the English Channel. This delayed association to the dream betrayed the skepticism about Freud's theories that lay, as Freud says, 'concealed behind [her] ostensible admiration' (1916–1917/1961: 119). The dream is discussed in *Seminar I* (S1, 1953–1954: 45–46). At the moment of resistance, manifest in her inability to follow the fundamental rule, Freud's presence rises up in her reluctance to reveal her true thoughts. Lacan (315, 6–7) links this case of forgetting arising from the presence in the imaginary of the other to the second, more famous case of forgetting: the 'Signorelli' example from Freud's *The Psychopathology of Everyday Life*. It relates to an incident in Freud's own life, his forgetting of the name 'Signorelli' while on a train trip to Bosnia-Herzegovina, which at the time was under Austro-Hungarian administration. I refer you to Freud's discussion of the example in *The Psychopathology of Everyday Life* (1901/1960: 1–7) for the necessary background to Lacan's analysis, which I discuss below. While in conversation with a fellow train traveler, Freud engages in an act of deliberate, conscious self-censorship (316, 1) when he refrains from pursuing a discussion whose themes he feels are too delicate to broach with a stranger, touching as they do on matters of sex and death, particularly in relation to Freud's capacity as physician and psychoanalyst. Then, turning to other, apparently more innocuous topics, such as the frescoes in the cathedral of Orvieto, Freud is unable to recall the name of the painter, Signorelli, even though he knows it very well. It is not just that the themes are delicate, but that they are also matters of deeply personal significance for Freud. Lacan discusses this example in similar terms in *Seminar I* (S1, 1953–1954: 46–49) and there is an important and detailed discussion of it in Chapters 2 and 3 of *Formations of the Unconscious* (Lacan, 1998/2017).

The suppression of the theme of death and sex, especially sexual impotence, led to the transient repression of the proper name, 'Signorelli'. Or, as Lacan puts it, by ceasing any further discussion with his counterpart in the train, Freud left the excised 'broken half...of the sword of speech' in his 'partner' (316, 1), that is, his imaginary semblable. In actual fact, it is not the entire name 'Signorelli' that disappears but only 'Signor', while '-elli' is retained in the name 'Botticelli', which comes to Freud's mind even as he is aware that it is not the right one. One should bear in mind that in Italian 'Signor', like the German 'Herr', is not merely an honorific equivalent to the English 'Sir' but is also used as the name of God, comparable to 'Lord' in English. And it is these words that form a syncope in Freud's thought and conversation. As Lacan will emphasize in *Formations of the Unconscious*, even if the names 'Botticelli' and 'Boltraffio' come to mind, there is initially a gap, a hole in discourse, around the name of our Lord on the topic of death. The structure of the phenomenon is identical to that of the stoppage that occurs in the associations of an analysand and which Lacan, following Freud, analyzed as resistance: the presence of a 'semblable' causes interference with the symbolic exchange via discourse. This is how we can understand Lacan's remark that 'the man who breaks the bread of truth with his semblable in the act of speech shares a lie' (316, 3). The situation is expressed in a minimalist form in the diagram known as Schema L. See, e.g. Lacan (S3, 1955–1956: 14) (Figure 7.1).

As we can see, the 'axis of poles' being 'crossed by a second dimension' which is 'not repressed but...a lure' (316, 6) is a precise reference to the symbolic and its interference by the imaginary.

Yet Lacan wonders whether this turning away from the topic of death in a conversation with a stranger in a train, and the consequent repression of 'signification', as he calls it, is the whole story (316, 4). He suggests that something has been 'excised' and not merely repressed. Now, the term 'excised' is the translation of '*retranché*' which reappears in Lacan's response to Hyppolite, where it is stated that '*retranché*' is how he chooses to translate Freud's '*Verwerfung*' (322, 7). Freud's term '*Verwerfung*' will subsequently be translated as the more familiar '*forclusion*', 'foreclosure', which, as Lacan explains, is a different mechanism from *Verdrängung*, repression, and will become

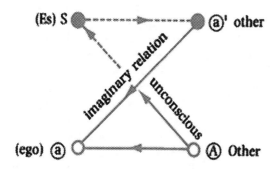

Figure 7.1 L-Schema. Image sourced from *Écrits: The Complete Edition* by Jacques Lacan (2006) © W.W. Norton & Company.

the central concept in Lacan's account of the mechanism underlying psychosis. See, above all, the seminar on the psychoses (Lacan, S3, 1955–1956) and the corresponding article, 'On a Question Prior to Any Possible Treatment of Psychosis', in *Écrits*.

Lacan (316, 4) then mentions the 'excised' speech, which consisted in the thoughts that Freud refrained from uttering about the striking anecdote according to which Turks place a higher value on sexual enjoyment than on anything else, and about how, in his experience, sexual disorders are likely to plunge them into despair in contrast with their resignation towards the threat of death (Freud, 1901/1960: 3). 'Being-toward-death' is possibly an allusion to what Freud called primal repression. Freud came to the view that repression proper, or secondary repression, in which material is rejected from consciousness, cannot occur unless there is repressed material already in the unconscious that has never been conscious and that acts to draw the repressed material to it. It seems that 'being-toward-death' is the name that Lacan gives here to this primal repression. Of course, 'Being-toward-death' is also a key concept in the philosophy of Heidegger, introduced in his 1927 *Being and Time* (Heidegger, 1953/1962, 279–311). But the term in Lacan should be regarded as a mere appropriation, rather than an indication of the significant influence of the philosopher on Lacan. There is no indication that Lacan ever embraced Heidegger's concept, with its threefold aspect of being-toward-death as non-relational, not to be out-stripped and unable to be understood through the death of others (Heidegger, 1953/1962, 299). Moreover, the term appears in *Écrits* in only one other text, 'Function of Field of Speech and Language in Psychoanalysis', where the mention is again brief and only vaguely Heideggerian. In the present context, the reference to 'being-toward-death' should, in my view, be understood as a gesture towards what will later become more apparent to Lacan as the inseparable link between sex and death. See, for one instance among many, his comment in *The Four Fundamental Concepts of Psychoanalysis*: 'The drive is profoundly a death drive and represents in itself the portion of death in the sexed living being' (Lacan, S11, 1973/1977: 205).

The final paragraphs of 'Introduction' (316, 5–326, 4) are Lacan's segue into Hyppolite's commentary on Freud's 'Negation' (Freud, 1925/1961: 235–239). Lacan mentions the relationship of death to negation, negativity and nonbeing, not in categorical terms but in terms that, because framed as questions, are at this point to be considered speculative and to be elaborated in what follows.

The tessera that Lacan mentions (316, 6) is the *tessera hospitalis* or *symbolum* that in Roman society was the material token of a sworn and sacred social bond of mutual hospitality between two parties and a guarantee to offer protection and support to one another in circumstances such as a court of law. The obligation was hereditary and for this purpose a die was often cast, broken in two and a part kept by each of the parties, potentially for later use by their descendants. It is a 'primordial image' in that it is one of the simplest symbols of a pact as well as being a concrete image of the Other. The second dimension referred to is the imaginary relationship, whose essential feature is one of being deceived by, primarily, the lure of an image or a decoy. The crossing of the dimensions (316, 6) refers to the crossing of the symbolic and imaginary axes in Schema L, above.

Let me make two minor comments and one more significant one on the discussion up to this point (316). The two minor comments are these: first, Lacan refers to the repression of 'signification' (316, 1). He will subsequently speak more accurately of the repression of signifiers. And second, the distinction between suppression, *Unterdrückung*, a more or less voluntary and deliberate act, and the unconscious mechanism of repression, *Verdrängung*, is drawn more sharply in later discussions such as in *Formations of the Unconscious* (S5, 1957–1958: 32).

The more important comment is that Lacan's remarks in this section are informed by his longstanding and enduring view that the presence of the analyst – and by extension the presence of any semblable – is a form of resistance. This is a view he will always maintain. In his very last written document, for instance, Lacan writes of resistance as the 'mirage of truth', from which 'only lies can be expected' (Lacan, 1977/2018: 25).

The text ends with some generous comments towards Hyppolite and an invitation for him to address the seminar.

What is most significant in this chapter is the analysis of resistance in terms of the difference between the symbolic and the imaginary. Resistance is analyzed as a form of interference by the imaginary in the symbolically mediated relationship to the Other. Because resistance is imaginary, it is an 'ego phenomenon' (311, 7). Moreover, while resistance is a concept that comes out of the experience of psychoanalysis, it is not confined to the clinical setting. The discussion of Freud's example of the forgetting of the name Signorelli demonstrates the continuity between resistance in a banal conversation with a casual stranger on a train and the intimate exchange between analysand and analyst in the consulting room. By contrast, there is no resistance from the unconscious, 'there is only a tendency to repeat' (Lacan, 1978/1988: 321). One should therefore avoid interpreting the resistance at the level of the ego, of ego-to-ego. To do so is to engage in a Hegelian struggle for prestige and mastery, the only possible conclusion of which is either submission or mastery, in other words, a deadlock in the imaginary ensnared, as he will say in 'The Freudian Thing', in 'the effects of prestige in which the ego asserts itself' (361, 3).

This position should, however, be viewed in the light of other remarks by Lacan that do not change but qualify the position adumbrated here. We should in particular bear in mind the comment made above, and often repeated, that 'there is no other resistance in analysis than that of the analyst' (314, 4, but also see, e.g. 497, 9; Lacan, 1978/1988: 228; Lacan, 1981/1993: 48), which I have already commented on. It should be borne in mind when considering Lacan's comments on analyzing the resistance in this chapter that the discussion is in part a polemic against ego psychology and his remarks should not be taken as an unreserved recommendation against interpreting resistance.

II Response to Jean Hyppolite's commentary on Freud's "Verneinung"

In the opening remarks of his response, Lacan (318, 1–3) thanks Hyppolite and then observes that, as Hyppolite has made clear, Freud's 'Negation' conveys a 'new emergence of truth', and that for this reason it is not to be read simply for what we can learn about the life and work of Sigmund Freud. To read it as a literary or historical text would be, he says, little more than a form of resistance.

Why does this amount to resistance? And what is being resisted? It amounts to resistance because a historical or literary reading would ignore the relevance of Freud's discoveries to the practice of psychoanalysis for Lacan and his contemporaries. We might note that Lacan's 'return to Freud' was a reaction to the banalisation of Freud's discoveries and to the growing tendency to treat Freud as a historical figure and read accordingly, and that this had contributed to a kind of repression of the truth of Freud's discoveries. What is being re-sisted is the challenges to the prejudices, mentioned above, that all analysts have by virtue of being human beings who, like the rest of humanity, live and breathe in the company of others. When Lacan (316, 3) says, 'The man who breaks the bread of truth with his semblable in the act of speech shares a lie', he includes analysts, and as these prejudices need to be challenged continuously, submitting Freud to 'our exegesis' should always be one of the components of our training. As we see, Lacan gives Freud's work a singular status, further describing it as '*une veritable parole*', with the connotation of 'true word' as in the true word of a prophet, 'true speech' as opposed to the din of empty talk.

To give Freud's work this place it has to be interpreted and interpreted using the same 'principles of comprehension' (319, 1) that the work itself carries. What these principles are Lacan does not say, but we can be confident that they are consistent with the 'transpsychological' nature of psychoanalysis. Lacan returns to the theme of the place Freud's work occupies in the training of analysts and remarks (319, 2) that Freud's texts are necessary reading for any prospective analyst as they expose him to a register without which even his own analysis is insufficient. As he adds (319, 3), the issue is that the analyst must be up to the task of grasping 'man' at the level at which an analyst operates and responds to the analysand. Moreover, he has to assume total responsibility for this task; no medical (or other) qualification or appeal to clinical experience can guarantee this.

Lacan then (319, 6) turns directly to Freud's 'Negation' (Freud, 1925/1961). He stresses the significance of the subject's introduction to a particular type of negation through *Bejahung*, or affirmation, as it is translated in the *Standard Edition*. The introduction of a subject to the concept of negation makes possible a fundamental distinction between being and reality. The allusion to Heidegger in the following paragraph (319, 7) suggests that 'being' is to be understood in the Heideggerian sense of the grounds of the possibility for the subject's 'opening' onto the domain of what can be thought or experienced, that is, reality. Being is not reality; it is what makes reality possible. Or, for Heidegger, being is what makes the world capable of being understood; it is the condition for any possible experience of the world.

In the allusion to Heidegger, Lacan (319, 7) observes – and this is a rare observation for Lacan – that Freud was 'far ahead of his time' and lacks nothing 'compared with the most recent aspects of philosophical reflection'. Because Freud arrives at this position on the basis of his clinical experience, and certainly not on the basis of a meditation on being and the 'deconstruction' of philosophy, which Freud never studied, it would be an aberration to say that Freud 'anticipates' the modern developments in the 'philosophy of existence' – the reference is to Lacan's contemporaries, the philosophers Maurice Merleau-Ponty (See Merleau-Ponty, 1945/1962) and Jean-Paul Sartre (1943/1984). Lacan places himself on the side of Merleau-Ponty in whose work the 'repercussions' of Heidegger's far-reaching meditation on being are uncovered, while in Sartre's they are, he believes, covered over.

These elliptical comments are further explained by the following paragraph (319, 8) in which Lacan says that Freud, on the basis of his clinical experience, is doing nothing more than raising anew the general questions that philosophy, more specifically metaphysics, has been interested in from the outset and to which Heidegger's philosophy has brought important clarification. Lacan concludes this reflection on Freud and philosophy by pointing out (320, 1) that for Freud, it was the issues arising from the clinical experience that frequently brought him back to what in philosophy takes the form of metaphysics.

'Metaphysics' is not a common term in Lacan's lexicon, and it mostly has negative connotations. Here, however, it is clearly laudatory, intended to convey that Freud's reflections are profoundly original and philosophical. Hyppolite himself is struck by this, even surprised by it. In his commentary (748, 4), he speaks of Freud's 'extreme philosophical subtlety' and of finding 'something truly extraordinary' that is 'of prodigious philosophical import' in Freud. Meanwhile, Lacan contrasts (320, 2) the profundity of Freud's thought with the superficial analysis of affects by the proponents of the 'new psychoanalysis', which almost certainly refers to Klein and the object-relations school. The problem as he sees it is that 'affect' has become a *qualitas occulta*, an obscure, hidden and unanalysable force, that leads to 'the notorious opposition between the intellectual and the affective', as he puts it in a helpful discussion in the seminar on Freud's papers on technique (Lacan, S1, 1953–1954: 57). The implication is that affects are experienced passively, occur spontaneously and are non-rational and possibly innate responses. The classic position on this view of affects is presented in Susan Isaacs' article on 'The Nature and Function of Phantasy' (Isaacs, 1948), which was republished in *New Directions in Psychoanalysis* in 1955 (Klein, Heimann, and Money-Kyrle, 1955), the year before the publication of 'Introduction' and 'Response'. Isaacs's paper was an explicit statement of Klein's views on fantasy, which she defines as 'the primary content of unconscious mental processes' and 'the mental corollary, the psychic representative, of instinct' (Isaacs, 1948, 81). According to Isaacs, unconscious fantasies are the mainspring and originary content of the unconscious. They include very early, prelinguistic forms of thought and are primarily experienced as nonverbal, visceral sensations and impulses. Unconscious fantasy includes the earliest forms of infantile thought and is the mainspring, the original and essential content of the unconscious mind.

Bruce Fink adds two variant translations of the paragraph (320, 3) in his 'Translator's Endnotes' (797, 2). I prefer a slight variant on the second: 'In this text by Freud, the affective is conceived of as what preserves the effects of a primordial symbolisation right down to the discursive structuration...', which I think makes more sense in the context. Lacan already has the concept of foreclosure in mind here and the discussion is laying the ground for its introduction. Also in the background is Lacan's explicit intention to demonstrate the relevance to Freud's work of his own distinction between imaginary, real and symbolic, and this of course has to be read into his analysis of 'Negation', given that Freud never thought in these terms.

What Lacan here calls 'intellectual' is not the polar opposite of the 'affective', but is a type of *Aufhebung* of the affective, which is preserved in the new, symbolic form of its negation. This is to follow the logic of Freud's account of "*Verneinung*" – which is *both* a negation *and* a disavowal – in which both 'yes' and 'no' function in ways that are interwoven. This means that this 'affective' continues to assert itself from inside the actual negations of conscious thought. The affective thus plays a role that is essential to negation, which is included in the destructive death drive whose origins lie in the affective. Hence Lacan's remark that the effects of a 'primordial symbolisation' are preserved 'right down to the discursive structuration' (320, 3). This primordial symbolization is only accessible through the intermediary of its effects, which arise at the intersection with the reality into which it, the primordial symbolization, expels what it has rejected. Primordial symbolization remains inassimilable to conscious thought and expelled from the ego insofar as the ego has put imaginary mechanisms of misrecognition in place. It is clear that the question of *Verwerfung* is on the horizon.

Lacan turns (320, 7) to two 'examples' to demonstrate to psychoanalysts and psychoanalysts in training attending his seminar what clarification the concepts of the imaginary, symbolic and real can bring to psychoanalysis – the first with respect to psychopathological 'structures', the second concerning some issues specific to the technique in clinical work.

The question of hallucination is first raised (320, 8–9) in connection with the excellent phenomenological study of hallucination in Maurice Merleau-Ponty's *The Phenomenology of Perception* (1945/1962), which is touched on again in *Seminar 3, The Psychoses* (Lacan, S3, 1955–1956: 74). Lacan is impressed by the 'displacement' of the question of hallucinations that Merleau-Ponty produced on the basis of a painstaking and detailed exploration of the psychiatric literature. He shows, in particular, that the approach which considers a hallucination a perception without an object is far too naïve and does not even do justice to the observable facts. However, there remains the problem that for phenomenology hallucinations are considered from the point of view of consciousness. And this is its ultimate stumbling block. Take, for example, the 'counterfeiting of consciousness' (320, 9), which refers to the assumption that it is consciousness that generates a hallucination, whereas a hallucination comes to the subject from the exterior and imposes itself upon his consciousness. Referring to the role phenomenology gives to the Cartesian cogito – to the idea that *I am thinking therefore I am* – as the guarantee of the certainty of conscious knowledge, Lacan objects that no adequate explanation of hallucinations can be based on the attributes of consciousness alone. From the point of view of a perceptual experience, so the phenomenologist reasons, there is no difference between a veridical perception and a hallucination – that is, where there is no object of perception. On this approach, as Descartes himself was aware, hallucinations are a challenge to the reliability of the senses. I could, at least in theory, experience a hallucination with exactly the same content as a veridical experience, and I could therefore not claim that my perception was ever 100% reliable. The phenomenologist Husserl captured this thought by saying that a hallucination and a perception that were indistinguishable from the point of view of the perceiver have the same *noema*. *Noesis*, on the other hand, refers to the act on the part of the subject, whether it be liking, desiring, judging, and so on, which then has a particular (noematic) content (Husserl, 1982). As Merleau-Ponty points out (1945/1962: 389–391), however, a person who is hallucinating is frequently capable of distinguishing their perceptions from their hallucinations, and he adds (1945/1962: 391) that 'according to the patient himself, hallucination has no place in objective being'. He speaks (1945/1962: 339), concerning hallucinations, of an original oneness of man and the world which is not abolished by everyday perception or objective thought, but repressed by it. The following sums up his position:

> The truth of perception and the falsity of illusion must be implanted in them [that is, in perception and illusion] in the shape of some intrinsic characteristic, for otherwise the testimony of the other senses, of later experience, or of other people, which would remain the only possible criterion, would then become unreliable, and we should never be aware of a perception or an illusion as such. If the whole being of my perception and the whole being of my illusion lies in the way they appear, then the truth which defines one and the falsity which defines the other must be equally apparent. There will be between them, therefore, a structural difference. A true perception will simply be true perception. Illusion will be no perception at all, and certainty will have to extend from the vision or sensation as conceived to perception as constitutive of an object. (1945/1962: 343)

The studied detail in Merleau-Ponty's analysis is commendable indeed, but it is too subtle, Lacan asserts (321, 2), to prevent the false explanations for the false problem into which psychoanalysts regularly fall: seeking an explanation for hallucinations as if they were a perception without an object. Explanations of this kind appeal to the loss of reality, absence of reality testing, or even the supremacy of the pleasure principle over the reality principle – a prime example of which we find in Raymond de Saussure (1950).

The easy objection to Saussure and others, Lacan comments (321, 3), would be to say that the content of hallucinations is not a function of what the subject finds satisfying. But this would miss the point, for the real issue lies elsewhere: not in the noema, or content, of the hallucination, but in the noesis, which is the 'act' of perception, and its relationship to the content. This is, however, to do no more – and indeed no less – than to lay out what is necessary for a 'true conversion' of the problem.

And indeed Freud's 'Negation' immediately takes us a step beyond this conversion. This is the point at which Lacan refers to a brief hallucinatory episode in the childhood of the Wolf Man. He had discussed this episode in his seminar the week before (Lacan, S1, 1953–1954: 42–44) where he reminds his audience that this case had been the subject of his seminar two years earlier (sadly, the stenographic transcription of Lacan's seminars only commenced in 1953). He refers to this episode in his seminar on the psychoses (Lacan, S3, 1955–1956) and in the article, 'A Question Prior to Any Possible Treatment of Psychosis'. The episode is described by Freud in the case of the Wolf Man (Freud, 1918/1955).

A brief discussion is called for here. Lacan zeroes in on the German noun '*Verwerfung*' (verb '*verwerfen*'), which he initially translates variously as *retranchement*, excision, *rejet*, rejection, or *refus*, refusal. At the end of the seminar on the psychoses he opts for *'forclusion'*, which is not a literal translation but a term drawn from *Grammaire de la langue française* by Damourette and Pichon (Damourette and Pichon, 1911–1922/1931). The French *'forclusion'* has been rendered as foreclosure in English. It should be noted that although Lacan is interested, as he says above (320, 7), in questions of psychopathology in this text and, we might assume, in questions of diagnosis, the diagnostic issue is not front and center at this moment. Lacan is concerned with the issue of hallucination, not with the difference between neurosis and psychosis, and there is no indication in this text that he considers *Verwerfung* to be a defining feature of psychosis. In 'Function and Field of Speech and Language' Lacan has already explicitly stated (256, 6–7) that a psychosis is triggered in the Wolf Man subsequent to and as a consequence of his treatment with Freud – though whether it was a result of his analysis is questionable. However, the foreclosure at issue here in the Wolf Man's hallucination of severing his finger is the foreclosure of castration and not the foreclosure of the Name-of-the-Father – and the thesis that the foreclosure of the Name-of-the-Father differentiates psychosis from neurosis, which is the key to Lacan's account of psychosis, does not come till his seminar on the psychoses (Lacan, S3, 1955–1956). For more on this see my chapter on foreclosure in *Lacan, Language and Philosophy* (Grigg, 2008, 3–24).

Lacan makes several paragraphs (321, 6–322, 5) of general remarks on the case of the Wolf Man and ends (322, 4–323, 1) with Freud's observation that while the Wolf Man's sexual life was genital, his unconscious fantasy life remained attached to the anal phase. Because he was in a feminine position, access to genital reality entailed the inevitable threat of castration, and Freud does not fail to note (SE 17, 84) the similarity with the delusional system of Schreber.

What interests Lacan (323, 2) is that Freud does not speak here of *Verdrängung*, repression, concerning the Wolf Man's castration, but of *Verwerfung*. Lacan quotes Freud's original German: *'er von ihr nichts wissen wollte im Sinne der Verdrängung'*, which James Strachey, Freud's English translator, renders as 'He would have nothing to do with it in the sense of having repressed it', except that Strachey adds a comma, not present in the original, which changes the meaning, or at least disambiguates it: 'He would have nothing to do with it, in the sense of having repressed it'. And then Freud adds, *'Er verwarf sie'*, that is, 'He foreclosed it', to follow Lacan's later terminology; there was no judgment upon its existence; it was as if it did not exist.[8]

The ensuing discussion (323, 3–324, 2) of *Bejahung*, affirmation, "*Verneinung*", negation, and *Verwerfung*, excision (which will later become foreclosure), is confusing, so let's spend some time clarifying it. The first thing to note is that there are crucial differences between Freud's text and Lacan's commentary. Freud (1925/1961: 236–237) distinguishes two types of judgment (*Urteil*). The first is the distinction between a judgment that affirms (*zusprechen*) and a judgment that denies (*absprechen*) that a thing possesses a particular attribute. Freud mentions *Bejahung* twice and each time opposes it to "*Verneinung*"; for Freud, therefore, to affirm and to negate something are opposites. Now, the attributes of a thing can – and let's just go along with Freud on this – be deemed good or bad. Those things deemed to possess good attributes are taken into the ego, which he calls the pleasure ego, while those with bad attributes are ejected from it. There is, then, a judgment that affirms or disaffirms/negates that something possesses a particular attribute; and on the basis of this judgment a decision is made to take that thing into the ego or expel it from the ego, according as it is deemed to be good or bad. That is the first step. Then there is a second judgment which, as it were, examines the objects taken into the ego and distinguishes between them on the basis of whether or not they can be refound in perception, which for Freud equates to reality; those that can be refound in perception are real and those that cannot are purely internal.[9]

Lacan, on the other hand, opposes *Bejahung*, not to "*Verneinung*", but to *Verwerfung*. It is Lacan that introduces this opposition, not Freud; it is an addition to Freud's paper on 'Negation'. I say this for two reasons. First, *Verwerfung* is not a concept in Freud in the full sense of the word; it is Lacan who forges it out of several places in which Freud uses the term. And second, in 'Negation' Freud (1925/1961: 235) uses it only once, in the verbal form *verwirft*, and even this instance is used merely in the sense of 'repudiating', which is how Strachey translates it. There is no other mention of *Verwerfung* in 'Negation'. What Lacan does, then, is extract the term '*Verwerfung*' from the case of the Wolf Man and substitute it for "*Verneinung*" in Freud's text. Lacan's discussion is confusing unless we grasp this fact.

This opposition between *Bejahung* and *Verwerfung* makes it possible for Lacan (323, 5) to speak of *Bejahung* as an original moment that is prior to, and makes possible, any judgment of attribution that affirms or disaffirms that a thing possesses a particular attribute. It is only by means of a *Bejahung*, indeed a 'primal *Bejahung*' (323, 3), that 'something from the real' can 'come to offer itself up to the revelation of being'; it is 'only afterwards that anything whatsoever can be found there as existent' (323, 5). For Lacan, this *Bejahung* is the 'primordial symbolization' (324, 1) that marks the entry into the symbolic order of important, even essential, signifiers. And where, for whatever reason, this primordial symbolization does not occur, Lacan speaks of *Verwerfung*, or foreclosure, as it will come to be known.

With this clarification, we can ask the question: what can be said about the foreclosed? The question arises because foreclosure is not without consequences; it is recognizable by its effects, which are different in kind from those of repression. The challenge, then, is to find the right way to describe these effects and what follows (323, 6–327, 8) is Lacan's way.

What has been foreclosed (excised, *verworfen*) from the symbolic 'will not be refound in his history' (323, 6) since it is only in the symbolic that one's history can be written. The nature of psychosis is that psychotic phenomena have no precedents in the subject's history prior to the onset of the psychosis. The *repression* of key signifiers in a person's history results in their return in disguised and symptomatic forms. Where *foreclosure* is concerned, the dynamics are different. Lacan (324, 1) puts it in these terms: 'What did not come to light in the symbolic appears in the real', a real that behaves 'erratically' (324, 2), which is to say in an unlawlike, random and unpredictable manner that is unlike the repressed which always returns in a manner whose laws can be understood, even if the return is disguised or displaced. Unlike a dream, a hallucination occurs without transference (324, 2). It is not a text (324, 2) but simply there, present in its brute existence or, rather, in its ex-existence, given that existence is the realm of mundane objects. The Wolf Man's hallucination illustrates the fact that the real 'does not wait for the subject' or expect anything 'from speech' (324, 3), because the subject experiences it in silence and is unable to communicate it to his nanny, even though she is his closest confidante and right there by his side. The symbolic is present in hallucinations as a noise in which everything and nothing can be heard – as a 'booming, buzzing confusion', to misquote William James. Lacan is emphasising the episodic, unpredictable and unlawlike character of the irruption of the real. Lacan writes that the real is there, 'ready to submerge in its fragments, what the 'reality principle' constructs there that goes by the name of the 'outside world' (324, 3).[10]

Lacan reiterates (324, 4) in a slightly different form his previous claim that, first, *Verwerfung*, or primal expulsion, forms the real and that at the second moment the 'representations', *Vorstellungen*, or ideas in Strachey's translation of Freud, form the symbolic by which reality is characterized as those things which one has experienced and *that can be refound* – at least in theory. Lacan is citing Freud on what looks like a rather crude criterion of reality, but if we take a generous approach, it could be made into something like a Kantian view of empirical reality as causally related enduring objects that have spatial properties. Of greater interest for our present purposes is the observation that the (foreclosed) real *'is already there'* (324, 4) in the empirical world, but as something that 'talks all by itself' and something of which appears in hallucinations – appears, that is, 'in the form of a thing which is far from being an object that satisfies him' (324, 4) (a dig at Raymond de Saussure) and which 'involves his present intentionality only in the most incongruous way' (324, 4–325,1), which is a critique of phenomenology. The issue here is hallucination, which Lacan regards as the appearance in the real, in almost pure form, of what has been foreclosed. It is, he says, radically different from the 'interpretive phenomenon' (325, 1) of paranoid delusions.

The value of Lacan's comments on Freud's description and discussion of the Wolf Man's childhood hallucination lies in the fact that his focus is on visual hallucinations in their purest, we might even say most phenomenological, form. This focus is why Lacan tells us not to be sidetracked by Freud's 'scrupulous' uncovering of the thematic and biographical connections and the 'whole symbolic richness' (325, 3) of the hallucination. Freud's analysis is not so much inaccurate as beside the point in that these connections inscribe the hallucination in the ambient symbolic framework. While this makes it possible to locate the hallucination in the Wolf Man's history and express and transmit the phenomenon in discourse, we should avoid being 'fascinated' by this semantic content and its associations. As Lacan says, it is 'not sufficient' to focus merely on the semantic content. By emphasizing the narrative, Lacan says (325, 5), we risk failing to take cognizance of the crucial fact that the Wolf Man is reduced to silence by the hallucination, incapable of speaking about it at the time. He is 'arrested' – could we say 'overwhelmed'? – by the 'strangeness of the signified', is incapable of communicating his feelings or anything else about it. As Lacan puts it, the real 'expects nothing from speech' (324, 3). Nor does he protest or react; he is incapable of uttering a word, despite the fact that his nanny is right there beside him. Furthermore, the hallucination is experienced outside of time, in a 'temporal funnel' (326, 1), or we might say a temporal sink, as if, like Alice, he is spiraling down into another dimension which he then returns from, and does so without having to make any effort on his part.

The instance of 'terrified mutism' (326, 2) mentioned by Freud and referred to by Lacan is worth quoting:

> At this point another recollection occurred to me, which has always been of the greatest importance to me, in so far as it is *one* of the three recollections which constitute all that I can remember of my mother, who died when I was very young. I remember seeing my mother standing in front of the washing-stand and cleaning the glasses and washing-basin, while I was playing in the same room and committing some misdemeanour. As a punishment my hand was soundly slapped. Then to my very great terror I saw my little finger fall off; and in fact it fell into the pail. Knowing that my mother was angry, I did not venture to say anything; but my terror grew still more intense when I saw the pail carried off soon afterwards by the servant girl. For a long time I was convinced that I had lost a finger – up to the time, I believe, at which I learnt to count.
>
> (Freud, 1914/1955: 206)

A very interesting comment follows about the hallucination as an emergence of the real, in connection with the 'temporal funnel' or 'temporal abyss' outside of 'ordinary time'. Referring (326, 4) to the Wolf Man's mistaken belief that he had already recounted the episode of the hallucination to Freud (1914/1955: 204–205), Lacan (326, 5) disagrees with Freud that it as a screen memory, since if it were it would be situated in the field of language and the symbolic, whereas what is at stake is something that has reappeared in the real. Lacan (326, 6) points to the fact that the Wolf Man himself (Freud, 1918/

1955: 85, fn. 2) corrects himself and tells Freud that the walnut tree, the same tree as in the wolf dream, has probably been brought in from his recollection of another hallucination in which the blood seeps, not from his finger, but from the tree itself. Lacan (326, 7) concludes that the atemporal character of these episodes reveals their origin in foreclosure and subsequent return in the real. Again, the hallucination is an indication of excision/foreclosure, just as a negative judgment is the hallmark of repression.

Lacan (326, 8) points to a complementarity between the (real) extra-temporality of the hallucination and the (imaginary) sense of déjà vu. The sense of déjà vu is an 'imaginary echo' that arises in response to 'a point of reality' that has been foreclosed from the symbolic (326, 9). Lacan then describes the sense of reality as 'exactly the same phenomenon as the sense of unreality' (326, 10). The difference is that one experiences something as real when it is 'produced inside the symbolic text that constitutes the register of recollection' (327, 1), which means that what makes the sense of reality is a series of symbolic articulations with one's experience, a process that Lacan refers to as 'recollection'. On the other hand, the sense of unreality 'corresponds to the immemorial forms that appear on the palimpsest of the imaginary when the text, leaving off, lays bare the medium of *reminiscence*' (327, 1, my italics). These forms are not 'immemorial' in the sense of 'from time immemorial' but in the sense of unable to be memorialised, and since to memorialize involves inscribing in the symbolic, these forms appear when the subject is unable to integrate his experience into a network of signifiers. The allusion to Plato's concept of reminiscence is made explicit when Lacan (327, 2) points out that Freud's thesis (1925/1961: 237) that the sense of reality arises when perception is of something that has previously been perceived will not do because the original experience is an arbitrary stopping point. What guarantees the reality of the initial perception? A perception only 'takes on the characteristic of reality' when its symbolic articulations are such that they are woven into myriad networks of signifiers that make a world.

The return of the foreclosed, which is what Lacan (327, 3) is here referring to, can carry no less a sense of reality, even though it does not exist, but ek-sists. Nevertheless, the massive symbolic meaning with which the episode is charged simply does not exist for the Wolf Man, because what does exist is the imaginary feminine position from which castration is foreclosed. Castration returns in the real, but drained of its imaginary ramifications.

Lacan completes this discussion of his first example with some important remarks on the differences between schizophrenia and paranoia, which he regards as the two poles of psychosis. This is the point of the remark that for the schizophrenic (as opposed to the paranoiac) 'all of the symbolic is real' (327, 6). The suggestion that nothing in the symbolic order has been symbolized, as if it has collapsed back upon or into the real, is a moot point and should, I would say, be taken to be describing something like an ideal type, and thus a claim about 'pure' schizophrenia. The point needs further discussion, and we should note that this is the single mention of schizophrenia in the entire *Écrits*. The important point, however, is the contrast between schizophrenia and paranoia, for Lacan goes on to observe that the elementary phenomena in paranoia are 'presignifying' – that is, not yet signifiers but capable of becoming so. The delusion of the paranoiac, always only 'partial', is the outcome of a 'long and painful' 'discursive organisation' (327, 7). This is a brief but suggestive observation whose implications are myriad. Should the aim of the treatment of schizophrenics be to establish the delusional system of the paranoiac, which has the capacity to stabilize the subject? How is it that some psychotics become paranoiacs while others always remain schizophrenic?

The second example (327, 9–end) is, as mentioned, the case made famous by Lacan of the 'fresh-brains man'. With this example, Lacan moves away from his response to Hyppolite and discussion of Freud's 'Negation'. The example is chosen because it illustrates the explanatory power, or 'fertile fields', of the categories of real, symbolic and imaginary that Lacan has imported into Freudian psychoanalysis. It is also intended, as he has already stated (320, 7), to contribute to an understanding of our clinical work and to shed light on the theory of technique.

This example is, then, like the first, one in which there is the interconnection between the symbolic and the real – and, most importantly, without the mediation of the imaginary – with the difference that in this instance the subject acts, '*agisse*', rather than passively experiences or undergoes, '*subisse*' (327, 9). It is a case of acting out – it was Lacan who introduced the English term into French and distinguished it clearly from *passage-à-l'acte*, the term by which it had previously been translated – that is taken from a paper by the ego psychologist, Ernst Kris (1951), which, as stated above, Lacan discusses on several occasions. Lacan (328, 1) also declares his intention to clarify the notion of acting out in the light of his basic categories of symbolic, imaginary and real.

Lacan (328, 2) cautions us not to expect that his analysis will go as far as the first, but this is because Kris's commentary on his case is not as rich as Freud's on the Wolf Man's hallucination. In fact, he is rather sarcastic about Kris for the 'wishy-washy notions' (328, 4) that the technical precepts his case is supposed to illustrate ultimately lead to. The sarcasm continues with the claim that Kris's 'masterful application' (328, 5) of the principles of ego psychology will provide an elegant resolution to the case. Clearly, Lacan is having fun. He lists these principles. They include: that one appeal to the subject's ego (at least the healthy part); that analysis starts from the surface (that is, analyze the defenses before unconscious material); and that the point of reference is reality (to which one adapts).

In the description Lacan gives of Kris's case (328, 6–329, 4), we learn that prior to seeing Kris the patient had been in analysis with Melitta Schmideberg, who mentions the case in a single short paragraph (1934/1938: 21). In his Translator's Endnotes Bruce Fink (798) points out some of the disparities between Lacan's account of the case and Kris's (1951) original paper. And the discussion (331–332) of Kris's article should be read in conjunction with Fink's notes which correct some mistranslations and misreadings by Lacan of Kris's text. Note, however, that they do not detract from the value of Lacan's discussion of acting out.

Kris refers to a patient obsessed with the idea of being a plagiarist whose fears, as reported by Lacan, Kris tries to demonstrate are unfounded by carrying out some investigations on his patient's behalf (329, 4). His efforts are described as 'quixotic' and doomed to fail when it comes to resolving the man's obsessive thought that he is a plagiarist.

Lacan goes on to make two relevant points. First, that there is of course no question of reassuring the patient that he is not a plagiarist by proving that his fears are unfounded 'from the outside' (329, 4); he must rather explore what the meaning of Kris's patient's self-accusation is. Second, the 'prohibition' against seeking evidence from outside the analytic setting to confirm or disconfirm a claim – in the present case the analysand's plagiarism – is 'more imaginary than real' (329, 7). The more significant issue is that such an approach overlooks the 'content' of the self-accusation, that is, what plagiarism means for the patient, especially as it brings about a corresponding inhibition that has a significant impact on him precisely because of his vocation as an academic (329, 8).

Lacan's discussion is for the most part descriptive and self-explanatory. The 'classic' comparison (331, 3) is of course over the size of the penis, while the more 'gallant' comparisons would presumably be rivalry over the mother and perhaps women in general.

Lacan (331, 5) is struck by the remarks by Kris's patient with which his vignette concludes: 'Every noon, when I leave here, before luncheon, and before returning to my office, I walk through X Street [a street well known for its small but attractive restaurants] and I look at the menus in the windows. In one of the restaurants, I usually find my preferred dish—fresh brains' (Kris, 1951: 23).

For Kris, this response shows the superiority of 'exploration of the surface' (24), that is, interpreting inhibitions and defenses, over analyzing the underlying oral drive. However, where Kris considers the patient's response to be confirmation of the soundness of his interpretation, for Lacan he is merely acting out, which indicates that the interpretation has missed the mark.

In speaking of an oral relation that is primordially 'excised' (333, 2) Lacan uses the term 'retranché', excised, which he has used earlier for Freud's 'Verwerfung' when discussing what has been excised from the symbolic and returns in the real in the case of the Wolf Man's hallucination. Since 'Verwerfung' will later become the operation specific to psychosis and contrasted with the operation of 'Verdrängung', repression, specific to neurosis, the question arises why Lacan speaks of a primordially *excised* oral relation here?

How does this compare with the return of the excised (foreclosed) in a hallucination?

To answer these questions, we need to go back to Lacan's stated reason for choosing these two examples, which is that they both illustrate the 'intersection of the symbolic with the real that...occurs without an *imaginary* intermediary, but...is mediated...by what was excluded at the first moment [*temps*] of symbolization' (320, 4). As Lacan sees it, the two cases of the hallucination and the acting out are examples where what is excluded from the symbolic reappears in the real with no mediation by the imaginary. Of course, there are differences, but it is the similarity of structure that Lacan demonstrates. In a hallucination, what is foreclosed reappears in the real. The fresh-brains man's action in response to Kris's interpretation shows that the interpretation has missed a vital signifier, which for the patient translates into an action he is incapable of understanding. To all intents and purposes, it is as if the signifier were foreclosed. The inability to understand the phenomenon in question indicates a bypassing of the imaginary. Lacan underscores the connection between the two cases when he says in his seminar on the psychoses, 'I treat acting out as equivalent to a hallucinatory phenomenon of the delusional type' (1981/1993: 78).

I know of no discussion by Lacan of hallucination equivalent to the detailed analysis in his response to Hyppolite. While the go-to references on Lacan's teaching on psychosis are the seminar on the psychoses (1981/1993) and 'On a Question Prior to Any Possible Treatment of Psychosis', where the discussion centers on the construction of delusion and the analysis of hallucinations in paranoid psychosis, Lacan gives something different in this chapter: an analysis of a hallucination that is on the side of schizophrenia rather than that of paranoia, a hallucination in which the emergence of the real is, as it were, unvarnished by the lucubrations of the paranoid subject of the likes of a Schreber. The linking of the Wolf Man's hallucination and the fresh-brains man's acting out encourages one to see acting out in a different and important light for clinical work. The discussion of Kris's patient returns in other places, as I have said, but what remains worthy of reflection here is the thesis that regards acting out as a hallucinatory phenomenon. The entire discussion is worth keeping in mind for underlining the fact that the Name-of-the-Father is not the only signifier susceptible to foreclosure, and that it is not foreclosure as such but foreclosure of the Name-of-the-Father that is the line of demarcation between neurosis and psychosis.

Notes

1 Compare E. Kris (1951, 16), "The precedence of technical over theoretical formulations extended throughout Freud's development."
2 See, for example, O. Fenichel (1945), *The Psychoanalytic Theory of Neurosis*, New York, Norton; D. Rapaport (1960), *The Structure of Psychoanalytic Theory: A Systematizing*

Attempt, New York, International Universities Press; J. Arlow and C. Brenner (1964), *Psychoanalytic Concepts and the Structural Theory*, New York, International Universities Press. All are still in print today.

3 See, for instance, his "Neuropsychoses of Defence" (Freud, 1894/1962).

4 Reading the first line of this paragraph differently. There is no reference to the patient in the French.

5 Kris (1951, 16): "His [Freud's] advice that analysis should start from the surface, and that resistance be analyzed before interpreting content implies principles basic in ego psychology."

6 The adjective "suspensive" applies to something that suspends or pauses an event or action in time and particularly to a legal action that suspends the course of justice. For Freud's remark, cited by Lacan (311, 5), that when the associations stop, the analysand has thoughts about the analyst, see his "The Dynamics of Transference" (Freud, 1912/ 1958: 101).

7 See Réginald Blanchet "What is Concealed by the So-Called Cht and Why" (Blanchet, 2019).

8 Freud's German is worth quoting in full: "Wenn ich gesagt habe, dass er sie verwarf, so ist die nächste Bedeutung dieses Ausdrucks, dass er von ihr nichts wissen wollte im Sinne der Verdrängung. Damit war eigentlich kein Urteil über ihre Existenz gefällt, aber es war so gut, als ob sie nicht existierte" (Freud, 1918/1955, 111).

9 Freud's reasoning cannot be taken seriously as a philosophical argument. For, whatever the value of his thinking, as a basis for a distinction between inner and outer experience, or subjective and objective, the argument is question begging, since it requires that I can already tell the difference between internal and external for me to know whether I am perceiving or imagining. It also faces the difficulty of entailing that an object which I have experienced once only is therefore purely internal, even if I have good grounds for knowing that I will never experience it again. This is all particularly pertinent in the context of a discussion of hallucination.

10 I now take the reference here to be to the fragmented appearance of the real, and so I read *"de ses éclats"*, not as roar, but as fragments, shards or slivers, which is what Lacan will later call *"bouts de réel"*, bits of real.

References

Arlow, J. and C. Brenner (1964) *Psychoanalytic Concepts and the Structural Theory*. New York: International Universities Press.

Blanchet, R. (2019) What Is Concealed by the So-Called Cht and Why. Available at: https://www.nlscongress2019.com/new-blog/what-is-concealed-by-the-so-called-cht-and-why

Breuer, J. and S. Freud (1893–1895/1955) Studies on Hysteria. In J. Strachey (ed.) *The Standard Edition of the Complete Psychological Works of Sigmund Freud*, Vol. 2. London: The Hogarth Press and the Institute of Psycho-Analysis.

Clausewitz, C. von (1832/1976) *On War*. M. Howard and P. Paret (eds.) Princeton, NJ: Princeton University Press.

Damourette, J. et E. Pichon (1911–1922/1931) *Des mots à la pensée: Essai de grammaire de la langue française*, 1911–1922. Paris: Arthrey.

Fenichel, O. (1945) *The Psychoanalytic Theory of Neurosis*. New York: Norton.

Freud, S. (1894/1962) Neuropsychoses of Defence. In J. Strachey (ed.) *The Standard Edition of the Complete Psychological Works of Sigmund Freud*, Vol. 3. London: The Hogarth Press and the Institute of Psycho-Analysis.

Freud, S. (1901/1960) The Psychopathology of Everyday Life. In J. Strachey (ed.) *The Standard Edition of the Complete Psychological Works of Sigmund Freud*, Vol. 6. London: The Hogarth Press and the Institute of Psycho-Analysis.

Freud, S. 1909/1955) Notes Upon a Case of Obsessional Neurosis. In J. Strachey (ed.) *The Standard Edition of the Complete Psychological Works of Sigmund Freud*, Vol. 10. London: The Hogarth Press and the Institute of Psycho-Analysis.

Freud, S. (1912/1958) The Dynamics of Transference. In J. Strachey (ed.) *The Standard Edition of the Complete Psychological Works of Sigmund Freud*, Vol. 12. London: The Hogarth Press and the Institute of Psycho-Analysis.

Freud, S. (1914/1955) Fausse Reconnaissance (Déjà Raconté) in Psycho-Analytic Treatment. In J. Strachey (ed.) *The Standard Edition of the Complete Psychological Works of Sigmund Freud*, Vol. 13. London: The Hogarth Press and the Institute of Psycho-Analysis.

Freud, S. (1916–1917/1961) Introductory Lectures on Psychoanalysis. In J. Strachey (ed.) *The Standard Edition of the Complete Psychological Works of Sigmund Freud*, Vol. 15. London: The Hogarth Press and the Institute of Psycho-Analysis.

Freud, S. (1918/1947) Aus der Geschichte einer infantilen Neurose. In *Gesammelte Werke*, Vol. 12. London: Imago.

Freud, S. (1918/1955) From the History of an Infantile Neurosis. In J. Strachey (ed.) *The Standard Edition of the Complete Psychological Works of Sigmund Freud*, Vol. 17. London: The Hogarth Press and the Institute of Psycho-Analysis.

Freud, S (1925/1961) Negation. In J. Strachey (ed.) *The Standard Edition of the Complete Psychological Works of Sigmund Freud*, Vol. 19. London: The Hogarth Press and the Institute of Psycho-Analysis.

Grigg, R. (2008) Foreclosure. In his *Lacan, Language and Philosophy*. New York: SUNY Press. Available at: https://www.sunypress.edu/pdf/61563.pdf.

Heidegger, M. (1953/1962) *Being and Time*. Trans. J. Macquarrie & E. Robinson. Oxford: Blackwell.

Husserl, E. (1982) *Ideas Pertaining to a Pure Phenomenology and to a Phenomenological Philosophy. First Book. General Introduction to a Pure Phenomenology*. Trans. F. Kersten. The Hague: Martinus Nijhoff.

Hyppolite, J. (1966/2006) A Spoken Commentary on Freud's "Verneinung" by Jean Hyppolite. In J. Lacan (ed.) *Écrits*. New York: Norton, 746–754.

Isaacs, S. (1948) The Nature and Function of Phantasy. *International Journal of Psychoanalysis*. 29, 73–97.

Klein, M., P. Heimann and R. Money-Kyrle (1955) *New Directions in Psychoanalysis*. London: Tavistock.

Kris, E. (1951) Ego Psychology and Interpretation in Psychoanalytic Therapy. *Psychoanalytic Quarterly*. 20, 15–29.

Lacan, J. (1956/2006) Function and Field of Speech and Language in Psychoanalysis. In his *Écrits*. Trans. B. Fink. New York: Norton.

Lacan, J. (1973/1977) *The Seminar. Book XI. The Four Fundamental Concepts of Psychoanalysis* (1965–1965). Trans. A. Sheridan. London.

Lacan, J. (1975/1988) *The Seminar. Book I: Freud's Papers on Technique* (1953–1954). Trans. J. Forrester. Cambridge: Cambridge University Press.

Lacan, J. (1978/1988) *The Seminar. Book II: The Ego in Freud's Theory and in the Technique of Psychoanalysis* (1954–1955). Trans. S. Tomaselli. Cambridge: Cambridge University Press.

Lacan, J. (1977/2018) Preface to the English Edition of *Seminar XI*. Trans. R. Grigg. *The Lacanian Review*. 6, 23–27.

Lacan, J. (1981/1993) *The Seminar. Book III. The Psychoses* (1955-1956). Trans. R. Grigg. NY: Norton.

Lacan, J. (1998/2007) *The Seminar. Book V. Formations of the Unconscious* (1957–1958). Trans. R. Grigg. Cambridge: Polity Press.

Lacan, J. (2013/2019) *The Seminar. Book VI. Desire and its Interpretation* (1958–1959). Trans. B. Fink. Cambridge: Polity Press.

Lévi-Strauss, C. (1978) *Myth and Meaning*. London: Routledge and Kegan Paul.

Merleau-Ponty, M. (1945/1962) *The Phenomenology of Perception*. Trans. C. Smith. London: Routledge & Kegan Paul.

Miller, J.-A. (2005) The Invention of Delusion. Trans. G. S. Marshall. *International Lacanian Review*, pp. 1–28. Available at: http://www.lacanianreview.com.br/index.asp.

Molière (1914) *The Doctor in Spite of Himself: A Farce in Two Acts*. Trans. Barrett H. Clark. New York: Samuel French.

Nacht, S. and S. Lebovici (1956) Indications et contre-indications de la psychanalyse chez l'adulte. In S. Nacht (ed.) *La Psychanalyse d'aujourd'hui*, Vol. 1. Paris: Presses Universitaires de France.

Rapaport, D. (1960) *The Structure of Psychoanalytic Theory: A Systematizing Attempt*. New York: International Universities Press.

Sartre, J.-P. (1943/1984) *Being and Nothingness: An Essay on Phenomenological Ontology*. Trans. H. Barnes. New York: Washington Square Press.

Saussure, R. de (1950) Present Trends in Psychoanalysis. *Actes du congrès international de psychiatrie*. 5, 95–166.

Schmideberg, M. (1934/1938) Intellectual Inhibition and Disturbances in Eating. *International Journal of Psycho-Analysis*. 19, 17–22.

Strauss, L. (1952) Persecution and the Art of Writing. In his *Persecution and the Art of Writing*. Glencoe, Illinois: The Free Press.

INDEX

Page numbers in *italics* refer to figures.

223

Printed in the United States
by Baker & Taylor Publisher Services